# The Family Tree of Queen Elizabeth II

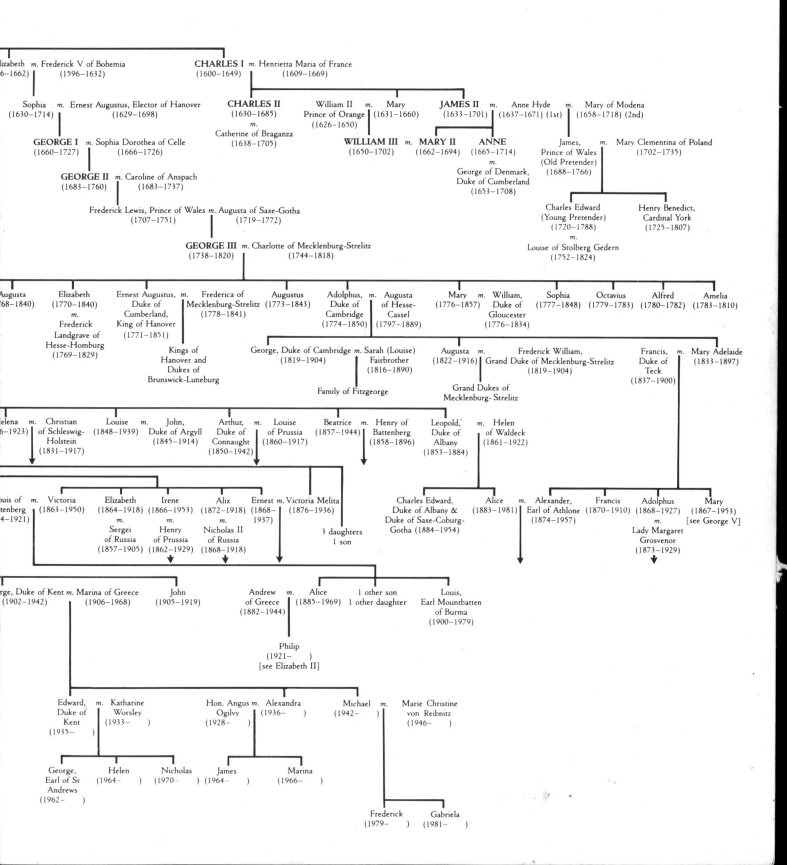

This book is dedicated to the
memory of Her Majesty Queen Mary,
whose love and appreciation of
fine jewels are reflected throughout
the royal collection.

LESLIE FIELD

# THE QUEEN'S JEWELS

## THE PERSONAL COLLECTION OF
## Elizabeth II

HARRY N. ABRAMS, INC., PUBLISHERS, NEW YORK

*Frontispiece:*
*The Queen arriving at Claridges for a State banquet given by*
*the Greek royal family in 1963. Behind her are*
*Prince Philip on the left and King Paul of Greece on the*
*right (see also page 140). The Queen is wearing*
*Queen Mary's 'Girls of Great Britain and Ireland' tiara,*
*Queen Mary's ruby cluster earrings, the King*
*George VI and Queen Elizabeth ruby bandeau necklace, and*
*a ruby and diamond Art Deco-style bracelet.*

Editors: Ruth A. Peltason, Felicity Luard
Designer: Dirk Luykx

Library of Congress Cataloging-in-Publication Data
Field, Leslie.
The queen's jewels.
Bibliography: p. 186
Includes index.
1. Crown jewels—Great Britain.   2. Elizabeth II,
Queen of Great Britain, 1926–    .   3. Great Britain—
Kings and rulers—Biography.   4. Jewelry—Private
collections—Great Britain.   I. Title.
DA112.F53   1987        739.27′0941        86–32187
ISBN 0–8109–1525–1

Published in 1987 by Harry N. Abrams, Incorporated, New York

Times Mirror Books

Printed and bound in Japan

# CONTENTS

ACKNOWLEDGMENTS *7*

PREFACE *8*

THE FAMILY JEWELS: VICTORIA TO ELIZABETH II 1837–1987 *9*

## *Amethysts* 20
THE KENT DEMI-PARURE

## *Aquamarines* 21
THE QUEEN'S CARTIER CLIPS

## *Coral* 24
THE QUEEN'S FIRST NECKLACE

## *Diamonds* 26
QUEEN MARY'S 'GIRLS OF GREAT BRITAIN AND IRELAND' TIARA      THE KING GEORGE III FRINGE TIARA      QUEEN ALEXANDRA'S
RUSSIAN KOKOSHNIK TIARA AND QUEEN MARY'S FLORET EARRINGS      QUEEN ELIZABETH THE QUEEN MOTHER'S SCROLL TIARA
PRINCESS ANDREW OF GREECE'S MEANDER TIARA      QUEEN MARY'S CLUSTER EARRINGS      QUEEN VICTORIA'S STUD EARRINGS
THE QUEEN'S PEAR DROP EARRINGS      THE KING GEORGE VI CHANDELIER EARRINGS AND FESTOON NECKLACE
QUEEN VICTORIA'S COLLET NECKLACE AND EARRINGS      THE KING FAISAL OF SAUDI ARABIA NECKLACE
THE KING KHALID OF SAUDI ARABIA NECKLACE      QUEEN VICTORIA'S BOW BROOCHES      THE QUEEN'S JARDINIÈRE BROOCH
THE QUEEN'S FLOWER BASKET BROOCH      THE QUEEN'S IVY LEAF BROOCHES      QUEEN ELIZABETH THE QUEEN MOTHER'S MAPLE LEAF BROOCH
QUEEN MARY'S DORSET BOW BROOCH      QUEEN VICTORIA'S BAR BROOCH      QUEEN MARY'S STOMACHER
QUEEN MARY'S TRUE LOVER'S KNOT BROOCH      PRINCE PHILIP'S NAVAL BADGE BROOCH      THE KING WILLIAM IV BROOCH
THE CULLINAN      THE LESSER STARS OF AFRICA BROOCH AND THE CULLINAN IX RING      THE CULLINAN V HEART BROOCH
THE CULLINAN VII AND CULLINAN VIII BROOCH      QUEEN VICTORIA'S WHEAT EAR BROOCHES
THE SWISS FEDERAL REPUBLIC'S WATCH      THE KING WILLIAM IV BUCKLE BRACELETS      QUEEN MARY'S LINK BRACELET
QUEEN MARY'S INDIAN BANGLE BRACELETS      THE QUEEN'S MODERN BAGUETTES AND BRILLIANTS BRACELET
THE QUEEN'S ENGAGEMENT RING AND THE PRINCE PHILIP WEDDING BRACELET

## *Emeralds* 86
THE CAMBRIDGE AND DELHI DURBAR PARURE      QUEEN MARY'S ART DECO BRACELET
QUEEN VICTORIA'S FRINGE EARRINGS AND THE GODMAN NECKLACE      QUEEN ALEXANDRA'S INDIAN NECKLACE

# *Gold* 97

# *Pearls* 98

THE QUEEN'S FIRST PEARL NECKLACE     THE KING GEORGE V JUBILEE NECKLACE     THE QUEEN ANNE AND THE QUEEN CAROLINE NECKLACES     THE QUEEN'S FOUR ROW CHOKER     THE EMPRESS MARIE FEODOROVNA OF RUSSIA'S NECKLACE     QUEEN ALEXANDRA'S BRACELET     QUEEN MARY'S BRACELET

# *Pearls and Diamonds* 110

THE CAMBRIDGE LOVER'S KNOT TIARA     THE GRAND DUCHESS VLADIMIR OF RUSSIA'S TIARA     QUEEN VICTORIA'S GOLDEN JUBILEE NECKLACE AND QUEEN MARY'S PENDANT EARRINGS     THE DUCHESS OF TECK'S EARRINGS     QUEEN VICTORIA'S DROP EARRINGS     QUEEN ALEXANDRA'S CLUSTER EARRINGS     QUEEN MARY'S BUTTON EARRINGS     QUEEN ALEXANDRA'S DAGMAR NECKLACE     QUEEN ALEXANDRA'S TRIPLE DROP BROOCH     QUEEN MARY'S 'WOMEN OF HAMPSHIRE' PENDANT BROOCH     QUEEN MARY'S BAR BROOCH     THE DUCHESS OF TECK'S CORSAGE BROOCH     THE DUCHESS OF CAMBRIDGE'S PENDANT BROOCH     QUEEN MARY'S KENSINGTON BOW BROOCH AND WARWICK SUN BROOCH     QUEEN ELIZABETH THE QUEEN MOTHER'S FLOWER BROOCH     PRINCESS MARIE LOUISE'S BRACELET

# *Rubies* 138

QUEEN MARY'S CLUSTER EARRINGS AND THE KING GEORGE VI AND QUEEN ELIZABETH BANDEAU NECKLACE     QUEEN ELIZABETH THE QUEEN MOTHER'S QUARTET OF BRACELETS     QUEEN MARY'S ROSE OF YORK BRACELET     THE QUEEN'S FIFTH WEDDING ANNIVERSARY BRACELET

# *Sapphires* 145

THE KING GEORGE VI VICTORIAN SUITE     THE PRINCE ALBERT BROOCH     THE EMPRESS MARIE FEODOROVNA OF RUSSIA'S BROOCH     QUEEN ELIZABETH THE QUEEN MOTHER'S LEAF BROOCH     THE QUEEN'S FLOWER SPRAY BROOCH     THE QUEEN'S SET OF FLOWER CLIPS     QUEEN MARY'S RUSSIAN BROOCH     THE QUEEN'S EIGHTEENTH BIRTHDAY BRACELET

# *Turquoises* 158

THE PRESIDENT AYUB KHAN OF PAKISTAN NECKLACE

# *The Crown Regalia* 160

THE KING GEORGE IV STATE DIADEM     THE IMPERIAL STATE CROWN, THE SCEPTRE AND THE ORB     ST EDWARD'S CROWN     THE ARMILLS AND THE CORONATION RING     THE SCOTTISH REGALIA     THE QUEEN'S 1937 CORONATION CORONET

# *Orders* 180

THE ROYAL FAMILY ORDERS     THE ORDER OF THE GARTER

GLOSSARY *185*

BIBLIOGRAPHY *185*

INDEX *189*

PHOTOGRAPH CREDITS *192*

# ACKNOWLEDGMENTS

I WOULD LIKE TO ACKNOWLEDGE my deepest gratitude to HER MAJESTY THE QUEEN for the help and guidance I have been given by Her Majesty's Household.

My grateful thanks to: HER MAJESTY QUEEN ELIZABETH THE QUEEN MOTHER; HRH THE DUKE OF EDINBURGH; HRH THE PRINCESS OF WALES; HRH THE PRINCESS ANNE, MRS MARK PHILLIPS; HRH THE PRINCESS MARGARET, COUNTESS OF SNOWDON; HRH PRINCESS ALICE, DUCHESS OF GLOUCESTER; HRH THE DUCHESS OF GLOUCESTER; HRH THE DUKE OF KENT; TRH PRINCE AND PRINCESS MICHAEL OF KENT; HRH PRINCESS ALEXANDRA, THE HON. MRS ANGUS OGILVY; LORD HAREWOOD; THE MARCHIONESS OF CAMBRIDGE; and LADY MARY WHITLEY for their help and corrections.

I am especially grateful to Anne Neal, Marcus Bishop and Charles Noble for their assistance.

And my appreciation to all the following: Sir Alastair Aird, Joseph W. Allgood, George Anderson, Sandra Ankacrona, Owen Arnot, John Asprey, Sir Simon Bland, Anne Beckwith-Smith, David Bennett, Sarah Brennan, Peter Brogan, Sir Richard Buckley, Teresa Buxton, Amar Singh Chhatwal, David Chipp, Daniel Cleary, Sir Robert Cooke, Tim Cooper, David Cottingham, Elizabeth Cuthbert, Gilbert and Jacqueline de Botton, Damon de Laszlo, Patrick de Laszlo, Frances Dimond, Elizabeth Dolan, Michael Doran, Allan Douglas, Michael Dover, Cedric Evans, David Evans, Oliver Everett, Colonel Michael Farmer, Susan Farmer, Robert Fellowes, Maurice Foster, Susie Friend, Margaret Godfrey, Paul Gottlieb, John Haslam, Sally Hine, Brenda Hodgson, Jennie Holden, Peter Hubble, Helen Hughes, Caroline and Anwar Hussein, Tim Jenkins, Geoff Katz, Amanda Kiddy, The Hon. Lady King, Fiona Koops, Ed and Julie Kosner, Laurence Krashes, Andreas Landshoff, Jane Langton, Carol Lemon, John Lloyd-Morgan, Felicity Luard, Fiona Lukes, Dirk Luykx, Barbara Lyons, Major-General Patrick MacLellan, Alistair S. McDavid, The Hon. Diana Makgill, Paul Marmin, Brigadier Kenneth Mears, Marilyn Meyers, Mona Mitchell, Geoffrey C. Munn, Hans Nadelhoffer, Cecilia Neal, Caroline Neville, Carley Newman, Nicholas Norton, Michael O'Mara, Anthony Oppenheimer, Lady Angela and Michael Oswald, Byron Ousey, Joan Parker, Fred Parkes, John Partridge, Ruth Peltason, Terence Pepper, Mark Piel, Leslie Ricketts, Liz Robbins, Daniel Roger, Kenneth Rose, John Sandoe, The Hon. Mrs Frances Shand Kydd, Michael Shea, John Shelley, Francesca Sherwood, David V. Thomas, James Todd, Heinrich Graf von Spreti, Clodagh Waddington, Robin D. G. Walker, Anne Wall, Philip Ward-Jackson, David Warren, Sir Francis Watson, Roger Wemyss-Brooks, The Hon. Mrs Jessica White, Patricia White, Marjorie Willis, Ronald Winston, Caroline Zubaida.

# PREFACE

DURING THIS CENTURY there have been probably a dozen truly great jewellery collections in the world. Today there is only one and that belongs to the Queen of the United Kingdom. The Queen's magnificent collection is unique not only because of its priceless value but because of its rare historical provenance dating back to the sixteenth century. Many of the pieces came from faraway places, often brought to Britain as a result of cataclysmic events such as civil wars, deaths and revolutions.

If I try now to remember my first fascination with the royal jewels multiple images spring to mind: the astonishing size of the pear-shaped drop diamond earrings worn by Queen Elizabeth the Queen Mother at a St James's Palace reception; the vivid hue of an enormous sapphire brooch pinned to the Queen's suit on a visit to the Courtauld Institute of Art in Portman Square; the blurred movement of the charms swinging from Princess Alexandra's gold link bracelet when she attended a charity lunch in a Pall Mall club; the staggering turquoise and diamond parure worn by the Duchess of Gloucester at a reception at Government House, in Melbourne, Australia; and the lustre of the Queen's pearl necklace at a drinks party given by Prince Philip at Buckingham Palace in honour of Bing Crosby.

Seven years of research and writing this book have done nothing to diminish the jewels' magical appeal. I sifted through 450,000 photographs in order to compile a complete catalogue of every jewel ever owned by any living member of the royal family. I read long-forgotten memoirs, royal diaries and biographies, and checked crumbling old newspapers and periodicals. I was surprised to find how many pieces have survived from the end of the eighteenth century and the early Hanoverian monarchs. It was interesting to trace changes in taste and fashion while examining pictures of seven generations of the royal family wearing the same jewels. And I came to realize that this is not a moribund museum collection, but that the royal jewels are constantly worn and have evolved according to each owner's taste and needs. Some of my discoveries were wonderfully exciting – where pieces had come from and how they became part of the royal collection – and occasionally I've been able to correct misinformation that had been repeated for decades. Illustrated here is the jewellery the Queen has inherited or been given as a family gift by her parents and her husband. But as the Queen is a link in a chain of historical continuity I've also shown jewels that she has given or loaned to her daughter and two daughters-in-law.

The Queen principally wears jewellery that belonged to her ancestors but she has added modern pieces to the royal collection, notably aquamarines and rubies, so decades from now her descendants will wear designs created during her reign. The royal jewels are historically important and reinforce the sense of stability that is the British monarchy's greatest strength. The Queen lives in three of the houses her great-great-grandmother Queen Victoria resided in. She travels to ceremonial occasions in horse-drawn coaches that Queen Victoria used. Yet perhaps the strongest chain of family continuity is forged by the personal collection of jewels that she wears, appreciates and of which she is lifelong custodian.

Leslie Field
London, 1987

# The Family Jewels

## VICTORIA TO ELIZABETH II
## 1837–1987

WHEN KING WILLIAM IV died at Windsor Castle at 2.12 am on 20 June 1837 William Howley the Archbishop of Canterbury, Lord Conygnham the Lord Chamberlain and the King's physician travelled by carriage through the night to Kensington Palace in London to awaken the eighteen-year-old Princess Victoria of Kent with the not unexpected news that her uncle was dead and that she had acceded to the British throne. Included in her inheritance were Windsor Castle, St James's Palace, Kensington Palace and Buckingham Palace as well as a priceless collection of paintings, art objects and furniture. As the Crown Regalia is the property of the State, Queen Victoria inherited in her own right the family collection of jewels, which included pearls bought by Queen Elizabeth I and diamonds that had belonged to King George III.

During his reign King William IV used stones from a number of old pieces in the royal coffers to create fashionable new jewels. These were worn by his wife, Queen Adelaide, and at his death she handed them on to her much loved niece, Queen Victoria. However, during the first year of Queen Victoria's reign, a disagreeable family fight denied her right to many of the jewels she had been given.

The root of the dispute dates back to 1714 when the Stuart line ended with the death of Queen Anne. She was succeeded by her second cousin the Elector of Hanover – King George I. Until 1837 the British kings ruled both Britain and Hanover. King George I and King George II each had divided their time between the two countries and were careful to keep the heirlooms of their two inheritances separate. When King George II died in 1760 he left half his personal collection of jewels to his grandson and heir, King George III, and the other half to his surviving son, William Augustus, Duke of Cumberland. In 1761 the Duke sold his share for £50,000 to King George III, who gave the jewels to his bride, Princess Charlotte of Mecklenburg-Strelitz, as a wedding gift. Queen Charlotte stored these jewels separately from the rest she owned and on her death in 1818 left them to 'the House of Hanover'.

Then came the cause of the dispute. In 1833 the Kingdom of Hanover passed new Salic laws conforming to the Germanic code that excluded women from the succession as long as any male members of the family survived. Therefore when King George III's son King William IV died in 1837 his successor, Queen Victoria, could not succeed to the Throne of Hanover and the two kingdoms were separated for the first time in 123 years. Instead, his brother Ernest Augustus, Duke of Cumberland, became King of Hanover and demanded a portion of the jewels left by King William as part of his inheritance, both as King of Hanover and as a son of Queen Charlotte. His niece Queen Victoria flatly denied the claim, basing her legal defense on the fact that whatever Hanoverian jewels she possessed, arguably those bought by King George III for Queen Charlotte in 1761, had anyway been purchased with English money. The Queen, whose collection of jewellery was equalled if not surpassed by those owned by the Duchesses of Bedford, Buccleuch and Sutherland, insisted on wearing the disputed pieces, not just because she sincerely believed she had the right but because she had few substitutes. King Ernest wrote sarcastically to a friend: 'I hear the little Queen is loaded with my diamonds, which made a very fine show.'

The wrangling continued for years. A Commission was appointed to investigate the matter, but just as it was about to report in 1846 one of its members died and it was disbanded without announcing a decision. The Queen bitterly referred to the dispute as 'the diamond question', and even after King Ernest died in 1851 his son, the blind

King George V, pressed on with the Hanoverian claim. Prince Albert proposed a compromise: let England buy the jewels from Hanover. However, an informal sounding-out of Parliament elicited the response that the Government would neither purchase the jewels nor loan the money to the Queen in order for her to do so. A second Commission was appointed and on 5 December 1857, twenty years after the dispute started, it found in favour of Hanover. In settlement of the claim jewels that included Queen Charlotte's diamond wedding crown, diamond stomacher, and a diamond necklace and cross were delivered to the Hanoverian Ambassador, Count Kielmansegge, on 28 January 1858.

During the sixty-four years of Queen Victoria's reign her collection of jewels probably increased ten-fold, tributes from her ever-expanding empire swelled the numbers and there were numerous gifts from her husband and later from their nine children. Her husband, Prince Albert, was extremely artistic and designed a number of pieces of jewellery for her – as has his great-great-grandson Prince Philip for the present Queen. But despite her magnificent diamonds, sapphires, rubies, pearls and opals, Queen Victoria was just as happy wearing trinkets that had a sentimental meaning.

Among the first of these keepsakes was a bracelet that had her fiancé's portrait as its centrepiece. Queen Victoria was wearing the bracelet on 23 November 1839 when she appeared before eighty-two members of her Privy Council in the Bow Room of Buckingham Palace to read out a Declaration of her impending marriage to Prince Albert of Saxe-Coburg-Gotha. She later confided to Lord Melbourne, her Prime Minister, that wearing Prince Albert's portrait on her wrist had given her the courage to face such an ordeal. She wore his portrait in this manner every day for the rest of her life.

Prince Albert later gave his wife a pair of bracelets on which were mounted miniatures of their nine children. Queen Victoria also wore gold lockets enclosing locks of her children's and grandchildren's hair. Writer Harold Nicolson recorded an extraordinary story that demonstrates the Queen's peculiar affection for her deceased husband. This event happened in Florence around 1887 or 1888:

> 'The façade of the Duomo had been repaired and the new frontage had been revealed. Policemen cleared the way for a little carriage. In it sat an old lady with a companion. It was Queen Victoria. She stopped the carriage, fumbled in her corsage, and drew out a locket which she held up to the façade. It was a miniature of the Prince Consort. She thought it would interest him to see how the Duomo looked after being repaired.'

Queen Victoria never for a minute forgot her position as the Monarch and Mother of the Empire. Although after Prince Albert's death in 1861 she dressed only in black, she wore her black bonnet or widow's cap as imperiously as her crown. She herself said:

> 'Dress is a trifling matter, but it gives also the outward sign from which people in general can, and often do, judge upon the inward state of mind and feeling of a person.'

There were times when Queen Victoria's people wanted to see her as a royal icon. Her children implored her to wear a crown and her velvet and ermine State Robe for the service of thanksgiving in Westminster Abbey for her Golden Jubilee on 21 June 1887. But she refused. Her Future Prime Minister, Lord Rosebery, told her that empires were symbolized by crowns and not by bonnets; Lord Halifax said that the people wanted 'gilding for their money'; Mr Chamberlain thought that a sovereign should be grand; and even one of the royal coachmen 'deplored' her driving to the Abbey 'with a bonnet on'. But a bonnet it was, though trimmed with white point d'Alençon lace and diamond ornaments. Around her neck were ropes of pearls and she wore all her Orders pinned to her Garter Riband.

Ten years later Queen Victoria celebrated her Diamond Jubilee. She was seventy-eight years old and so crippled that a service was held outside St Paul's Cathedral during which the Queen remained seated in her open carriage. This time her bonnet was of black lace trimmed with jet, white acacia flowers, ostrich feathers and a diamond aigrette. Her moiré silk dress had been embroidered with silver roses, shamrocks and thistles, the national symbols of England, Ireland and Scotland. This was the Queen's last major public appearance in England; in April 1900 she made a State visit to Ireland, where she was greeted in Dublin's Phoenix Park by fifty-two thousand children. After this her health gradually declined and she died on 22 January 1901 at Osborne House on the Isle of Wight.

Royal wills are never made public so exactly how Queen Victoria divided her vast private fortune among her descendants cannot be known for certain. However her will included a schedule of jewels that were to be considered 'as belonging to the Crown and to be worn by all future Queens in right of it'. This list included those Hanoverian jewels which Queen Victoria had kept after the resolution of the court case in 1858, the King George IV State Diadem, which now became part of the Crown Regalia, and a number of pieces of jewellery that she had been given by Prince Albert or that they had designed together from stones already in the royal collection. The rest of her jewellery was divided among her children and grandchildren.

Queen Victoria's daughter-in-law, Alexandra, was fifty-seven when she became Queen Consort on the accession of King Edward VII. She had been Princess of Wales for thirty-seven years from 1863 to 1901. She was Queen Consort for nine years from 1901 to 1910 and then Queen Mother from 1910 until her death on 20 November 1925. Queen Alexandra epitomized the popular concept of a queen clothed in a shimmering haze of precious gems. During the day a *sautoir* and small brooch on her collar sufficed, but at night she glittered with jewels. She wore a tiara, a high pearl dog-collar and rows of sparkling diamond chains, while pinned to her low-cut bodice were brooches – stars, crescents, butterflies and flowers – and possibly a stomacher as well. She also wore earrings and a multitude of bracelets over her long white kid gloves.

On State occasions Queen Alexandra appeared to be covered in jewels from the top of her head to the hem of her skirt. When she entered Westminster Abbey for her Coronation on 9 August 1902 one spectator reported that she looked as if she was 'ablaze with light'. Gladys Deacon, the future Duchess of Marlborough, was struck by her relaxed and natural manner, despite her gold net gown, heavy State Robe and the quantity of her jewels.

Queen Alexandra was not oblivious to the effect she created. When Edward became King a grand function was scheduled for the last day of official mourning. Queen Alexandra was asked by her ladies if for this occasion they could exchange their black dresses and jet beads for the pale colours of half-mourning. She refused to give a ruling on the matter, knowing that without her permission her ladies wouldn't dare appear in anything but black. Queen Alexandra then wore white, and sparkled with jewels.

Undoubtedly Queen Alexandra was a remarkably beautiful woman. Prime Minister Herbert Asquith's outspoken wife, Margot, said that 'she always made other women look common'. The words 'divine' and 'dazzling' appear repeatedly in the memoirs of her contemporaries. The American multimillionaire Cornelius Vanderbilt Jr wrote that she 'was known to possess the world's most perfect shoulders and bosom for the display of jewels'. And when the internationally famous painter Philip de Laszlo painted portraits of the Queen and King Edward at Windsor Castle he wrote:

> 'I particularly admired the grace of her movements. Personally I should have liked to have had the
> opportunity of painting her in evening dress, for she had very well constructed shoulders and bust,
> but I had to do the portrait in ordinary day dress, with a high lace collar and pearls.'

Because Queen Victoria retired from society after Prince Albert's death in 1861 her daughter-in-law was very much in the public eye during the many years that she was Princess of Wales. This period also coincided with the appearance of photographs in the national newspapers. Thus even more than Queen Victoria, Queen Alexandra was a familiar figure to people who had never seen her in person.

Queen Victoria had found opulent displays of wealth objectionable and cautioned her children against them, but Queen Alexandra loved her jewels and gowns and King Edward was so proud of his wife's beauty that he enjoyed seeing her wearing his gifts. Queen Alexandra truly personified the glamour of the Edwardian era.

Queen Alexandra's successor, Princess May of Teck, was born at Kensington Palace on 26 May 1867. In 1893 she married Queen Alexandra's second son, the Duke of York. She was Duchess of York until 1901 when she succeeded her mother-in-law as Princess of Wales. In 1910 Princess May's husband became King George V and she became Queen Mary. After King George V's death in 1936 Queen Mary was Queen Mother until her own death on 24 March 1953.

Despite their great fondness for each other, Queen Mary could not have had an easy time of it as Queen Alexandra's daughter-in-law. She spent thirty-two years in the shadow of a woman whose reputation as a great beauty lasted long after her looks had faded, and who was such a possessive mother that at her own insistence her grown-up children still called her 'Motherdear'. Her overwhelming charm made other women seem gauche by comparison. An underlying problem in their relationship was that Princess May of Teck had first been engaged to the eldest son, Albert, Duke of Clarence, and Queen Alexandra had never fully recovered from his sudden death from influenza on 14 January 1892. When her second son, George, was crowned King at Westminster Abbey on 22 June 1911 Queen Alexandra lamented to her lady-in-waiting that this should have been Albert's Coronation day and not George's.

After her marriage Queen Mary soon developed her own unique style of dress that never conformed to the dictates of fashion and so gave her a remarkably timeless quality. Although she seemed tall and imposing this was due more to her perfect posture than to her height, which was 5 feet 6 inches, exactly the same as her husband. She dressed in pale colours, white, cream and her favourite pale blue, so that she could be picked out in a crowd, and her legendary toque hats were chosen to allow people a clear view of her face. According to a lady-in-waiting the line of Queen Mary's neck and shoulders was flawless and her skin pure alabaster. When she was young her hair was a golden honey colour, but because it was very fine she customarily wore a hairpiece – in those days called a 'transformation' – which made it easier and more comfortable to attach a tiara. Queen Mary wore a tiara and evening gown every night for dinner, even if she and the King were dining alone. He wore a tail coat and his Garter Riband.

In Queen Mary's dressing room stood a dressmaker's dummy, made to her exact measurements, and after she had decided what to wear the garment was placed on the dummy while she chose which jewels, hat and gloves to wear with it. She never carried a handbag, but invariably had a parasol to match her dress. Most of her parasols had Fabergé handles. At night she always carried one of her vast collection of valuable jewelled fans. Her evening dresses all had reinforced buckram bodices to bear the weight of her massive jewelled stomachers. It was said of Queen Mary that no other woman in the world could wear jewels as she did. One of her contemporaries wrote in 1936 shortly before King George died:

> 'I now come to Queen Mary... the past twenty-five years she has been one of the handsomest women in Europe. Her quarter of a century on the throne has given her whole personality poise and her manner assurance. I have never known any Empress or Queen who could wear a quantity of superb jewels with such ease and simplicity and without appearing in the least overladen. Queen Alexandra could successively wear a great many jewels, but I have sometimes thought her slight figure a little overborne by them; it is never so with Queen Mary.'

Queen Mary was a royal matriarch in a way that Queen Alexandra never was. In later life she was described as 'stately', 'imposing' and 'other-worldly'. She became more beautiful as she grew older, with her white hair crowning a still youthful complexion. 'Ablaze, regal and overpowering', she epitomized the traditional splendour of the monarchy.

The 1920s and 1930s – the years between the First and Second World Wars – were difficult decades for Britain and the royal family. Yet the King and Queen's unvarying style and way of life established a safe, stable traditional atmosphere that enabled the royal family to withstand every social and political upheaval. Much of this aura of stability was created by Queen Mary, who had reacted against her own very unstable background.

Queen Mary's mother, Princess Mary Adelaide of Cambridge, was a granddaughter of King George III and Queen Victoria's first cousin. Although extremely pretty and sweet-tempered, she was monumental in every sense of the word being tall, very stout – nearly fifteen stone – and with an expansive personality. In 1866 at the age of thirty-two, despite family fears that because of her size she would end up an old maid, she married the German-born Prince Francis of Teck, created Duke of Teck by the King of Württemberg in 1871. He was extremely handsome but because of his parents' morganatic marriage was only a 'Serene Highness' and not a 'Royal Highness'. In the protocol-ridden hierarchy of nineteenth-century royal circles this made their only daughter's marriage prospects a difficult proposition, for Princess May was supposedly not royal enough to find a royal husband and too royal to marry a member of the nobility. It was Queen Victoria who bluntly said this was stuff and nonsense, and Princess

May's youngest brother, Prince Alexander, later married the Queen's granddaughter Princess Alice of Albany.

Despite the undoubted happiness of the Tecks' marriage the Duke was embittered by not being given a proper job to do, and spent his time decorating, gardening and helping his wife who worked indefatigably for numerous worthy causes. The Tecks also had severe money problems. The Duke had a small income, while Princess Mary Adelaide was given £3,000 a year by Parliament and small allowances by both her mother and her brother, the Duke of Cambridge. Queen Victoria provided the couple with two 'grace and favour' residences, an apartment in Kensington Palace and White Lodge, Richmond Park. But the Tecks had expensive tastes; they filled their houses with beautiful furniture and pictures and required a sizable staff to look after them. Princess Mary Adelaide, despite her size, dressed in the height of fashion and loved wearing her fine collection of jewellery, some of which she had inherited from her aunt the Duchess of Gloucester in 1857. The Tecks practised the fine art of brinkmanship, running up large bills and living on credit. The Cambridge family helped them out financially on more than one occasion but in 1883, when Princess May was sixteen, an emergency family conference decided that in exchange for the payment of all their debts the Tecks must give up their residence at Kensington Palace, close up White Lodge, and live abroad observing the strictest economy.

There were tears and arguments but the Cambridges, supported by Queen Victoria, were adamant. The Duke and Duchess of Teck, accompanied by Princess May and her three brothers, went to live in Florence. They had been forced to leave their homes, publicly auction off their furniture from Kensington Palace, retrench in every possible way, but the one thing the strong-willed Princess Mary Adelaide refused to do was to pawn or sell her diamonds.

The hazardous financial insecurity of her youth does a great deal to explain Queen Mary's need for order and her passion for collecting precious jewels and valuable objets d'art. For her they represented a tangible form of independence – she'd never be the poor relation again.

It is due to Queen Mary's careful planning that the royal family's collection of jewellery exists in its present form today. Queen Alexandra died intestate in November 1925. Excluding those pieces which Queen Victoria specifically listed in her will to be worn by future queens, all Queen Alexandra's jewellery had been her personal property. On 9 January 1926 King George and Queen Mary and two of Queen Alexandra's three daughters, Queen Maud of Norway and Princess Victoria of Wales (Princess Louise, the Princess Royal, was at her home in Scotland), assembled at Sandringham House in Norfolk, Queen Alexandra's home since her marriage in 1863, to divide her possessions into four equal shares. The King and Queen specifically included in their share those jewels that in 1863 had been wedding gifts to Queen Alexandra from her husband, the then Prince of Wales, Queen Victoria and civic bodies, as well as the jewellery that Queen Victoria had left to Queen Alexandra as personal bequests in 1901.

Queen Mary had herself received an immense amount of jewellery as wedding gifts in 1893. In 1897 her mother died and she inherited some of her diamonds. In 1901 and 1905 she and her husband, as Princess and Prince of Wales, made long tours of the Empire and received princely tributes. When King Edward VII died in 1910 Queen Alexandra had passed on to Queen Mary the jewels Queen Victoria had left to the Crown. In that year too Queen Mary was given the 102 cleavings of the Cullinan diamond as a gift by the South African Government. Her brother Prince Francis died in October 1910 and she inherited from him their mother's Cambridge emeralds. In 1911 there were magnificent gifts to celebrate King George's Coronation in June, and in December at the Delhi Durbar the King and Queen were given fabulous treasures from the vaults of the Maharajahs. But it was in 1929 that Queen Mary bought some of the most beautiful jewels worn by the royal family today.

It is fair to say that at the beginning of the twentieth century there were no jewellery collections anywhere in the world comparable to those of the many members of the Russian royal family. On public occasions the Romanov women bedecked themselves from head to toe with the most stupendous jewels, which had been handed down from generation to generation. In 1917, the year of the Russian Revolution, the imperial jewel collection and some fifteen million pounds in gold were stored in Moscow's Imperial Bank. At 2 am on the night of 6 November a truckload of Bolshevik Red Guards surrounded the building and their commander told the head of security that his men were taking control of the imperial treasure in the 'name of the people'. There was no resistance and within minutes it was all over. In 1927 the Soviet Government was so short of foreign currency and essential supplies that they offered some of these royal treasures for sale through Christie's, and a large number of jewels and Fabergé ornaments ended up in the hands of rich foreigners, many of them Americans.

The Tsar's mother, the Dowager Empress Marie Feodorovna, was formerly Princess Dagmar, daughter of King Christian IX of Denmark and younger sister of Queen Alexandra of England. In November 1866 she married the immensely tall Tsarevitch, later Tsar Alexander III, and they had five children. Although never considered as great a beauty as her sister, Alexandra, the dark-eyed Empress was extremely attractive and captivated people with her sense of humour and charismatic personality.

Empress Marie Feodorovna had originally been engaged to the elder brother, Nicholas, but when he died she married Alexander instead. She loved parties, clothes, jewellery – her husband was furious with her when the bills poured in – and all the public adulation that her position gave her. Her husband died in November 1894 when she was only forty-seven and was succeeded by their eldest son, Nicholas. She never had an easy relationship with her daughter-in-law, the Empress Alexandra, who was one of Queen Victoria's Hessian granddaughters. By the time the Great War began in 1914 she and the rest of the royal family were virtually estranged from Nicholas and Alexandra, a rift caused by the monk Rasputin's influence over the imperial couple because of their only son's haemophilia.

On 15 March 1917 the Provisional Government forced Tsar Nicholas's abdication. The Dowager Empress insisted on remaining at her palace in the Crimea for the next two years under the protection of the White Army, which remained loyal to the monarch. The civil war raged until the spring of 1919 when there could no longer be any doubt that the Bolsheviks would triumph. In July 1918 news began to filter out of Russia that the Tsar and his family had been slaughtered at Ekaterinburg. Although the Empress claimed until her dying day that they had in fact secretly escaped, King George V now insisted that she leave Russia, which she did aboard the British warship HMS *Marlborough* in April 1919.

When she arrived in England, she stayed with Queen Alexandra at Marlborough House in London, and was reunited with her two married daughters, the Grand Duchesses Xenia and Olga, both of whom had also managed to escape with their husbands and children. But England was not home and in 1920 the Empress decided to return to her native Denmark, accepting an invitation from her nephew King Christian X to move into one wing of the Amalienborg Palace in Copenhagen.

There can be no question that the seventy-three-year-old Empress was a difficult woman to deal with. For fifty years, from her marriage until the Russian Revolution, she had led a life of unparalleled luxury and power. She was mourning the deaths of numerous relatives, friends and staff. The bitterest pill of all was that so much of this devastating debacle could be laid at the feet of her son and daughter-in-law.

Though a refugee the Empress was not penniless or dependent on the charity of others. She had brought with her valuable objets d'art and a large leather case filled with her jewels. Her Danish nephew was pleased that she was returning to Denmark. Xenia's estranged husband, her son-in-law the Grand Duke Alexander, had a plan for her to open a paper factory in France so that all the exiled Romanovs could derive a decent income from it. The Empress's nephew King George V assured his 'dear Aunt Minnie' that if she needed any help in managing her affairs his own advisors would be only too happy to be of assistance and his private secretary, Sir Frederick Ponsonby, arranged for Captain Andrup of the Danish Navy to look after her finances.

Everyone was full of suggestions for the future because it was taken for granted that Empress Marie Feodorovna would sell her jewels as required and there would be enough money for everyone. But they didn't take into account the Empress's own plans. She would live in Denmark, but as her nephew's guest; she would support her daughters, but in return they must act as her companions; and the one thing she certainly would not do was sell any of her jewels.

Life in Denmark was fraught with domestic strife: the Empress and King Christian fought incessantly, he appalled by her extravagance, she affronted by his complaints. On one occasion he sent a footman across the courtyard to her drawing room with a request that she should turn off the lights as the latest electricity bill had been excessive. Speechless with fury, she summoned her own footman and ordered him to turn on every light in her wing of the palace. The Grand Duchess Xenia found the atmosphere so disagreeable that she moved first to Paris and then to England where King George gave her Frogmore Cottage in Windsor Great Park and a pension of £2,400. King

George also provided the Empress with an annual pension of £30,000, and the Grand Duchess Olga and her family lived with her.

King Christian constantly nagged the Empress to sell some of her jewels so that she could reimburse the money he was expending on her behalf. To avoid his lectures she occasionally escaped to Hvidøre, the small seaside summer villa that she and Queen Alexandra had bought years earlier, but after her sister died in November 1925 the Empress aged rapidly and rarely left Copenhagen.

During the last months of her life the Empress was completely bedridden and clung to her leather box of jewels – all that remained of her former life. As her eyesight failed she had the case moved closer and closer to her bed, obsessed with the idea that everyone was trying to take her jewels from her. Her two daughters stayed by her side. She was in a coma for the last three days and death came as a merciful release on 13 October 1928. She was eighty-one years old.

All the while the Empress was so gravely ill, the jewels became a ticking time bomb. The Empress had assured her daughters that after she was gone the jewels would be divided between them to secure their financial futures. But King Christian claimed a share to reimburse him for his aunt's upkeep, and other of her Romanov relatives felt that she also had an obligation to provide for them. There were even rumours that the Soviet Government would claim the jewels as State property, not to mention gossip that international jewel thieves were just waiting to make their move.

Since 1919 Sir Frederick Ponsonby, Keeper of the Privy Purse, had been intimately concerned with sorting out the problems besetting the Russian royal family. They had never in their lives had to worry about money or business affairs and were thoroughly incapable of dealing with either. The Grand Duchess Xenia had already lost most of her own jewellery collection to a con man who had taken them to sell on consignment and then promptly disappeared.

Peter Bark, an anglicized Russian, had been the last Imperial Finance Minister, from 1914 to 1917. Bark was trusted by the two Grand Duchesses and agreed to look after their affairs. When word of the Empress's approaching demise reached London Sir Frederick and the King discussed how best to protect the Grand Duchesses' interests. It was agreed that Bark should act as an intermediary and he left for Copenhagen taking with him a letter from King George to the Grand Duchesses suggesting that after the death of their mother the jewels be brought by diplomatic courier to London, where they could be safely stored in a bank vault until they decided how to dispose of them. He also suggested that Bark be appointed trustee of the Empress's estate.

Once in Denmark Bark ascertained that none of the interested parties would make their move until after the Empress's funeral. Going to see Olga and Xenia at the Amalienborg Palace he convinced them that there was no time to be lost in getting their mother's jewels out of the country and back to England. The jewels were packed up in a stout box and carefully sealed. A courier from the British Legation immediately travelled to London and delivered the box to Sir Frederick Ponsonby who deposited it in the basement strongroom at Buckingham Palace. In 1929 Peter Bark was given a Knighthood in recognition of his efforts.

Shortly after all this cloak and dagger manoeuvring King George became seriously ill and was unable to deal with anything for some months. So when the Grand Duchesses themselves arrived in England Queen Mary said she would loan them any money they needed until the jewels could be sold.

In February 1929 Mr Hardy from Hennell & Sons, London jewellers who had had a long association with the royal family, was asked to make a complete inventory of the jewels and then to sell them in as discreet a manner as possible. One reason for this secrecy was that so many Russian jewels had come on to the market in the decade following the Revolution that they were often sold for sums well below their true value. Before the box was opened Queen Mary accompanied the Grand Duchess Xenia to verify that the seals were untouched since she had last seen them in Copenhagen the previous October. Sir Frederick Ponsonby described what he saw when the box was opened:

> 'Ropes of the most wonderful pearls were taken out, all graduated, the largest being the size of a big cherry. Cabochon emeralds and large rubies and sapphires were laid out.'

After Mr Hardy had appraised the jewels the Grand Duchesses each selected some to keep and then the rest were sold. Queen Mary bought a number of them herself which are today still worn by her descendants. The proceeds from the sale supposedly amounted to £350,000, but the Grand Duchess Olga always claimed that she never received her fair share. However Sir Frederick wrote in his memoirs that King George V saw that the money, minus expenses, was deposited in a trust fund for the benefit of his two cousins, and there is no reason not to believe his account.

By 1930 Queen Mary had amassed a greater collection of priceless jewellery than any previous Queen of England. For the marriages of her children – her daughter, Princess Mary, the Princess Royal, in 1922, the Duke of York in 1923, the Duke of Kent in 1934 and the Duke of Gloucester in 1935 – she assembled parures of jewels from her collection for each bride so that today each line of her descendants owns jewellery going directly back to their Hanoverian forbears.

She rewrote her own will after her husband's death, King George V, in January 1936, after the abdication of her son King Edward VIII in December 1936 and, lastly, after the death of her second son, King George VI, in February 1952. I believe that when she died the list of jewels she left to the present Queen, her granddaughter, probably established which jewellery will continue to be the property of the future Queens of the United Kingdom. There is no law governing this matter but Queen Victoria and Queen Mary both made very clear which jewels they wished to belong to the monarch.

King George VI succeeded his brother King Edward VIII in December 1936 and his consort, Queen Elizabeth, took over the jewels that Queen Victoria had stipulated should be worn by all future queens, and chose from all the jewels in storage any other pieces that she herself wanted to wear. Queen Mary's own jewels were her personal property so she kept them until her death in 1953. Queen Elizabeth selected from jewels that had formerly belonged to Queen Victoria and Queen Alexandra – some of which were the same ones that King George and Queen Mary had chosen as their share when Queen Alexandra died in 1925. So the informal family system was working: by convention certain jewels were worn by the Queen, while others remained a queen's personal property to be bequeathed in any way she desired.

The new Queen had been Lady Elizabeth Bowes-Lyon until her marriage in 1923 to the Duke of York. She was Duchess of York until her husband's accession in 1936 when she became Queen Consort. Since King George VI's death on 6 February 1952 she has been known as Queen Elizabeth the Queen Mother.

For six years out of the fifteen that her husband reigned Britain was at war, fighting for its very survival. The post-war years were almost as grim as the country slowly recovered. Queen Elizabeth was a very different personality from her mother-in-law. In many ways one might describe her as theatrical, although she says it is untrue that she refers to her clothes and jewels as 'my props'. It is rare to see her without either a hat or a tiara, depending on the time of day. She moves slowly, with little gliding steps, and as she passes a crowd of people everyone there is certain that they've received a very special look from her bright blue eyes. As she stops to speak to someone she'll often touch her necklace or pat her hair, beguiling intimate little gestures.

The Duchess of York had to develop her own style when she unexpectedly became Queen. She felt that she was not photogenic and it is true that photographs rarely do her justice. But she was helped by an inspiration of her husband's. Norman Hartnell had been chosen to make the Queen's clothes for the royal couple's first State visit which was to Paris. When Mr Hartnell came to Buckingham Palace the King took him to see Winterhalter's romantic portraits of royal ladies. 'This might suit the Queen don't you think', was the King's soft suggestion. The idea was planted. Hartnell designed magical nineteenth-century ballgowns with enormous embroidered crinoline skirts and flatteringly low necklines, perfect for displaying regal jewels. Queen Elizabeth's new style was to captivate the world for half a century.

The King and Queen visited Canada and the United States for the first time in 1939 and stayed at the White House as the guests of President and Mrs Roosevelt. Harry Hopkins was a special adviser and personal assistant to the President. He had an eight-year-old daughter who had been bitterly disappointed to see the royal couple arrive dressed in ordinary clothes. This was mentioned to Queen Elizabeth who suggested that if the child waited in the hall as they left to host a dinner at the British Embassy the situation might be rectified. Mrs Roosevelt was with the King and Queen as they descended the graceful curved staircase and came through an oval archway into the main hall. The Queen was wearing a shimmering, billowing ballgown with the blue Riband of the Order of the Garter, Queen

Victoria's diamond collet necklace and earrings and the Hanoverian fringe tiara sparkling in the light from the massive chandeliers. The little girl curtsied to the Queen, spellbound, ignoring the King completely. The royal couple paused to talk to her and as they moved out to the waiting cars she turned to her father and said: 'Oh, Daddy, Daddy! I have seen the Fairy Queen.' It's a story that well illustrates Queen Elizabeth's appeal. Later that same year at the Opening of Parliament on 28 November she wore trailing black velvet, furs and pearls, and the MP Sir Henry 'Chips' Channon commented: 'I have never seen her so regal and beautiful. She was dressed to perfection. Everyone remarked on it.'

When Queen Elizabeth was young, she liked jewelled clips on her cloche hats, brooches pinned to her pochette handbags, long pendant earrings and ropes of pearls. Today she wears large hats, usually trimmed with veils and feathers and her clothes are of floating fabrics; at night her handbag matches her gown. Everything is soft and sumptuous. But Queen Elizabeth never had the passion for jewels that Queen Mary did. Instead she enjoys collecting pictures and Chelsea china, and has gained much pleasure from buying and restoring the derelict castle of Mey.

Queen Elizabeth the Queen Mother now wears the same few pieces of jewellery constantly – a brooch of Queen Victoria's, a necklace of Queen Alexandra's, the diamond brooch that was one of her husband's wedding gifts in 1923.

Her daughter the present Queen is very like her. She wears the same family jewels repeatedly because she is fond of them and because they have a sentimental connection. But one has the impression that if she were awakened by a fire in the middle of the night the only thing the Queen would rush to save is the diamond engagement ring Prince Philip designed for her forty years ago.

There has been endless speculation about the value of the Queen's jewels but this is incalculable; because of their unique provenance they are literally priceless. Although there are a number of widely varying estimates as to the extent of the collection, there is no complete inventory, either official or unofficial. But my own research shows that the Queen owns, or has worn – and these are not quite the same thing as some pieces have never been worn, while others were loaned to her when she was young by Queen Elizabeth the Queen Mother – fourteen tiaras, thirty-four pairs of earrings, ninety-eight brooches, forty-six necklaces, thirty-seven bracelets, five pendants, fourteen watches and fifteen rings.

Until 1947 the Queen, then Princess Elizabeth, owned only two pearl necklaces, half-a-dozen brooches, one pair of pearl and diamond earrings, a few wrist watches and a sapphire bracelet. But on 21 April 1947 she became twenty-one and among her gifts were diamond earrings, a necklace, a pair of clips and a floral spray brooch. On her marriage to Prince Philip that November her grandmother Queen Mary gave her nine pieces of jewellery including her first tiara. There was more jewellery from King George and Queen Elizabeth, from Prince Philip, from his mother, Princess Andrew of Greece, and from various dignitaries and organizations.

Princess Elizabeth received further gifts of jewellery as she fulfilled an increasing number of public engagements and when she succeeded her father, King George VI, on 6 February 1952 she became the custodian of the jewels left to the Crown by Queen Victoria in 1901. On 24 March 1953, ten weeks before the Queen's Coronation, Queen Mary died, the only Queen in British history to have seen a granddaughter become Queen. She left the new Queen a unique bequest of several dozen pieces of jewellery, chosen for their historic connection with the monarchy.

In every royal home there are reinforced strong rooms where precious objects and jewellery can be stored. The vault at Buckingham Palace is deep underground in an old air-raid shelter and is wired up to the Palace police station. There is a safe in each of the Queen's dressing rooms in her different homes. These are under the jurisdiction of her dresser – as a royal lady's maid is called – Miss Margaret 'Bobo' MacDonald, who has been looking after the Queen since 1926. This security is in great contrast to Queen Alexandra's day, when the Queen's jewellery was kept on display in glass cases in her dressing room.

Many of the present Queen's jewels are kept in their original flat cases, the leather scratched with age, the velvet scruffy and discoloured. Some have the original gift card still nestled inside the lid. A number of her brooches are stored in one case in which there is a tray for each type of stone – diamonds, emeralds, sapphires. This case sounds rather grand until one remembers the Nizam of Hyderabad who had a blue safe for his sapphires, a red safe for his rubies, and a green safe for his emeralds. There are also special domed leather cases for the tiaras, lined with satin or velvet. When the Queen travels, whether it be to Sandringham or Balmoral or on a State visit abroad, her jewellery is packed into a special leather case protected by a canvas cover. During the journey this case is the responsibility of her personal footman who delivers it back to the dresser once their destination is reached.

On the Coronation tour of the Commonwealth in 1953-4, the Queen was on the New Zealand leg of her trip when her jewels disappeared. She had already left for Wellington when it was discovered that the case was missing. Finally someone suggested that it might inadvertently have been taken with the rest of the luggage. By the time her staff arrived at the airport the baggage aeroplane was already airborne. When they arrived in Wellington the luggage was on its way to Government House. One can only imagine their feelings when they finally reached the residence to find that the case had indeed travelled unguarded with the hundreds of other suitcases belonging to the royal household and was there waiting for them.

It may seem surprising that a woman with such a stupendous collection of jewels is given still more, but when the Queen launches a ship, opens a factory or makes a State visit the event is often marked by the presentation of a valuable piece of jewellery. It is quite in order for members of the royal family to receive such gifts, which become their private property. However a company is not supposed to present its own products to the Queen or any other members of the royal family as a means of gaining publicity. Over the years the Queen has been given numerous jewelled badges by charities of which she is patron or by the many regiments of which she is colonel-in-chief. Prince Charles supposedly owns an enormous collection of presentation gold boxes, and Queen Mary once remarked that she had more than four hundred gold and silver keys that had been given to her at official occasions of one kind or another.

Some gifts are accepted on behalf of the Crown and are considered State property, such as the Koh-I-Noor diamond, given to Queen Victoria in 1850, the Cullinan diamond, presented to King Edward VII in 1907, and the 'Ladies of India' emerald necklace, which was made for Queen Mary in 1911. But all other gifts are considered to be personal. Any gift, whether given on a State visit or presented by a group such as the Girl Guides, is carefully catalogued by one of the Queen's ladies-in-waiting so that it can be produced on the next occasion that the Queen visits that country or organization. For the Queen is well aware of how much pleasure it gives people to see her wearing their gifts.

The exchange of gifts is an important part of every State visit. The Queen's own gifts vary according to the taste of the recipient and are carefully chosen to suit her host or guest of honor. Other gifts she bestows during a visit are similar to those her great-grandmother Queen Alexandra gave a hundred years ago – signed photographs in silver or leather frames, cuff links, wallets, silver boxes, brooches or powder compacts. They all bear the Queen's cypher, ER II, and are given to everyone who has looked after her or made the arrangements for the visit in strictly hierarchical order. The other members of the royal family give similar gifts embossed with their own cyphers.

Were she a private citizen the Queen would wear her pearl button earrings, three-strand pearl necklace and a shoulder brooch and be thoroughly content. But her public role often requires her to wear a glittering tiara, precious jewels, ornate robes and lavish gold braid. Many of us carry within ourselves the concept of royalty as a graven image and we don't really want to see the Queen dressed in ordinary attire. Even today it is rare for the Queen to make a public appearance without some small child plaintively asking, 'Why isn't she wearing her crown?'

Children write letters to the Queen asking if her crown is comfortable, if it is easy to take off, if she wears it in bed and how many jewels are set in it? If she arrives slightly late for a public engagement they understand perfectly because it must 'take her some time putting her crown on properly'. They worry terribly that it might be too heavy for her to wear when she comes to visit their school. Even on the Queen's 1986 historic visit to China, the world's largest egalitarian society, the children waiting to greet her in Peking knew that if she was a queen she would of course be wearing a crown. They were greatly disappointed when her elegant red coat was topped by a matching red straw hat.

A monarch's special status is somehow implicit in his or her manner of dress. Although the Queen goes among us dressed in ordinary clothes, on public occasions she always wears a hat, the substitute for a crown. Covering the head is a sign of authority and formality. When everyone else is bareheaded a covered head is the focus of attention and represents leadership.

Jewels are an important part of the royal image. The traditional picture of a British queen is of a woman in a heavily embroidered full-length evening gown, with a sparkling tiara and wearing the blue Garter Riband from left shoulder to right hip. The Queen assiduously avoids being ostentatious but she knows people love to see her richly jewelled and it gives her pleasure to fulfil their expectations. During her first tour of the Commonwealth after her Coronation in 1953 on ceremonial occasions she wore her Coronation gown, weighing thirty pounds, however great the heat, because she knew how much it would please people to see it.

A king must be seen to be king. On State occasions the Queen has a duty to be regal, for these events are part of the national heritage and there is splendour and glory in their observance. The royal jewels are beyond fashion. The Queen is not a movie star, an image that horrifies her, but for ceremonial events her appearance is inevitably theatrical. Pageantry is an indispensable part of royalty; one of the joys of monarchy is the spectacle we associate with it. Even at the end of the twentieth century the majesty of the Queen's office and high estate is as palpable as it was in her namesake Queen Elizabeth I's more flamboyant time.

# Amethysts

AMETHYSTS WERE A FAVOURITE STONE of the Queen's great-grandmother, Queen Alexandra, who often wore them after the death of her eldest son, Duke of Clarence, in January 1892. She was usually seen in the pastel colours of half-mourning – lilac, mauve, lavender, grey and violet – whose misty shades were the perfect background for amethysts as well as for her swags of pearls and diamonds.

Amethysts are one of the four most desirable coloured gemstones in the world, and, at their most valuable, are a rich purple colour. Muted tones seem to typify the Edwardian era, but it was the Victorians, with their strict social conventions, who made the amethyst popular. During the first six months of mourning only jet and onyx jewellery could be worn, but amethysts were permissible during the next three months of half-mourning. The birthstone for February, amethysts were said to represent sincerity and sobriety.

The Queen owns another amethyst necklace in addition to the Kent demi-parure (page 22), but appears to have no special affection for the stone, as she has worn the Kent suite only twice in public and the second necklace never. This necklace was a wedding gift from Queen Alexandra to Queen Elizabeth the Queen Mother in 1923 and was given to the Queen after her marriage. Shortened and redesigned since 1923, the necklace now consists of three rows of small pearls interspersed with eight large oval amethysts, each surrounded by brilliant-cut diamonds. Hanging from the front largest cluster is a heart-shaped amethyst pendant surrounded by brilliants, and from the four side clusters hang oval amethyst drops surrounded by brilliants.

The Queen's other amethysts are set in a brooch presented to her in October 1960 when she opened the Queen's Bridge at Perth in Scotland. The brooch is a miniature flower bouquet with seven amethyst buds surrounded by white and yellow gold ferns and grasses, with a central group of twelve freshwater mauve-tinted pearls from the River Tay.

# Aquamarines

ONE OF THE QUEEN'S most magnificent parures is fascinating not just because it is her only completely modern suite of jewels, or because the jewels are so well matched that it took more than a decade to collect them, but because the evolution of the complete parure also reflects the Queen's own changing taste.

In 1953 the President and people of Brazil presented the Queen with a Coronation gift of a necklace and matching pendant earrings of aquamarines and diamonds. It had taken an entire year to collect the perfectly matched stones. The necklace had nine large oblong aquamarines each in a diamond scroll setting with an even bigger oblong aquamarine pendant drop. The simple diamond setting of the pendant was echoed by the pendant aquamarine earrings. The Queen has since had the pendant drop reset in a more ornate diamond cluster and it is now detachable from the necklace. Her Majesty was so delighted with the set that in 1957 she had a relatively simple tiara made to wear with it. This was a diamond and aquamarine bandeau surmounted by three vertically set oblong aquamarines. In August 1958 the Brazilian Government added to their original gift with a bracelet of seven large oblong aquamarines set in clusters of small diamonds. There was also a brooch to match the original setting of the pendant, a single large square aquamarine in a simple diamond setting.

In 1968 the Queen and Prince Philip made their first State visit to Brazil and the Governor of São Paulo presented the Queen with a V-shaped 'hair ornament', as it was described at the time, also made of aquamarines and diamonds. In 1971 the stones from this were used to make four scroll-shaped motifs for the tiara, positioned around the three upright oblongs; a collet aquamarine was placed on the tip of each of the seven vertical ornaments. The Queen wore the Brazilian parure when she gave an official dinner aboard *Britannia* during her 1986 State visit to China; her pale blue lace evening dress was a perfect foil for the aquamarines.

Other aquamarines in Her Majesty's collection include a second brooch, a large square aquamarine set in two curved diamond branches; a square aquamarine ring with diamond shoulders; and two bracelets, one a 1950s design of a double row of small square aquamarines separated by pavé-set diamond bars, and the second of diamonds surrounding four round aquamarines.

Another member of the royal family to wear aquamarines was Queen Elizabeth the Queen Mother. In the 1930s she had a pair of curved diamond and aquamarine clips. She was wearing these in 1935 when she brought her two daughters to Norman Hartnell's salon in Bruton Street to have a fitting for their bridesmaid's dresses for the marriage of Princess Alice, Duchess of Gloucester. In the 1950s she wore an aquamarine and diamond tiara that had pine-flower scroll motifs separated by single oblong-cut aquamarines, mounted on an aquamarine and diamond band. Queen Elizabeth the Queen Mother gave this to Princess Anne as a wedding gift in 1973 when she married Captain Mark Phillips. The Queen had a pair of aquamarine and diamond pine-flower cluster earrings made to match as one of her gifts to her daughter.

# THE KENT DEMI-PARURE

The Kent demi-parure is the oldest set of jewellery in the royal collection, and was owned by Queen Victoria's mother, the Duchess of Kent, who, as the widowed Princess of Leiningen, had married King George III's fourth son in 1817. When she died at Frogmore on 16 March 1861, aged seventy-five, she left all her property to the Queen, and Prince Albert was named sole executor of her estate. In the nineteenth century amethysts were very popular and as a result quite valuable, and in her 1901 will Queen Victoria left these jewels to the Crown. The set consisted of a necklace, three brooches, a pair of earrings and a pair of hair combs.

ABOVE, LEFT: *In this engraving after the 1839 miniature by Sir William Ross, the Duchess of Kent wears only the brooch.*

ABOVE, RIGHT: *Queen Elizabeth also wore only the brooch as she, the King and the two Princesses looked over the itinerary for the royal couple's forthcoming visit to the United States and Canada in 1939.*

RIGHT: *The Queen wearing the demi-parure on her State visit to Portugal in 1984. The central pendant with its small diamond drop matches the earrings, and the sunray design of diamonds surrounding the two side stones in the necklace is the same as that around the brooch.*

# THE QUEEN'S CARTIER CLIPS

ABOVE: *The idea of clip brooches came to French jeweller Louis Cartier*
*as he idly watched a peasant woman hanging out her washing*
*with wooden clothes pegs, and he popularized his idea in the 1930s by*
*designing brooches so that they could be worn as a single brooch*
*or as two matching clips. These aquamarine and diamond clips were*
*given to the Queen in 1944 by her parents as an eighteenth-*
*birthday present, and are a typically 1940s design, combining baguette,*
*oval and round stones.* ABOVE, RIGHT: *In 1958 the Queen wore*
*them as separate clips.* RIGHT: *In 1965, as she and Prince Philip*
*attended Royal Ascot, the Queen wore them as a brooch. The*
*Royal Meeting at Ascot, a racecourse founded by Queen Anne in 1711*
*on land close to Windsor Castle, is held annually in the third*
*week of June. The Ascot racecourse still belongs to the Monarch.*

# Coral

CORAL BECAME FASHIONABLE in England in the early 1800s. It was mostly imported from Naples, and British jewellers carved it into berries, flowers and leaves and used it for the most extravagant suites of jewellery. A string of coral beads became a popular christening gift for girls; the future Queen Victoria was painted in 1831 at the age of twelve wearing a white muslin frock and coral necklace, according to her governess, Baroness Lehzen.

There was a tradition in Scotland that coral brought beauty and prosperity to little girls. Queen Elizabeth the Queen Mother, youngest daughter of the Earl and Countess of Strathmore, was given her beads as a child, and continuing the tradition she passed them on to her first-born daughter.

Most recently, the Princess of Wales wore a string of coral beads on her honeymoon in 1981, and the present Duke of Gloucester designed a wide ring of silver and coral for the Duchess, which she wore before their marriage.

# THE QUEEN'S FIRST NECKLACE

As a nine-month-old baby in December 1926, Princess Elizabeth's jewellery collection was started in the same unostentatious manner as that of any other daughter of the aristocracy. Not for the royal family a gaudy display of nouveau-riche wealth with strings of diamonds or sparkling clips from fashionable Bond Street jewellers. Instead, the first-born child of the young Duke and Duchess of York was given a delicate string of her mother's own childhood pink coral beads just before her parents had to leave her behind for six months while they represented King George V on a goodwill tour of Australia and New Zealand.

After they sailed in HMS Renown, the baby Princess often stayed with her grandparents, and Queen Mary, knowing how painful it was for her son and daughter-in-law to miss their daughter's first tooth, step and words, had photographs taken of her every month and sent out to them. The Princess wore her coral necklace for these and in most of her childhood pictures until 1940. ABOVE: Queen Elizabeth the Queen Mother, aged two, in August 1902, wearing her coral bead necklace. ABOVE, RIGHT: The Queen in 1927. Pearls have been added to the coral beads, and she plays with an ivory-handled rattle given her by Queen Mary. RIGHT: Princess Anne photographed with her mother to mark her first birthday in 1951. She is not only wearing the same necklace and playing with the same rattle, but the picture was taken by the same photographer, Marcus Adams.

# Diamonds

THE MOST TANTALIZING QUESTION about diamonds – and one for which there is no single answer – is why should something that in its natural state looks like a dull glass pebble and is technically no more than a crystal formed out of carbon, the hardest substance on earth, have had such a magical power to inspire the minds of men for more than two thousand years?

Diamonds are 140 times harder than rubies or sapphires and 180 times harder than emeralds. To this day they are weighed in carats, a system that dates back to ancient times, when dealers used the seeds of the carob tree as weights for their scales because they were all uniform.

The word 'diamond' derives from the Greek *adamas*, meaning unconquerable, and the ancients regarded diamonds with awe, investing them with mystical properties. Early superstitions held that diamonds were splinters of stars fallen to earth or that they were hardened dewdrops formed during a rare conjunction of the planets at dawn. The Greeks believed that the fire in the heart of the stones reflected the constant flame of love; they were also treasured as talismans that would guard against poison, intrigues, lunacy and the spells of witches. Warriors wore diamonds trusting that their hardness would give them courage and protection in battle while maidens believed that the diamond's purity symbolized their own virtue. The realization that every diamond in the world was unique only added to their magical appeal.

Diamonds were first found in India in about 600 BC, the greatest mines being discovered at Golconda in Hyderabad. Their scarcity gave them great value and for many centuries only kings and the nobility were allowed to wear them, their possession being seen as a sign of wealth and position. For fifteen hundred years diamond trading was restricted to regions of the Far East and the Mediterranean, but during the Crusades as Christian rulers returned home to Europe after fighting the Saracens in the Holy Land, European trading routes were established via Venice and the demand for diamonds increased. The gems available were often large but crudely cut as it was not until the end of the fifteenth century that lapidaries discovered the art of symmetrical faceting which brought out the diamond's full beauty. Once the Portuguese explorer Vasco da Gama had opened a direct sea route between Europe and the Indian subcontinent in 1498 Antwerp became the centre of the diamond-processing industry.

Historically diamonds had been reserved primarily for male adornment, and it was only in 1477 when the Archduke Maximilian of Austria gave a gold ring set with a large diamond as a betrothal gift to Princess Mary of Burgundy that the tradition began of exchanging diamonds as tokens of eternal love.

The diamond deposits in India were nearly depleted when new sources were accidentally discovered in 1725 by gold-miners in Brazil. The increased flow of stones and ever-improving cutting methods made diamonds even more popular. The greatest of the gems were still the prerogative of kings but smaller stones were now available to anyone who could afford them.

During the nineteenth century English taste in jewellery underwent a number of changes. By the 1860s as Victorian designs both in clothing and interior decoration became more florid, coloured gems and semiprecious stones such as amethysts, coral and turquoises were much used by jewellers who displayed them to advantage in diamond settings. So many new fortunes were made during the Industrial Revolution that rich men draped their wives with diamonds as a way of proclaiming their success and prosperity. The one blot on the horizon was the overworking of the Brazilian mines which caused a shortage of stones and so pushed prices to record levels.

Then came the discovery of the first South African diamond, appropriately called the 'Eureka'. It was found near Kimberley in 1867 by a boy named Erasmus Jacobs, and soon the Great Diamond Rush brought fortune-hunters flocking. The opening of what became the greatest mines in the world and the subsequent increased number of stones available made diamonds accessible to a whole new market. Ironically by the 1880s the brilliant glare of the new electric light was making coloured stones look too garish for refined taste. By 1886 the sale of diamonds in Birmingham, for instance, was twenty times greater than it had been in 1865. By the 1890s coloured stones had virtually gone out of fashion but the start of the Boer War in 1899 cut off the supply of diamonds to Europe and jewellers desperately tried peridots, topazes, tourmalines and zircons in their search for substitutes.

When eighteen-year-old Queen Victoria acceded to the throne on 20 June 1837 she inherited the Hanoverian treasure-trove of jewels, which comprised a number of fine diamonds, many of which had been reset by King William IV between 1830 and 1837. At her wedding, on 10 February 1840, in place of a crown or tiara she wore a simple wreath of orange blossoms with 'a very few diamonds studded into her hair behind, in which was fastened her veil of Honiton lace'. She also wore what she referred to in her diary as 'my Turkish diamond necklace and earrings', a personal gift from the Sultan of Turkey and which she did not consider to be part of the royal collection. At her death in 1901 she left the necklace to her third son, Arthur, Duke of Connaught, the infant in the Winterhalter painting (page 41) and the present Queen's godfather.

Queen Victoria credited Prince Albert with assembling her various pieces of jewellery into impressive matching parures and redesigning some old-fashioned ornaments to make them more wearable. She loved heavy pendant earrings, especially the girandole style such as the Queen wears today (page 56), necklaces with pendant drops, clusters of different brooches and rings on every finger. Until Prince Albert died in 1861 she often wore King George IV's diamond diadem at grand functions (page 163), and in 1858 she had the magnificent new diamond collet necklace and earrings made (page 54). In the most endearingly feminine manner she often chose the colour pink for her evening gowns because, as she confessed, it showed off her diamonds so splendidly.

In 1850 Queen Victoria was presented with the Koh-I-Noor diamond by Lord Dalhousie on behalf of the East India Company at a levee to commemorate the 250th anniversary of its founding by Queen Elizabeth I. A new diamond diadem was designed in 1853 to display the jewel. Until the Cullinan was discovered in 1905 the Koh-I-Noor was the largest known diamond in the world and it had an extraordinary provenance. Supposedly from the Golconda mine in Hyderabad, it had probably been discovered many centuries before the first record of it in 1112, when it was reported to have weighed 793 carats in the rough. It belonged to the Indian Rajah of Malwa's family for many generations until in 1304 it came into the possession of Sultan Ala-ed-din. In 1526 the Sultan Baber, first of the Mogul emperors, defeated the Rajah of Gwalior in battle and gained all his treasures, among which was the Koh-I-Noor. He had it cut in 1530 to 186 carats. The stone, along with many other precious gems, was inherited by each succeeding Mogul emperor, including Shah Jahan who built the Taj Mahal to honour his deceased wife, Mumtaz Mahal.

When North-West India was conquered by the Persian Nadir Shah in 1730 all the jewels and valuables in the treasury were seized, but the most valuable, the Koh-I-Noor, had disappeared. Delhi was pillaged and burned but still Mohammed Shah, the last Mogul emperor, claimed to know nothing of the gem's whereabouts. He was finally betrayed by one of the concubines in his harem, who reported to Nadir Shah that the Emperor always kept the diamond hidden in his turban. The devious Nadir Shah announced that he was returning home and held a great farewell banquet, during which he restored Mohammed Shah to his throne. He then suggested that as a gesture of reconciliation and friendship the Emperor and he should exchange their national headdresses. The Emperor could do nothing but agree and handed Nadir Shah his simple linen turban in what seemed an unequal trade for a richly jewelled Persian headdress. When Nadir Shah was alone in his tent he swiftly unwound the turban and found the stone. 'Koh-I-Noor', he exclaimed (which means 'mountain of light'), and from then on the stone was always known by that name.

The superstition that the stone brings bad luck to any male owner and can only be worn safely by a woman dates from this time, for as it was passed from man to man its history became a saga of murder and bloodshed. Nadir Shah was assassinated by a member of his bodyguard in 1747; his son, Rukh Shah, was deposed in a rebellion; his successor, Ahmed Shah, who founded the Durani Afghan dynasty, died and the Koh-I-Noor was inherited first by his eldest son, Timur Shah, and then by his grandson, Zaman Shah. Zaman was soon imprisoned and blinded by his brother, Shuja Shah, but he managed to hide the Koh-I-Noor in the mud walls of his cell. Then, by a fluke of fate, the mud plaster peeled away and exposed the gem to his jailors. Shuja Shah was also overthrown and blinded. The two brothers, sentenced to exile in 1833, fled to Lahore, taking with them many precious gems including the Koh-I-Noor. They sought sanctuary at the court of Maharajah Ranjit Singh, the 'Lion of the Punjab', and in exchange for his protection were forced to sell him the diamond. Ranjit Singh wore it first in a bracelet and then had it set surrounded by small rubies in a gold armlet, which he wore constantly on his right arm until his death in June 1839.

Ten years of civil unrest followed, and during the second Sikh war of 1849 the British annexed the Punjab. It was then governed by the East India Company, which maintained its own army and navy and imposed its own taxation system. In the 1849 Treaty of Lahore the eleven-year-old Maharajah Duleep Singh, Ranjit Singh's son, renounced for himself and his heirs any claim to the Punjab, and the property of the state was confiscated, including the Koh-I-Noor. The specific clause read: 'The gem called Koh-I-Noor . . . shall be surrendered by the Maharajah of Lahore to the Queen of England.' The English Governor General, Sir John Lawrence, later Lord Lawrence and Viceroy of India, was entrusted with the task of conveying the diamond to England. He absent-mindedly left the stone in a pocket of his clothes, which were removed by his Indian servant to be washed. When Lawrence realized what must have happened he summoned the dhobi and asked, 'Did you find a piece of glass in my pocket?' The servant, who had put it in his button box, produced it at once and it was safely delivered to the East India Company's London office.

Duleep Singh also came to England where he became a great favourite of Queen Victoria. He was given a handsome pension. (In 1863 he bought Elveden Hall in Suffolk, which he transformed into an Indian palace. He devoted his life to sybaritic pleasures and shooting, and is buried in the grounds of Elveden.) On his arrival in England Duleep Singh was shown the Koh-I-Noor by Queen Victoria and he made a graceful little speech thanking her for saving him from possible assassination by his enemies and assuring her that he was happy, as her loyal subject, to see her wear the Koh-I-Noor. However one of his relatives, the putative heir to the Punjab, was not so gracious and said that the Queen had no more right to the Koh-I-Noor than he had to Windsor Castle, and churlishly referred to her as 'Mrs Fagin', after the character Fagin in Charles Dickens's novel *Oliver Twist*, who was a receiver of stolen goods. Queen Victoria had told the East India Company that she accepted the Koh-I-Noor not as a personal gift but as 'belonging to the Crown and to be worn by all future queens in the right of it'. A century later, in 1985, members of India's Janata Party were still demanding the return of the stone to India declaring that it was a national treasure that had been confiscated illegally.

On 1 May 1851 Queen Victoria arrived in an open carriage for the opening of the Great Exhibition at Paxton's Crystal Palace in Hyde Park – which had been masterminded by the Prince Consort – dressed in pink and silver and with a small crown and two feathers on her head. The Koh-I-Noor in a brooch setting was pinned on her breast. She described it as:

> 'the happiest, proudest day in my life, and I can think of nothing else. Albert's dearest name is immortalised with this great conception, his own, and my own country showed she was worthy of it.'

Following the opening the Queen allowed the Koh-I-Noor to be put on display in a specially constructed glass case under the jurisdiction of Her Majesty's Commissioners. The day before the exhibition closed on 15 October 1851 the Lord Chamberlain wrote to his head clerk, Mr T.C. March, conveying the Queen's express command that the Koh-I-Noor was to be returned immediately to her at Windsor Castle. Mr March delivered it in person to Prince Albert, whose private secretary, General Charles Grey, signed a receipt for it.

When the 186-carat Koh-I-Noor diamond was cut in 1530 it was done in the Indian manner, the oldest form of diamond cutting known. This method served to retain the shape of the stone, covering its surface with numerous facets that unfortunately also exposed all the diamond's flaws, so that despite its size, the Koh-I-Noor lacked fire and sparkle. In the summer of 1852, the chief cutter from Coster's in Amsterdam, Mr Voorsanger, was summoned to London to reset the stone and installed in the crown jeweller's workroom under the supervision of the Prince Consort. Both Prince Albert and the Duke of Wellington were present on the day Mr Voorsanger began work, and thirty-eight days later he had completed his task of recutting the Koh-I-Noor into a 108.9-carat brilliant. The Koh-I-Noor, which now measured 1¼ by 1⁷⁄₁₆ inches, was too shallow to achieve the perfect proportions that a deeper stone might have had, but it was infinitely improved. An oval brooch and a diadem were made with detachable settings to display the Koh-I-Noor. The diadem was set with more than two thousand diamonds in a design of fleurs-de-lys, crosses pattée, quatrefoils and Greek honeysuckle ornaments. However, in February 1986 the stone was remeasured by the new metric carat weight, and it is now officially 106 carats.

Queen Victoria often wore the Koh-I-Noor brooch, such as on a State visit to Paris, at the weddings of her children or at the Opening of Parliament (page 51). After she died in 1901 the stone was designated a Crown jewel and set in the consort's crowns made for Queen Alexandra in 1902, Queen Mary in 1911 and Queen Elizabeth in 1937. Both Queen Alexandra and Queen Mary continued to wear the Koh-I-Noor as a brooch, and Queen Mary sometimes had it removed from its setting and attached in the centre of Queen Victoria's enormous three-part stomacher, making this piece even more impressive by hanging large oval diamonds from it as pendant drops (page 126). Since 1937, however, the Koh-I-Noor has been on display in the Jewel House at the Tower of London set in the platinum crown of Queen Elizabeth the Queen Mother.

Although it is well known that from the date of Prince Albert's death in December 1861 to her own in January 1901 Queen Victoria wore only black, she should not be imagined as an old crone dressed in musty fusty widow's weeds. She had always loved fashion and even if her gowns, cloaks, shawls and bonnets were sombre they were made from the most sumptuous materials. Most certainly the gowns she wore at night or on ceremonial occasions were embroidered with thousands of jet beads and embellished with pleats, ruffles and bows (page 51). Her snow-white cuffs and collars were of the softest silks and organzas, and the long flowing veils she wore trailing from her widow's cap or under a sparkling tiara were made of priceless Alençon or Honiton lace or *crêpe lisse*. For her daughter Princess Helena's wedding at Windsor Castle on 5 July 1866 she wore a black moire antique dress interwoven with silver. For the State banquet at Buckingham Palace on 21 June 1897 to celebrate her Diamond Jubilee or, as she herself put it, 'the 10th anniversary of my fifty Years Jubilee', the entire front of her dress had been worked in gold by Indian embroiderers.

Whatever the occasion Queen Victoria was splendidly bedecked with jewels; she wore diamonds around her neck and on her ears, brooches outlining her bodice, a wide diamond bracelet on her left wrist, and on her right a four-row diamond collet bracelet with a large oval portrait of Prince Albert as its centrepiece. Whether she was wearing a tiara or a bonnet, numerous large collet diamonds would be pinned among the folds of the long translucent veil that was firmly attached to the crown of her head with a diamond-studded 'Alice-band'. A dummy head, of the type used in milliner's shops, was kept in the Queen's dressing room and the veil and headdress she had chosen to wear were arranged first on this before her dresser carefully positioned them on the Queen's head. Her Majesty made sure herself that they were comfortable and securely fastened, sometimes tucking another diamond chain among the folds of the veil or positioning the small diamond crown she had had made in 1870 smack on top.

Queen Victoria received many gifts of jewellery during her reign, but none so impressive as those she received from India in 1876. On 1 May the Royal Titles Bill became law and Queen Victoria also became Empress of India – *Victoria Regina et Imperatrix*. The bill had been a personal gift from Prime Minister Disraeli to his 'faery queen'. The proclamation of Queen Victoria's new title took place in Delhi on 1 January 1877 and the Queen gave a banquet at Windsor Castle to celebrate the occasion. She greeted her guests literally covered with Eastern jewels that were obviously gifts sent to her from the fantastically rich Indian rulers. When the Prime Minister, newly created Lord Beaconsfield, complimented her on her splendid appearance she teased him that she could impress him with far more than this small display and sent a servant to fetch three large leather cases that were filled with princely tributes of priceless jewels.

For Queen Victoria's Golden Jubilee in 1887 and her Diamond Jubilee in 1897 gifts arrived from across the Empire but there was also an enormous outpouring of public affection from the people of Britain, which both surprised and touched the Queen. As the presents piled up she confided to a member of her Household that when she had married Prince Albert in 1840 they had not received one gift from 'the country' and now just look at all this.

Queen Victoria's new Empire had an influence on fashion. The irregularly shaped Indian stones, the lack of mechanical precision in their settings, and their decorated clasps in place of concealed ones all seemed natural and spontaneous and led to an immediate vogue for Indian jewellery.

Diamonds from the new South African mines added to Queen Victoria's collection. The first of many South African presentations to members of the royal family came in January 1881. Mr Porter Rhodes, on behalf of the Kimberley mine owners, delivered a selection of stones to Queen Victoria at Osborne House on the Isle of Wight. The Queen chose two large brilliants which she had mounted in a bracelet. Her Majesty sent Mr Rhodes an engraved watch as a thank-you and instructed her private secretary to tell him that, 'H.M. highly appreciated the loyal feeling which prompted you to offer them for her acceptance.'

Queen Alexandra's slim ethereal figure was deceptively fragile for she could load it with an abundance of sparkling diamonds that would have made most women look vulgar. She was the Edwardian romantic ideal with her long neck, beautifully modelled head and graceful lilting walk, the result of a slight limp that had persisted after a severe attack of rheumatic fever in 1866.

Princess Alexandra's first valuable diamonds were wedding gifts in 1863. A necklace of thirty-eight large graduated brilliants costing £10,000 was given by the Lord Mayor and Corporation of the City of London. The Prince of Wales gave her a diamond tiara, part of a pearl and diamond parure. The circlet, formed of three rows of brilliants, was surmounted by scroll motifs and Greek devices that could all be detached and worn as separate ornaments (page 128). There was a diamond bracelet from the 'Ladies of Leeds' and a large cross set with eleven fine brilliant-cut diamonds suspended from a row of pearls given by the 'Ladies of Liverpool'.

An exhibition of all the wedding gifts at the South Kensington Museum began a new royal tradition. One report claimed that:

> 'The crush of ladies was so great, that it was said that some of the fair sex had their crinolines torn off while they were standing lost in admiration of the Princess's jewels.'

The Princess of Wales's diamond dog-collar made fashion news, and when she wore a set of eight large diamond stars scattered across the bodice of her black evening gown or pinned down the length of her skirt like buttons they were copied in paste and sold in thousands. She also favoured diamond brooches in the shape of arrows, crescents, butterflies and flowers.

There was a great development in jewellery design with the introduction of lightweight platinum. It first appeared in the manufacturing records of Cartier in 1853, but it was not until around 1900 that platinum began to replace gold and silver, which because of their weight limited jewellers to bulkier settings and less delicate designs. Platinum was so flexible that invisible settings could be made that enhanced the brilliance of the stones. Lacy patterns for brooches and necklaces were introduced. The eighteenth-century garland style came back into fashion, and a platinum honeycomb mesh studded with diamonds that looked as if they were floating on air was used for the first *collier résille* necklaces (page 45, top right). Queen Alexandra acquired two of these necklaces from Cartier between 1901 and 1910.

In addition to her own personal collection of jewels Queen Alexandra wore those that had been bequeathed to the Crown by Queen Victoria, most of which are still worn today by the Queen or by Queen Elizabeth the Queen Mother. Queen Alexandra adapted her mother-in-law's jewellery to suit her own style, for example wearing Queen Victoria's diamond bordure as a girdle for the Opening of Parliament in January 1902 (page 95). Her style gradually evolved as fashion changed. By 1910 dog-collars were beginning to be considered old-fashioned and long diamond chains were worn, forerunners of the 1920s *sautoir* – multiple strands of pearls or beads usually waist-length and often ending in a tassel. During the day Queen Alexandra would wear just one chain with a simple brooch pinned on the front of her high collar, while at night she wore several in addition to heavy elaborate necklaces.

Until her marriage Princess May of Teck, the future Queen Mary, had only the usual debutante's collection of small pieces of diamond jewellery, family gifts for her confirmation and birthdays. Her first large diamonds were given to her by the Prince and Princess of Wales on 27 February 1892, the day that had been fixed for her marriage to the late Duke of Clarence. They asked her to stay with them at Compton Place, Eastbourne, where they gave her the rivière of diamonds that was to have been their wedding gift along with the handsome fitted dressing case that Albert had ordered for her. Rereading her diary of 1892 thirty-five years later, Queen Mary noted how much their gift had meant to her at such a time of grief.

Princess May wore the Wales's diamond necklace when she married Albert's younger brother, George, Duke of York, on 6 July of the following year. She also wore a diamond tiara (which could be converted into a necklace) that Queen Victoria had given her at Buckingham Palace a few days earlier. It framed a small wreath of orange blossoms, myrtle and white heather from which fell the short veil of Honiton lace that her mother, Princess Mary Adelaide, had worn at her own wedding in June 1866. Her only brooch was a gift from the bridegroom: a diamond anchor set with two small sapphires. The Duke of York had been educated in the training ship *HMS Britannia*, and always looked back on his days in the navy as among the happiest of his life.

Princess May and the Duke of York were overwhelmed with gifts; fifteen hundred arrived in the first few weeks after their engagement was announced and the total collection was said to be worth more than £300,000. The gifts were briefly exhibited at the Teck home, White Lodge in Richmond Park, the jewellery set out in a large glass-topped cabinet at the end of a long corridor. On 5 July, the day before the wedding, they were moved to the Imperial Institute in London where they were displayed to the public to raise money for the widows and orphans of a marine disaster, the sinking of HMS *Victoria*.

The presents ranged from the most humble home-made items to magnificent silver garnitures, antique furniture, paintings, crystal, porcelain and numerous clocks from official bodies. Daily reports in the newspapers kept the public informed about each new arrival. Princess May was also given many pieces of jewellery, including four diamond tiaras, two diamond necklaces and numerous brooches and bracelets. Queen Mary passed on some of the most valuable of these gifts – from the 'Girls of Great Britain and Ireland', the counties of Hampshire, Dorset and Devon and the 'Inhabitants of Kensington' – to the present Queen, ensuring that the nation's gifts should be worn by future queens of the United Kingdom.

Queen Mary's collection of diamonds steadily increased. In 1901 as Duke and Duchess of York, she and her husband made a nine-month tour of the Empire and while in South Africa De Beers Consolidated Mines presented her with a casket of unset diamonds. In 1910 the Union of South Africa gave her the 102 cleavings from the Cullinan from which were made three brooches and a ring (pages 73, 74, 76, 77). Her husband gave her many presents of jewellery to mark special occasions, such as the pink topaz and diamond pendant that was his Christmas gift to her in 1928 when he was recuperating from a serious illness. In 1929 Queen Mary further added to her collection by purchasing a number of jewels from the estate of the Dowager Empress Marie of Russia.

Queen Mary's diamonds were amazing not just for their quantity and quality but for their versatility. Most of her diamond tiaras could be transformed by using different coloured stones as centrepieces or by adding stones set on spikes on top (pages 91 and 114). Her high diamond dog-collars divided into separate collet rivières, many of her necklaces divided into bracelets and her stomachers broke up into separate brooches (pages 67 and 92, top left). Her collection of large oval diamond drops all had invisible hooks and could be attached as pendants to her diamond necklaces, or to Queen Victoria's bow brooches (page 59, top centre), or to the King William IV diamond brooch (page 70, top right). Enlarging them in this way turned brooches into corsage ornaments, and by pinning a cluster of brooches in a triangular pattern she created new stomachers. Once Queen Mary had tired of a piece of jewellery or no longer had any use for it as fashions changed, she often removed the stones from their settings in order to have something new made.

Queen Alexandra and Queen Mary were the last of the great nineteenth-century *grandes dames*. When the Duchess of York became Queen Consort in December 1936 she brought in an entirely new style, which was like a breath of fresh air. No less majestic than her mother-in-law, with whom she had always had a warm and loving relationship, she too was seen at a gala or Court reception dripping in diamonds, but unlike Queen Mary she was never formidable or untouchable. When the writer Virginia Woolf saw her in the royal box at the theatre one night she described her as:

> 'A simple, chattering, sweet-hearted, little round-faced young woman in pink, but her wrists twinkling with diamonds and her dress held on the shoulder with diamonds.'

Queen Elizabeth had received a number of beautiful pieces of diamond jewellery for her marriage in 1923. Her father, the Earl of Strathmore, had given her a platinum and diamond bandeau tiara, made by Messrs Catchpole and Williams of Oxford Street. Its design was of five large roses separated by diamond sprays and it could be broken up to form separate brooches. One of King George V's wedding gifts had been a lacy diamond ribbon-bow brooch. Queen Elizabeth still often wears this for the annual Festival of Remembrance at the Albert Hall, using it to attach her red silk poppies to her left shoulder. The Duke of York had given his bride a diamond replica of his naval cap badge and a large diamond cluster corsage brooch in a floral design with three dangling diamond pendants hanging from a V-shaped platinum chain. Queen Elizabeth wears both of these brooches, but has never been seen in public wearing another of the Duke of York's wedding gifts, a diamond necklace with a Greek key design and seven large V-shaped festoon drops. Other wedding gifts had been a diamond brooch from her godmother Mrs Arthur James, a diamond and emerald arrow from the Hon. James Stuart and a watch with a platinum and diamond bracelet strap from the 'City of Belfast'. She wore this in August 1982 at the christening of her great-grandson Prince William.

Prior to the York's wedding at Westminster Abbey on 26 April many of the gifts were placed on view in large glass cases in the picture gallery on the first floor of Buckingham Palace. On 24 April the King and Queen gave an evening reception for six hundred family friends who were able to inspect the presents. As previously done in 1863 and 1893, the newspapers ran daily lists of who had given what.

During the next ten years when, one must remember, the Duchess of York was Queen Mary's only daughter-in-law, the Queen gave her a number of jewels. These included a small diamond horseshoe brooch that she herself had worn as a young woman, and a wedding gift that she had received from Miss Alice de Rothschild, a diamond lover's knot brooch from which hung a small round diamond scent bottle. The Duchess also acquired her first diamond collet rivière and a scroll tiara (page 46).

Shortly after King George VI's accession in December 1936 Queen Mary offered Queen Elizabeth the jewels that Queen Victoria had left to the Crown in 1901. Together they inspected the royal collection, which when not being used was kept safely in storage. From all these jewels the new Queen chose the following: a diamond snake bracelet that Queen Alexandra had worn in the 1890s (page 96); a diamond waterfall brooch that was given to Queen Victoria in 1876 and which Queen Elizabeth later wore at her daughter's Coronation in 1953 (page 64, top right); Queen Victoria's wide diamond cuff bracelet (page 55); the King George III diamond fringe tiara (page 43); Queen Victoria's diamond collet necklace and earrings (page 55); Queen Victoria's diamond bow brooches (page 59); Queen Victoria's diamond bar brooch (page 64); the King William IV diamond brooch (page 70); and the King William IV buckle bracelets, which Queen Mary and Queen Elizabeth both wore at their Coronations (page 80).

When Princess Victoria of Wales, King George V's sister, died on 3 December 1935 (seven weeks before the King), she left the Duchess of York a diamond fringe necklace. Of early-nineteenth-century design, it is similar to one Princess Elizabeth was given as a wedding gift in 1947 from dignitaries of the City of London (page 66).

King George VI delighted in giving his wife jewellery. Among his gifts were five rivières of perfectly matched large diamond collets, the first two of which were the King's Coronation present to Queen Elizabeth. The five necklaces could be worn together or separately. There was also a pair of drop flower earrings, each flower having eight single marquise-cut diamond petals and a brilliant-cut diamond centre, a Cartier diamond curved-leaf clip and one of the most spectacular brooches ever created by Cartier, a diamond floral spray that was nearly a foot long. Another handsome diamond brooch with a sentimental attachment was a spray of Scottish thistles and leaves, which Queen Elizabeth has worn during the last fifty years.

In July 1939 Cecil Beaton took the first of his enormously successful Winterhalter-style photographs of Queen Elizabeth. When he arrived at Buckingham Palace they discussed the various evening gowns she might wear and what rooms they should use as backdrops. The photographer suggested that Queen Elizabeth should wear as much jewellery as possible. But despite what to most women would seem to be an inexhaustible collection she smiled apologetically and replied, 'The choice isn't very great you know!' Beaton, who described the diamonds around her neck as being as large as 'robins' eggs', was slightly nonplussed.

The King and Queen toured South Africa in 1947 with Princess Elizabeth and Princess Margaret. They were asked if during the trip they would visit the Kimberley mines to promote 'the romantic allure of diamonds'. The diamond trade had fallen off sharply during the war and needed reviving, so the Government were anxious to find ways of encouraging people to buy diamonds again. The tour seemed a heaven-sent opportunity to publicize the royal family's interest in diamonds. When this was suggested to the King and Queen they agreed to spend a day, 18 April, at the Big Hole mine, hoping that the publicity attached to their visit would have useful sales results. Before they left Kimberley Queen Elizabeth was presented with a marquise-cut diamond of 8.5 carats that she subsequently had set in a ring. The King was given 399 diamonds to use in a new Garter Star; Princess Elizabeth received the 6-carat blue-white brilliant-cut diamond that is now set as the central stone in the bracelet made from her 'best diamonds' (page 49); and Princess Margaret was given a 4.5-carat blue-white emerald-cut diamond set in a ring.

After the royal family's return to England – and the marriage of Princess Elizabeth and Prince Philip that November – Queen Elizabeth began planning a new tiara for herself. Queen Mary had passed on to her a large number of diamonds that she herself had been given by De Beers in 1901 when she and her husband had visited South Africa during a nine-month tour of the Empire. Once back in London, Queen Mary had the diamonds set in a high tiara of seven egg-shaped arches with a small diamond floral spray in the centre of each. Although she wore it as Princess of Wales, when she became Queen in 1910 it disappeared from view. The design which Queen Elizabeth chose used the diamonds from this tiara as well as others from the royal collection to make a modern diadem with a geometric honeycomb design (page 64). It had three horizontal rows of pentagonal motifs each framing three brilliant-cut diamonds. When it was completed the top row had a straight edge making the tiara appear slightly top-heavy and cumbersome. A few years later Cartier altered it by replacing every other motif on the top row with a small diamond triangle of six brilliant-cut stones.

Since the late 1960s Queen Elizabeth the Queen Mother has worn only two tiaras, of which the Cartier diamond tiara is one and Queen Victoria's ruby and diamond tiara the other. She usually wears the Cartier tiara with her diamond collet necklaces or with Queen Alexandra's pearl and diamond festoon necklace, and a spectacular pair of pendant earrings that she had made around 1953. These have triangular diamond studs from each of which is suspended an emerald-cut diamond and an immense pendant oval drop. The stones are so heavy that they noticeably pull down her ear lobes (page 64). Although Queen Elizabeth the Queen Mother dislikes dwelling on the past she has a strong sentimental attachment to her jewellery and wears the same pieces over and over again. Unlike Queen Mary she doesn't convert them into different shapes, and the idea of hanging pendant drops on everything has never occurred to her. She occasionally wears a ring set with an emerald-cut solitaire diamond next to her plain Welsh gold wedding band, and at the 1986 Royal Variety Performance a large diamond oval pendant brooch that Queen Victoria's granddaughter Princess Marie Louise had left her in 1957 suddenly reappeared (page 137).

The Queen, then Princess Elizabeth, was presented with her first diamond brooch on 1 December 1944 when, aged eighteen, she undertook her first solo public engagement. In a northern port, unidentified at the time for security reasons, she launched the largest British battleship yet built, HMS *Vanguard*. For the first time her personal standard was flown. At the luncheon following the launching Lord Aberconway, Chairman of Messrs John Brown and Co., the ship's builders, presented her with an antique diamond brooch in the shape of an English rose with a small bow at the base of the stem. In her maiden speech she said: 'This will always serve to remind me that the first important public duty I ever undertook was a naval occasion.'

Princess Elizabeth celebrated her twenty-first birthday on 21 April 1947 while the royal family were on their official visit to South Africa. She was given a platinum brooch set with three hundred diamonds as a birthday present from forty-two thousand Southern Rhodesian school children, who had each donated a week's pocket money after an interracial appeal. The brooch was in the shape of a flame lily, the Rhodesian national flower. In order to make a perfect replica of the lily, which varies in colour from pure yellow to dark purple red, a flower had been specially flown to South Africa where an artist worked against time to complete reference drawings of it before it wilted.

A representative delegation of children was invited to present the gift to the Princess at Government House in Salisbury. Dressed in their best clothes, the girls wearing white gloves and the boys in carefully buttoned formal suits, they posed for a photograph on the steps of Government House after the presentation. The Princess was already wearing the brooch on her left shoulder, a personal touch that was greatly appreciated and drew admiring comments in the press the next day. King George VI died on 6 February 1952 while Princess Elizabeth and Prince Philip were in Kenya. They arrived back in London the next day, and when the new Queen disembarked from the aircraft in the early evening dusk the diamond flame lily brooch was pinned to the lapel of her black coat.

DIAMONDS

33

Following her daughter's Coronation in June 1953 Queen Elizabeth made her first Commonwealth tour as Queen Mother, accompanied by Princess Margaret. On 3 July she opened the Rhodes Centenary Exhibition in the Queen's Ground, Bulawayo. Sir Ellis Robbins, Chairman of the Exhibition Board, presented Queen Elizabeth the Queen Mother and Princess Margaret with diamond and platinum flame lily brooches made in Johannesburg and exact replicas of the one the Queen had been given in 1947. Queen Elizabeth immediately removed her brooch from its case and pinned it to her dress, giving it an admiring little pat as she did so, which elicited a cheer from the enthusiastic crowd. These brooches are the only identical pieces of jewellery owned by the Queen, her mother and her sister.

Since 1944 the Queen has acquired some twenty diamond brooches, most of them worn only for a period and then put away. Some of the brooches, although principally of diamonds, are also set with other stones. A floral spray brooch was another twenty-first birthday gift, presented by the Girl Guide Movement. Its three trefoil flowers (symbolizing the Guide badge) were set with diamonds, rubies, sapphires and topazes and tied with a diamond bow. Every Brownie, Ranger and Girl Guide in the Empire had donated a penny to pay for it. In 1947 the fifty-eight thousand members of the Over-Seas League gave Princess Elizabeth a jewelled clip of their emblem, a galleon in full sail, as a wedding gift. Made from Canadian platinum, it was set with diamonds and rubies from South Africa, sapphires from Ceylon and rubies from Burma. When Princess Elizabeth launched the airliner *Elizabeth of England* for the British Overseas Airways Corporation, they presented her with a diamond brooch of their flared-wing emblem, the wings accentuated by two lines of sapphire baguettes. For a time she wore the brooch whenever she flew from London Airport. In November 1952, the first year of her reign, the Queen laid the foundation stone for the new headquarters of Lloyds of London and was given a diamond brooch of the frigate *Lutine*. The *Lutine* was a warship that sank off the coast of Holland in 1799. Its cargo of gold and silver, said to be worth at least £250,000, was insured by Lloyds, who were entitled to keep anything that could be salvaged from the wreck.

In 1947 the Queen was only the third woman to receive the Freedom of the City of London, her immediate predecessor being Florence Nightingale. This occasion was marked by the gift of a diamond brooch depicting a lily. The 'Women of New Zealand' gave the Queen a diamond fern brooch as a Christmas present in 1953 during her Coronation tour of the Commonwealth. Other diamond brooches in the Queen's collection are a large frosted-gold sunflower with a diamond cluster centre and a diamond set in each of its twenty-one petals; a mythical sea creature, wearing a gold crown, covered in pavé-set diamonds and with a cabochon ruby eye; two different diamond rose sprays set in gold; a six-petalled diamond flower with a large collet centre; a Greek soldier dressed in native costume set with diamonds; and a diamond Scottish thistle surmounted by a carved amethyst 'brush'.

In 1981 the Queen was left a late-Victorian diamond star brooch by Lady Jardine, which she has worn on many occasions. It has a collet diamond on a knife-wire between each of its eight points. Another brooch that the Queen has worn since she received it was presented by the Australian Prime Minister Mr Menzies at a State banquet in Canberra in February 1954. The brooch is a spray of wattle nearly four inches long with three tea tree blossoms in the centre. The wattle, which resembles the mimosa, is Australia's emblem; tea trees are a Polynesian species with edible roots. The brooch is set with 150 diamonds: rare yellow diamonds form the wattle, blue-white diamond baguettes are set on the leaves and a 5-carat diamond is set in the centre of each tea tree flower. On her sixtieth birthday in April 1986 the Queen wore it on the shoulder of her yellow coat when she appeared on the balcony of Buckingham Palace before thousands of school children all singing and waving daffodils to celebrate her birthday.

Other diamond pieces include a Cartier platinum ring set with a 6.6-carat marquise-cut diamond given by the Government and people of Sierra Leone in 1961. The diamond, which in the rough weighed 19.5 carats, was cut by the London firm of Briefel & Lemer; Prince Charles went to watch the work being done. The Queen also has a cluster ring and two rings set with yellow diamonds, one round and one square, none of which have been seen in public. Finally, there is a delicate narrow link bracelet with floral motifs, which has not been seen in public, and a modern triple-row brilliant-cut diamond bracelet, which the Queen wears at evening functions.

Princess Margaret owns many fine pieces of diamond jewellery, a number of which had belonged to her grandmother Queen Mary. These include a large hollow oval brooch, and a pair of heart-shaped clips that Queen Mary sometimes wore on one of her legendary toque hats. Unlike the Queen who only pins her brooches on her left shoulder, Princess Margaret follows her grandmother's style and sometimes wears brooches centre front on her collar – an example is a diamond Rose of York brooch that Queen Mary gave as a wedding gift to Queen Elizabeth the Queen Mother, who passed it on to her younger daughter. Another family heirloom is a long diamond wheat ear brooch, probably made around 1880, which the Princess wore a great deal in the 1950s. One of her most beautiful and impressive diamond brooches was a wedding present from her mother in 1960. This is a spray of three large flowers that Queen Elizabeth first wore at the end of the war and which may well have been a gift from King George. During their marriage Princess Margaret and Lord Snowdon redesigned a number of her more old-fashioned pieces of jewellery into modern styles, just as Queen Victoria and Prince Albert had done 125 years earlier.

When she was eighteen Princess Margaret borrowed a tiara from her grandmother Queen Mary. This diamond bandeau had lozenge-shaped motifs and was originally surmounted by thirteen large oval oriental pearls set on spikes. By 1946, however, Queen Mary had removed the pearls. In September 1948 the eighteen-year-old Princess wore it when on one of her first official engagements she represented King George VI at the Inauguration of Queen Juliana of the Netherlands in Amsterdam, the Dutch equivalent of a coronation. Princess Margaret also borrowed a diamond scroll tiara for a number of years from her sister, the Queen (page 46). However, at a Sotheby's auction in 1959, she bought the Poltimore tiara for around £5,000, sold by the fourth Baron Poltimore's daughter, the Hon. Lady Stucley. This high diamond diadem of scrolls, leaves and flower clusters is set on a row of small diamond collets. Most ingeniously it can be converted into a necklace or taken apart to form two large corsage brooches, each with a floral spray framed by two scroll motifs. When worn as a necklace the diamond collet base of the tiara becomes a choker from which the seven vertical sprays hang like a bib. Princess Margaret wore the tiara at her wedding, her hair in a chignon beneath her white silk tulle veil, which was made by Claude St Cyr of Paris.

In the 1950s the Princess set a number of fashions in jewellery: diamond butterfly brooches worn in her hair for a visit to the ballet at the Royal Opera House, Covent Garden; matching diamond clips pinned on her hat, or one on her hat and one on her lapel; the initial 'M' set in diamonds on her handbag; and a twenty-first birthday gift from her father, a rivière of diamond collets. All these were later imitated.

Princess Anne was seventeen when she first wore a diamond tiara while accompanying the Queen to the Opening of Parliament in 1967. This was the Queen's scroll tiara, which Princess Margaret had also worn and which Princess Anne now borrowed for a number of years (page 46). For Princess Anne's eighteenth birthday the Queen gave her an antique diamond festoon necklace with ribbon bows and pendant drops, and a pair of pendant earrings to match. Around 1972 the Princess was also given the meander tiara that had belonged to her paternal grandmother, Princess Andrew of Greece (page 47). In 1971 the Queen took out of storage for Princess Anne a delicate Edwardian necklace that Queen Alexandra had worn in 1917. This was a black velvet choker on which a narrow diamond chain was caught up in two swags by three diamond circles. That December Princess Anne received a unique gift of coloured diamonds, or 'fancies', from the De Beers Company when she visited their London headquarters. She later had them set in a round brooch. In 1972 her parents gave her an important necklace of unusual design. At the front twenty-one triangular clusters with large collet drops are suspended between two looped motifs; at the back is a chain of diamond collets. Princess Anne often wears it with a pair of pendant cluster earrings.

In 1973, the year of her marriage to Captain Mark Phillips, Princess Anne received a small avalanche of diamonds. The World Wide Shipping Group gave her a delicate antique festoon tiara topped with single diamond collets when she launched their tanker *World Unicorn* (page 107). The Queen's wedding gifts to her daughter included a pair of diamond flower-cluster earrings and a large 18-carat gold stalactite clip brooch set with brilliant-cut diamonds. Princess Margaret and Lord Snowdon gave her a pair of gold flower earrings set with diamonds, and the Prince of Wales's present was a diamond bow brooch of five ribbon loops with a central cluster and two long ribbon tassels. Captain Phillips, who was in the Queen's Dragoon Guards, gave his bride a copy of his regimental brooch set with diamonds and rubies. This follows a long-standing army tradition. It was Queen Mary's close friend and lady-in-waiting Mabell, Countess of Airlie, who in 1886 had been the first to wear such a brooch. Princess Anne's wedding gifts, 1,524 in all, including the jewellery and other family presents, were exhibited in aid of charity in the State Apartments of St James's Palace and attracted more than fifty thousand visitors.

Lady Diana Spencer was only nineteen when she became engaged to the Prince of Wales in February 1981 and had very little jewellery of her own. Her mother, the Hon. Mrs Shand Kydd, loaned her for the entire period of her engagement the triangular diamond pendant earrings that she wore on her wedding day as her 'something borrowed'. Mrs Shand Kydd had bought them for herself with money that she had been left as a legacy. Lady Diana also borrowed an antique diamond necklace and matching chandelier earrings from Collingwood to wear with an emerald-green taffeta evening dress for the official engagement photographs taken by Lord Snowdon at Highgrove House. Collingwood, who have been the Spencer family jewellers since Lady Diana was a girl, had wanted to present her with the diamond set as their wedding gift, but Palace officials ruled that such a valuable present would be improper. The necklace and earrings were subsequently offered for sale by an Iranian jeweller in Düsseldorf, Genio Hakimi, who claimed they were Spencer heirlooms that had been sold to pay for the wedding. He had bought them from an unscrupulous dealer who offered the engagement photograph as proof that the jewels were Spencer property.

The Spencer tiara unquestionably does belong to the family. A second tiara owned by the Spencers, which had belonged to Queen Marie Antoinette of France, is worn by the present Countess Spencer. Lady Diana wore the Spencer tiara on her wedding day, as had her two older sisters, Lady Sarah McCorquodale and Lady Jane Fellowes on theirs. Dating from the early nineteenth century, it has a design of swirled arcs of leaves and flowers. The Princess has continued to wear the tiara ever since her marriage, although it remains Spencer property.

The only diamond necklace that the Princess of Wales owns is the solid chain of brilliant-cut diamonds set in gold that was part of the sapphire and diamond suite she received as a wedding gift from the Crown Prince of Saudi Arabia. Its large sapphire pendant is detachable and the Princess also wears the chain with the diamond Prince of Wales feathers' pendant that Queen Elizabeth the Queen Mother gave her just after her engagement was announced. This oval pendant, which has a detachable cabochon emerald drop, had been a wedding gift to Princess Alexandra of Denmark from the 'Ladies of Bristol' when she married the future King Edward VII in 1863. Another wedding gift to the Princess of Wales was a diamond evening watch from Sheikha Fatima Bint Mubarak al-Nayiyan of the United Arab Emirates. The Prince and Princess of Wales received more than twelve thousand wedding gifts of which a thousand were exhibited in aid of charity, attracting 207,000 visitors. The Princess allowed her wedding dress and shoes to be put on show, but none of the jewellery given by the two families or their personal presents were included in the exhibition or listed in the official catalogue.

The Princess of Wales enjoys wearing a certain amount of costume jewellery, including various pairs of fake diamond earrings, for example, oval 'diamond' drops set in silver gilt, 'diamond' hoops and a pair of large gold discs each set with a round 'diamond'. The Princess emphatically explains that she loves the fun of glitzy fake jewellery and that in today's world it is just as much fashion as are the clothes she chooses. When the Princess and Prince of Wales visited King Fahd of Saudi Arabia in 1986 she wore a pair of pendant 'diamond' earrings in the shape of crescent moons as a tribute to him. The Princess had purchased the earrings at Butler & Wilson in London.

The newest royal princess, the Duchess of York, received her first grand diamonds as a wedding gift from the Queen and Prince Philip. They gave her a modern suite of earrings, necklace and bracelet with a cluster design. When she entered Westminster Abbey on her wedding day Sarah Ferguson's veil, like Queen Victoria's in 1840, was held in place by a floral wreath, in this case cream roses, gardenias, lily petals and lilies of the valley. But when she and Prince Andrew re-emerged from the vestry behind the altar after signing the register, the flowers had been removed and a diamond tiara, borrowed from a close friend of the Ferguson family, glittered above her beaming smile. Like her sister-in-law, the Princess of Wales, she too wears a number of sparkling 'diamond' earrings that are costume jewellery from Butler & Wilson or Ken Lane.

Princess Alice, Duchess of Gloucester, has a wonderful collection of diamond jewellery, most of which she shares with her daughter-in-law, the present Duchess. It includes four diamond tiaras, two pairs of diamond earrings and two diamond necklaces, one of which has a pink beryl centrepiece that matches a detachable stone in one of the tiaras (page 81, top left). There is also a matching bracelet and brooch. Princess Alice gave Birgitte, her future daughter-in-law, a square diamond brooch as an engagement gift. It had been given to her by her own husband after the birth of the present Duke. Princess Alice was given a set of four matching diamond link bracelets, which can be connected to form a necklace, as a wedding gift in 1935; she and her husband gave them to the present Duchess as a wedding gift in 1972. A beautiful diamond tiara, in the style of a Russian Kokoshnik, was a bequest to the present Duke in 1957 from Princess Marie Louise, Queen Victoria's granddaughter.

Princess Marina of Greece, who married the Duke of Kent in 1934, was the granddaughter of the Grand Duchess Vladimir of Russia whose jewellery collection was second only to that of the Dowager Empress Marie Feodorovna. The Grand Duchess's daughter, Princess Nicholas of Greece, lived in exile in Paris and sold many of the jewels she had inherited from her mother, including a pearl and diamond tiara that the Queen owns today (page 117). But she had a great deal left to pass on to her three daughters.

One of the most spectacular of the Romanov jewels, a pair of antique diamond chandelier earrings, was left to the present Duchess of Kent in 1968. These long earrings are so fragile that on more than one occasion the Duchess has had to scramble around to find a diamond drop that had fallen off. Princess Marina also had three magnificent rivières of diamond collets, one of which had been a wedding gift from King George V. She left one necklace to each of her three children, Princess Alexandra, the Duke of Kent and Prince Michael of Kent.

Until Princess Marina's wedding it had been traditional for royal brides to follow Queen Victoria's example and wear a floral headdress. But Princess Marina had received a diamond fringe tiara as a wedding gift from the 'City of London' and wore this to anchor her white tulle veil. The tiara, which was almost identical to the King George III fringe tiara, had been purchased from the Ranee of Pudukota. As it happened, her wedding day, 29 November, was darkened by a real pea-souper fog. But as Princess Marina travelled to and from Westminster Abbey she sat well forward in her carriage and the sparkling glitter of her tiara could be seen by the watching crowds even through the gloom. Princess Alexandra wore the tiara for her marriage in 1963 to the Hon. Angus Ogilvy, and Princess Michael of Kent wore it at the evening reception that followed her civil marriage in Vienna in 1978.

The present Duchess of Kent wore a narrow diamond bandeau tiara at her wedding in 1961. The tiara, which had been a wedding gift from Princess Marina, had originally belonged to Queen Mary, who had had oval cabochon emeralds set on spikes along the top rim. But these had been removed before she left it to Princess Marina in 1953. Princess Marina loaned it for a time to her daughter, Princess Alexandra. The Duchess of Kent has also inherited from Princess Marina an oblong diamond brooch with a square cluster centre and link ends, which she had been given by Queen Mary as a wedding gift. Princess Marina wore it pinned to her Paris wedding dress just below the point of her V-neckline. She also had on the rivière of thirty-six large diamonds that King George V had given her.

Queen Mary gave Princess Marina three other diamond brooches on different occasions. The first, a large oval diamond cluster brooch, had been one of the pieces of jewellery bought from the Dowager Empress of Russia's estate in 1929 (page 51, bottom left). It is worn today by Princess Michael. The second, a diamond three-leaf clover with a central brilliant-cut diamond and an emerald set in the middle of each leaf, was a wedding gift to the future Queen Mary from Sir Frederick and Lady Milner in 1893. It also now belongs to Princess Michael. The third, a large rectangular brooch with curved ends, is worn today by Princess Alexandra. The Princess used to wear a set of three pointed diamond stars that Princess Marina had worn in the 1930s, pinned in her hair, on jacket lapels or at the waist of a ball gown.

Princess Michael has three fourteen-petalled diamond daisy brooches, one large and two small, that Princess Marina had in 1948. The two smaller daisies can also be worn as earrings. Princess Marina used to clip a pendant drop pearl to the large daisy, and often wore the two small ones pinned on her hat or on a five-row pearl necklace. Princess Michael also has Princess Marina's large diamond hoop earrings, which date from the early 1950s. They can be worn with single diamond or sapphire centres that hang from small collet diamonds. These centre stones can be worn on their own as drop earrings. Princess Michael's collection also includes Princess Marina's diamond bracelet set with brilliant-cut and oval stones, and a 1930s 'cocktail'-style wide diamond-set ring.

'Great diamonds are rare and tend to take the breath away by their sheer magnificence,' wrote the Deputy Governor of the Tower of London, Brigadier Kenneth Mears, in a letter to *The Times*. Kenneth Mears keeps the Crown Jewels under his watchful eye. All the age-old superstitions about them – that they represent purity and innocence, make one merry, prevent fear of the dark and guarantee married happiness – may be true, but part of their magic stems from the mystery of how such fire and brilliance can be created from rough pebbles.

# Queen Mary's 'Girls of Great Britain and Ireland' Tiara

*In 1893 a committee was formed by Lady Eve Greville to raise money from the 'Girls of Great Britain and Ireland' to purchase a wedding gift for Princess May of Teck, the future Queen Mary. They collected more than £5,000, and after buying a diamond tiara from Garrard, the surplus money was given, at Princess May's request, to a fund that had just been set up to aid the widows and orphans of the men lost after the sinking of HMS Victoria. In her thank-you letter, dated 4 July 1893, Princess May wrote:*

*'I need scarcely assure you that the tiara will ever be one of my most valued wedding gifts as a precious proof of your goodwill and affection.'*

*The tiara was a diamond festoon-and-scroll design surmounted by nine large oriental pearls on diamond spikes and set on a bandeau base of alternate round and lozenge collets between two plain bands of diamonds.*

PAGE 38, ABOVE LEFT: *Queen Mary, then Duchess of York, wearing the tiara shortly after her marriage. The ornate diamond and pearl necklace, which could also be worn as a tiara, was another wedding gift, presented by 'Some Ladies of England'.* PAGE 38, ABOVE RIGHT: *By 1920 Queen Mary had removed the bandeau base and the upright pearls, replacing them with large collet diamonds. This photograph was taken in 1930.* PAGE 38, BELOW: *Around 1921 she wore the bandeau as a simple headband.* PAGE 39: *This is how the tiara looked in 1947 when Queen Mary gave it to the Queen, then Princess Elizabeth, as a wedding present. Its broken spiky line emphasized by diamond collets, the tiara has the great advantage of being exceptionally lightweight. At the exhibition of 2,660 wedding gifts held in the State Apartments of St James's Palace and opened to the public in aid of charity, the tiara and the bandeau were displayed separately on curved velvet stands.* ABOVE, RIGHT: *This photograph taken in 1949 shows the Queen wearing her first tiara, which she still affectionately calls 'Granny's Tiara'. She is also wearing the smallest watch in the world, made by Cartier. The dial measured only ³/₁₆ inch across and was set in a bracelet of thirty-two miniature platinum squares. Her father and mother, on a State visit to France in 1938, accepted it on her behalf from the President of the French Republic, Monsieur Lebrun, as a gift from the French people. Princess Elizabeth was then twelve years old. She wore it almost daily – even at her wedding and Coronation – until 13 January 1955 when she lost it while out walking the dogs at Sandringham. Despite an intensive search by the police, farm workers, Boy Scouts and even soldiers with mine detectors, it was never found. In 1957, when she herself made a State visit to France, the Government presented her with a replacement that was nearly as small, only this one was set in a diamond and platinum bracelet strap. This photograph also records one of the rare times that Her Majesty wore coloured nail varnish.* ABOVE, LEFT: *In 1969 the Queen had the bandeau and the tiara reassembled, as is seen here in 1981 at the Royal Variety Performance.*

# THE KING GEORGE III FRINGE TIARA

*The diamond fringe tiara — a graduated circle of vertical rows of diamonds — was made in 1830 as a necklace from brilliant-cut stones that had belonged to King George III (page 42). Although designed to be worn either as a collar or mounted on a thin wire band as a tiara, it is as a necklace that its sunray design is most apparent. Queen Victoria first wore it as a tiara when she paid an official visit to the Opera in 1839.* ABOVE: *In Winterhalter's painting* The First of May, *made in 1851, she wears it as she holds Prince Arthur, the future Duke of Connaught, while his godfather the Duke of Wellington presents him with a jewel-studded gold box and Prince Albert looks on. In her will,*

*the necklace was one of the items Queen Victoria left to the Crown, and it was then described as a diamond fringe necklace.* OPPOSITE, ABOVE LEFT: *It was inherited by Queen Mary when she became Queen Consort in 1910, and she in turn gave it to her daughter-in-law the new Queen in 1937.* OPPOSITE, ABOVE RIGHT: *When Queen Elizabeth, now the Queen Mother, first appeared in it at the Duchess of Sutherland's Coronation Ball at Hampden House, MP 'Chips' Channon noted disparagingly in his diary that she wore white, and 'an ugly spiked tiara'. She wears it here in 1953.* OPPOSITE, BELOW LEFT: *She loaned it as the 'something borrowed' to her daughter Princess Elizabeth for her wedding in 1947. As the Princess was getting dressed in her second-floor room at Buckingham Palace before leaving for Westminster Abbey, the frame snapped and the court jeweller, who was standing by in case of any emergency, rushed to his workroom with a police escort. Queen Elizabeth reassured her nervous daughter that it could be repaired in time, and it was.* OPPOSITE, BELOW RIGHT: *Queen Elizabeth the Queen Mother loaned it again to her granddaughter Princess Anne for her marriage to Captain Mark Phillips in 1973. The Princess wore with it the diamond flower-cluster earrings that had been a wedding gift from her mother, the Queen.*

# Queen Alexandra's Russian Kokoshnik Tiara and Queen Mary's Floret Earrings

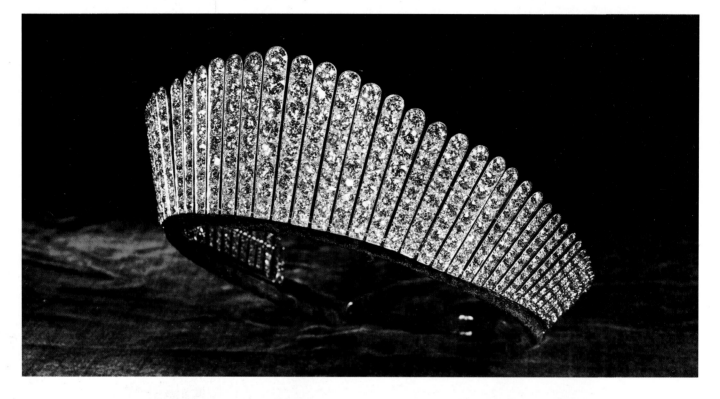

OPPOSITE, ABOVE: *On 10 March 1888 the Prince and Princess of Wales celebrated their silver wedding anniversary at Marlborough House. Before they hosted a large family dinner party, Princess Alexandra received Lady Salisbury, who presented her with this diamond tiara on behalf of 365 peeresses of the United Kingdom. As Princess May wrote to her Aunt Augusta, the Grand Duchess of Mecklenburg-Strelitz:*

*'The presents are quite magnificent.*
*The ladies of society gave a lovely diamond spiked*
*tiara.'*

*In fact, Princess Alexandra had specially requested that the tiara be in the fashionable Russian style of a peasant girl's headdress, the Kokoshnik design she knew well from her visits to her sister, the Empress of Russia, who had an identical one. The tiara was made by Garrard, supervised by the Marchionesses of Ailesbury and Salisbury and the Countesses of Cork and Spencer. It is formed of sixty-one platinum bars graduating from the centre in the eighteenth-century manner and totally encrusted with 488 diamonds, of which the two biggest are 3.25 carats each.* OPPOSITE, BELOW: *These floret earrings have a large centre diamond surrounded by seven slightly smaller ones and were bought by Queen Mary.* ABOVE, LEFT: *Queen Alexandra in about 1890. The elaborate diamond and pearl necklace she is wearing beneath the rows of chokers was her wedding present from the Prince of Wales. Queen Elizabeth the Queen Mother currently wears the necklace, but without the bottom row of drops and tassels, which have been removed (page 129).* ABOVE, RIGHT: *Queen Mary in the official portrait to celebrate her eightieth birthday on 26 May 1947 is also wearing Queen Alexandra's diamond collier résille made by Cartier in 1904 (page 64, above right).* RIGHT: *The Queen photographed in the Blue Drawing Room of Buckingham Palace in 1961.*

# Queen Elizabeth the Queen Mother's Scroll Tiara

ABOVE, LEFT: *The scroll tiara was one of about half-a-dozen tiaras that the Duchess of York wore between her marriage in 1923 and her accession to the throne in 1936. This photograph, with the Duke, was taken just weeks before King Edward VIII's abdication. Queen Elizabeth still wears the diamond and pearl drop earrings, which she has had since shortly after her marriage. The diamond tiara, with its fan-shaped motifs, was given to the Queen, but she has never worn it in public.* ABOVE, RIGHT: *She loaned it for a number of years to her sister, Princess Margaret, seen here in 1962, and then to her daughter, Princess Anne, who wore it for this 1973 portrait by William Narraway (left).*

# PRINCESS ANDREW OF GREECE'S MEANDER TIARA

The word 'meander' derives from the River Maiandros, which in ancient Greece inspired a classical design of regular lines set at right angles to each other that was often used both in architecture and works of art. It began to be popular in modern jewellery design around the turn of the century. The design is commonly known as the key pattern, which is how Prince Philip says he has always known this tiara. This meander tiara also incorporates a central wreath of leaves and scrolls on either side. It was a wedding gift to the Queen from her mother-in-law, Princess Andrew of Greece, born Princess Alice of Battenberg, Queen Victoria's great-granddaughter. The Queen has never worn it in public and gave it to Princess Anne around 1972. Princess Anne wears it here in 1973 with her diamond and sapphire engagement ring and a diamond brooch – a six-pointed star with diamond collets that she received when she launched HMNZS Canterbury at the Yarrow shipyard in 1970.

# QUEEN MARY'S CLUSTER EARRINGS

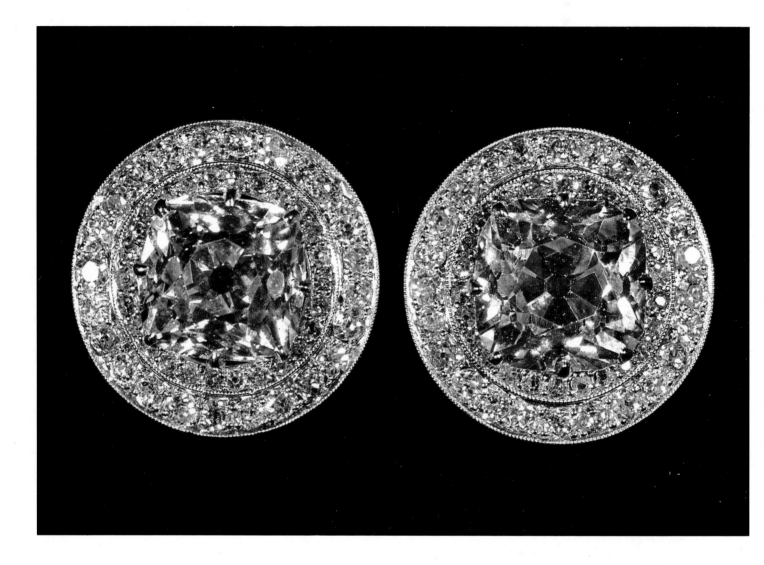

ABOVE: *Each of these unusual earrings has a large, brilliant-cut diamond sunk into two concentric circles of small diamonds set in platinum with a millegrain edge.* OPPOSITE, LEFT: *Queen Mary wore the earrings in 1948. Her diamond cluster brooch with a pearl centre was left to Princess Alice, Duchess of Gloucester, and is now worn as the centrepiece of a four-row pearl necklace by her daughter-in-law, the present Duchess.* OPPOSITE, RIGHT: *The Queen, in 1953, making her Christmas broadcast from Auckland, New Zealand, during her six-month-long Coronation tour of the Commonwealth. She is also wearing the necklace and bracelet made from her very first diamonds. In 1947 King George VI and Queen Elizabeth took their daughters to South Africa on a post-war tour, to express their appreciation to the people who had fought so valiantly. Princess Elizabeth's*

birthday, 21 April, was declared a public holiday throughout the Union of South Africa and that night a Young People's Ball was given in her honour at Government House in Cape Town. The King and Queen did their best to stay in the background as, dressed in a white tulle evening gown sparkling with diamanté and sequin embroidery, Princess Elizabeth was presented by Field-Marshal Smuts with her gift from the Government: a silver casket containing a long chain necklace of twenty-one large diamonds that had been cut and polished in Johannesburg, the largest of which was 10 carats. Forming connecting links between each of the twenty-one main stones were two small brilliant-cut diamonds mounted on either side of a baguette diamond. The casket was handed to Princess Elizabeth as she stood by a microphone and the entire nation heard her gasp of delight when she saw the necklace. From that night on, she has always called them 'my best diamonds'. Five years later, shortly after the Queen acceded to the throne, she decided to have the necklace shortened and it was cut down to fifteen large stones, the other six with their connecting links being made up into a matching bracelet. During their South African tour, the royal family had visited the Big Hole, the first and greatest of the Kimberley diamond mines, and the Princess had been given a superb round-cut, 6-carat, blue-white diamond, presented by little Mary Oppenheimer, daughter of the Chairman of the De Beers Corporation. In 1952 this stone was added as a centrepiece to the new bracelet. The Queen has continued to wear the set throughout the years, from her eve-of-wedding ball at Buckingham Palace to the Royal Opera House gala to celebrate her sixtieth birthday in 1986.

# Queen Victoria's Stud Earrings

ABOVE: *Two perfectly matched, large, brilliant-cut diamonds, which Queen Victoria had set as ear studs.* OPPOSITE, ABOVE LEFT: *She wore them in this portrait taken in 1873 when she was fifty-four. The huge diamond set in the brooch on the bodice of her dress is the 106-carat Koh-I-Noor.* OPPOSITE, ABOVE RIGHT: *Queen Alexandra in 1901.* OPPOSITE, BELOW LEFT: *Queen Mary in 1950. The oval brooch set with diamonds pinned to her collar belonged to Empress Marie Feodorovna of Russia before the turn of the century, when it also had three large oval diamond drops. Queen Mary bought it from her estate in 1929, and on her death in 1953 left it to Princess Marina, Duchess of Kent. It now belongs to Princess Michael of Kent.* OPPOSITE, BELOW RIGHT: *The Queen in 1961, visiting Freetown, Sierra Leone. Her modern gold brooch set with pavé diamonds has seven curved sprays of baguette diamonds and an arc of graduated square rubies. Her four-row necklace was made from family pearls.*

# THE QUEEN'S PEAR DROP EARRINGS

LEFT: *These modern, gold-set diamond stud earrings with large pear-shaped drops were made from family stones.*
BELOW, LEFT: *The Queen and Prince Philip at a film premiere in 1968.* BELOW, RIGHT: *In 1983 the Queen loaned the earrings to the Princess of Wales who was making her first official visit to Australia. At a banquet she wore the earrings with the Spencer family diamond tiara and the string of pearls with a diamond and sapphire clasp she received as a wedding present.*

# THE KING GEORGE VI CHANDELIER
# EARRINGS AND FESTOON NECKLACE

ABOVE: *These long chandelier earrings ending in three drops show examples of every known modern cut of diamond. They were a wedding gift to Princess Elizabeth in 1947 from King George and Queen Elizabeth, but it was not until she had her ears pierced that she was able to wear them. When it was noticed that she had done so, doctors and jewellers found themselves inundated with women anxious to have their ears pierced as well.* ABOVE, RIGHT: *In 1947 King George wanted to make some jewellery from 239 loose diamond collets that he had inherited, and in 1950 105 of them were set in this three-row festoon necklace with triangle motifs.* RIGHT: *In 1962 the Queen attended a Gilbert and Sullivan gala wearing the earrings and necklace.*

# Queen Victoria's Collet Necklace and Earrings

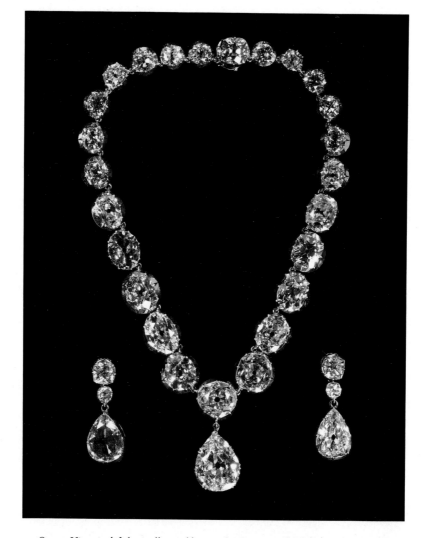

ABOVE: *Queen Victoria left her collet necklace and earrings to the Crown in 1901. They were made in 1858 from twenty-eight collet stones that she had had removed from a Garter Badge and a ceremonial sword; she wore them when Winterhalter painted her portrait in 1859. The necklace added up to 161 carats, the nine largest stones weighing between 8.25 and 11.25 carats each. The pendant stone, known as the Lahore diamond, and the drops in the earrings come from the Timur ruby necklace, taken from the Treasury of Lahore and presented to Queen Victoria by the Honourable East India Company in 1851.*
OPPOSITE, ABOVE LEFT: *This was Queen Victoria's official 1897 Diamond Jubilee Portrait, although the photograph had actually been taken in 1893. Her wide diamond bracelet is now worn by Queen Elizabeth the Queen Mother.* OPPOSITE, ABOVE RIGHT: *Queen Mary wore Queen Victoria's necklace as the bottom row of her diamond collar for her Coronation in 1911, and she wore Queen Victoria's stud earrings instead of the collet drops. The diamond stomacher on her bodice originally belonged to Queen Victoria. Queen Elizabeth the Queen Mother wore just the centre portion at her Coronation in 1937. Queen Mary's crown was made for her and is set only with diamonds, including the*

*106-carat Koh-I-Noor, which can be seen in the front. In 1937 Queen Elizabeth removed the detachable Lahore pendant from the collet necklace, had it cut down to 22.48 carats and wore it inserted in her new crown for the Coronation, wearing the necklace as a plain collet chain. At the same time she took out two of the large stones, replacing them with three smaller ones from another Crown collet necklace, and made another pair of earrings. Today there are twenty-nine collets and the three pendants from the Timur ruby necklace in the set of necklace and earrings.* ABOVE, LEFT: *Queen Elizabeth photographed in 1940. Her second chain of forty-five collets was also left to the Crown by Queen Victoria.* ABOVE, RIGHT: *The Queen wore the necklace and earrings at her Coronation in 1953, and here, in 1961, at a formal ceremony on an official visit to Sierra Leone.*

# THE KING FAISAL OF SAUDI ARABIA
## NECKLACE

# THE KING KHALID OF SAUDI ARABIA
## NECKLACE

OPPOSITE, ABOVE: *King Faisal of Saudi Arabia bought this fringe necklace of drop diamonds set
with brilliants and baguettes made by the American jeweller Harry Winston and
presented it to the Queen in 1967 on a State visit to England. The Queen wore it on the
last night of his visit when he gave a banquet at the Dorchester Hotel in her honour.*
OPPOSITE, RIGHT: *In 1979 the Queen wore the necklace to a film premiere together with a pair
of antique diamond girandole earrings, a triple-pendant design that Queen Victoria
had been very partial to more than a hundred years earlier.* OPPOSITE, LEFT: *In 1983 the Queen
loaned the necklace to the Princess of Wales for her visit to Australia.*
ABOVE, LEFT: *Another gift from Saudi Arabia, this modern collar of round and pear-shaped
diamonds in a sunray design made by Harry Winston, was given to the Queen by
King Khalid when she made a State visit to his country in February 1979. She wears it here
to a film premiere in 1982.* ABOVE, RIGHT: *She loaned it to the Princess of Wales to
wear on at least three occasions during 1982 and 1983. Here the Princess wears it with a
pair of ornate diamond and pearl drop earrings, which were given to her as a wedding
present by the Amir of Qatar.*

# QUEEN VICTORIA'S BOW BROOCHES

ABOVE: *Bow-knot brooches have been popular since the seventeenth century, and in May of 1858 Garrard made a set of three bow brooches, two large and one small, out of 506 diamonds supplied by Queen Victoria. Although it seems that there is no pictorial record to prove that Queen Victoria ever wore them herself, Queen Alexandra and Queen Mary both wore them at their Coronations.* OPPOSITE, ABOVE LEFT: *Queen Alexandra, in mourning for Queen Victoria at the first State Opening of Parliament of the new reign in 1901, wore the bow brooches on her skirt, and suspended from each one a chain of round diamond clusters, usually joined together as a necklace, with a large oval diamond drop on the end of each. She also wore the small diamond crown covered in 1,300 diamonds that Queen Victoria had had made in 1870, as she found the Imperial State Crown uncomfortably heavy to wear (page 64, top left). The diamond waterfall brooch on her collar and the wide diamond bracelet were both worn by Queen Victoria and are owned by Queen Elizabeth the Queen Mother at present.* OPPOSITE, ABOVE CENTRE: *For this formal photograph in 1912, Queen Mary wore all three of the bow brooches. From the top one is suspended the pear-shaped Cullinan III diamond and from the bottom two bows she has hung two large oval diamond drops. Directly above the bows is the 106-carat Koh-I-Noor diamond in a brooch setting.* OPPOSITE, ABOVE RIGHT: *Queen Elizabeth the Queen Mother wore just one bow in 1938, along with her signature rows of large lustrous pearls, although she sometimes wore the two big brooches as a set.* OPPOSITE, BELOW LEFT: *The Queen only ever wears one, as here in 1971.* OPPOSITE, BELOW RIGHT: *It is a tradition that members of the royal family who are staying at Balmoral for their summer*

holidays attend the annual Braemar Highland Games. In September 1986, just two months after her marriage to Prince Andrew, the Duchess of York came to the Games for the first time, where she is pictured here with Prince Charles. Pinned at the collar of her white blouse is one of the bows, a loan from the Queen. Her traditional pearl and diamond button earrings were a wedding gift.

# The Queen's
## Jardinière Brooch     Flower Basket Brooch

ABOVE, LEFT: *This small Art Deco platinum and diamond basket brooch overflowing with cabochon ruby berries, carved pale Indian emerald leaves and sapphire flowers, was a typical design of the 1930s, and variations of it were produced by Cartier in large numbers.* LEFT: *It was a present to the Queen from her parents in 1941, and she wears it here bicycling at Royal Lodge, Windsor, on 11 April 1942.*

ABOVE, RIGHT: *Bigger and more sophisticated than the jardinière brooch, this has a more naturalistic design with its simple garden-basket shape and spray of ruby, diamond and sapphire flowers. This style of brooch was sometimes known as a* giardinetti – *'little flower garden'. It was given to the Queen in November 1948 by her parents to mark the birth of Prince Charles, and she wore it a month later for his first official photographs.* RIGHT: *The Queen in 1973.*

# THE QUEEN'S IVY LEAF BROOCHES

ABOVE: *The royal family were on their official visit to South Africa at the time of Princess Elizabeth's twenty-first birthday on 21 April 1947, but her parents had come prepared with this twin pair of Cartier ivy leaf brooches, each covered with pavé-set diamonds and a large round brilliant in the centre.* RIGHT: *The Queen in 1951 wearing them as lapel brooches; she also wore them on her hat, or to accentuate the corners of a square neckline.*

# QUEEN ELIZABETH THE QUEEN MOTHER'S
## MAPLE LEAF BROOCH

ABOVE, LEFT: *When the King and Queen visited Canada in 1939, Her Majesty was presented with a large diamond-encrusted maple leaf brooch, the national emblem, which she wore constantly during the war pinned to her shoulder, hat or even on the side of a pochette bag. She wears it here at Royal Lodge, Windsor, in 1940. The gift followed a long tradition: in 1901 Queen Mary, then the Duchess of York, visited Canada as part of a seven-month-long tour of the Empire and she was given an enamel maple leaf spray by the ladies of Montreal. In 1923, Queen Elizabeth, then the Duchess of York, received as a wedding gift from the Canadian Legion of the British Empire Service League a gold maple leaf brooch set with diamonds.* ABOVE, RIGHT: *In 1951 Princess Elizabeth and Prince Philip toured Canada for the first time and the Princess borrowed her mother's brooch to wear during the trip.*

OPPOSITE, ABOVE: *This fancy ribbon-bow brooch set with fine brilliants was made by Carrington and Company and presented as a wedding gift to Queen Mary in 1893 by the 'County of Dorset'.* OPPOSITE, LEFT: *Queen Mary, then the Duchess of York, wearing the brooch in 1898. Her diamond tiara had been a wedding gift from Lord and Lady Iveagh. She left it to Princess Alice, Duchess of Gloucester, who has given it to her daughter-in-law the present Duchess.* OPPOSITE, RIGHT: *Queen Mary gave the brooch to Princess Elizabeth as a wedding present in 1947. She wears it for this formal portrait with Prince Philip in the drawing room of their home, Clarence House, in 1952.*

# Queen Mary's Dorset Bow Brooch

# QUEEN VICTORIA'S BAR BROOCH

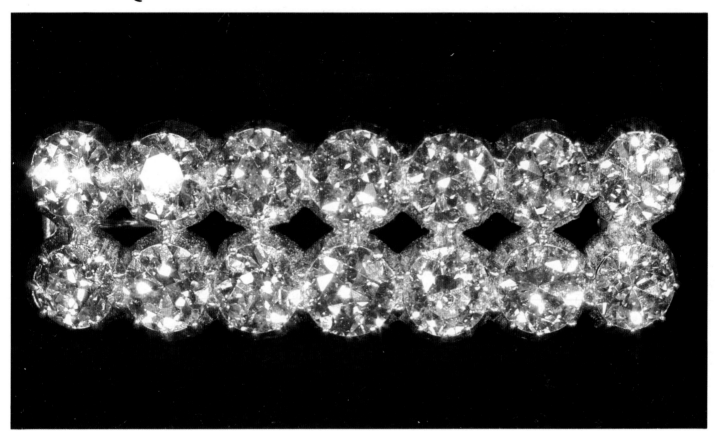

ABOVE: *In 1839 Queen Victoria wore two bar brooches of collet diamonds, pinned about three inches apart, to keep her Garter Riband securely in place (page 151, above left). Later she had them reset as a double bar brooch, which she left to the Crown in her will, its description tucked away in a long list of jewelled Orders.* OPPOSITE, ABOVE LEFT: *Queen Victoria photographed in 1893 as Empress of India.* OPPOSITE, ABOVE RIGHT: *Queen Alexandra photographed in about 1908. The beaded net of her dress was woven for her in India and the circlet is the one that Queen Victoria had made in 1858 to display the 106-carat Koh-I-Noor diamond, set in the front cross pattée and detachable. Queen Alexandra's waterfall brooch had belonged to Queen Victoria.* OPPOSITE, BELOW LEFT: *Queen Mary is wearing the bar brooch with the 'Cambridge sapphires' – a parure of tiara, necklace, stomacher, earrings and two bracelets that the Duchess of Cambridge, Queen Mary's grandmother, gave to her eldest daughter Augusta in 1843 when she married the Grand Duke of Mecklenburg-Strelitz. The Grand Duchess left these on her death in 1916 to her niece and goddaughter, Queen Mary, who in turn gave them to her goddaughter Princess Marina of Greece when in 1934 she married Queen Mary's fourth son, the Duke of Kent. Part of the set is presently worn by the Duchess of Kent. (For the necklace in the parure see page 114, above right.)* OPPOSITE, CENTRE: *Queen Elizabeth the Queen Mother wearing the brooch for her official eightieth-birthday portrait in 1980. She has pinned it vertically instead of horizontally. Her diamond tiara was made in the 1940s but was slightly altered by Cartier in the early 1950s when the triangle motifs were added. The necklace is the one that Queen Alexandra was given for her wedding (page 129).* OPPOSITE, NEAR LEFT: *The Queen wore the brooch at the annual Ghillies Ball at Balmoral in 1972.*

Stomachers first became popular in the fifteenth century and were designed to cover the front of the bodice; as fashions changed, so did the shape of the stomacher. When the waistline disappeared altogether in the early 1920s, stomachers quickly sank into oblivion and were either divided into smaller, more wearable brooches, or the stones used for completely new pieces of jewellery. OPPOSITE: *Queen Mary gave this eight-inch-long Victorian stomacher to the Queen as a wedding gift in 1947. Designed as a series of intersecting circles and half circles, it has ten diamond drops, and divides horizontally into three separate brooches.* ABOVE, LEFT: *Queen Mary with King Albert and Queen Elizabeth of the Belgians in 1922, when she and the King were paying them a State visit. In addition to the stomacher, she is also wearing the diamond diadem that she had made in 1911 to wear at the Delhi Durbar. Originally there were cabochon emeralds set on top, but they had been removed by this date. In the front are the third and fourth Cullinan stones, which replace part of the original delicate scroll design. In 1947 Queen Mary lent the diadem to Queen Elizabeth for the official trip to South Africa, which included opening Parliament. The Cullinans had been removed and the original setting restored. That was the last occasion on which this tiara has been seen.* ABOVE, RIGHT: *The Queen in the Green Drawing Room at Buckingham Palace in 1953. She is wearing the bottom, smallest part of the stomacher only, and has never worn the complete brooch. Her early-nineteenth-century diamond fringe necklace, a traditional Russian design, is threaded on silk and was a wedding gift from the Lord Mayor and Aldermen of the City of London, the Governor of the Bank of England, the Chairmen of the Stock Exchange, Lloyds and the Baltic Exchange and the Committee of the Crown Clearing Banks.*

# QUEEN MARY'S
# TRUE LOVER'S KNOT
# BROOCH

# PRINCE PHILIP'S NAVAL BADGE BROOCH

OPPOSITE, ABOVE RIGHT: *A large diamond bow in a 'true lover's knot' design with scalloped edges and pendant tassels.* OPPOSITE, LEFT: *Queen Mary painted by Sir Oswald Birley in April 1934. He painted the King at the same time, and when Queen Mary went to inspect the two portraits in the painter's studio on 4 May, she judged them as 'good'. In addition to the lover's knot brooch, she is wearing a diamond choker necklace that she gave to Queen Elizabeth the Queen Mother, who has shortened it into a bracelet (page 181).* OPPOSITE, BELOW RIGHT: *The Queen in July 1986 at a State banquet at Buckingham Palace. She inherited the brooch from Queen Mary in 1953. Here she wears with it the new tiara – a wreath of flowers made from Burmese rubies and diamonds – that she commissioned Garrard to make in 1973. The earrings are miniature flowers, the rubies edged with a circle of brilliant- and baguette-cut diamonds. Her necklace of round rubies surrounded by diamonds, with an ornate diamond centrepiece and three oval ruby drops surrounded by more diamonds, was acquired in the early 1960s. The stones for the tiara and earrings came from the Queen's private collection. She had been given a necklace of ninety-six rubies set in gold by the people of Burma as a wedding gift. The number ninety-six is significant because there is a Burmese tradition that there are ninety-six diseases that can affect the human body, and each of the rubies symbolized a charm against an illness, so that 'the recipient will be as impervious to the ninety-six diseases as is the lotus leaf to water'. The diamonds came from a tiara the Queen had been given as a wedding gift by the Nizam of Hyderabad and Berar (page 82, right).*

RIGHT: *Prince Philip was still a serving officer in the Royal Navy at the time of his marriage to Princess Elizabeth in November 1947. One of his first gifts to her was this miniature naval badge brooch set in diamonds. She wears it here in September 1950 as she poses in her sitting room at Clarence House for Princess Anne's first photograph, one month after her birth.*

# THE KING WILLIAM IV BROOCH

ABOVE: *In 1830 King William IV took six large brilliants and a number of smaller stones from a diamond-studded Badge of the Order of the Bath that had belonged to his father, King George III, and had this brooch made using the six large stones set in a circular frame around a cluster centre.* OPPOSITE, ABOVE LEFT: *This eleven-foot-high marble statue commemorates Queen Victoria's Golden Jubilee and was unveiled on 24 May 1889 at the Royal College of Physicians Examination Hall on the Embankment by the Prince of Wales, who in his speech said that there was 'nowhere a finer statue of the Queen'. The sculptor was Francis John Williamson. The brooch is pinned on her bodice just below the Crown collet necklace. In 1901 Queen Victoria left the brooch to the Crown.* OPPOSITE, ABOVE CENTRE: *Queen Alexandra wore the brooch in 1901 pinned at her waist.* OPPOSITE, ABOVE RIGHT: *Queen Mary in 1929 attached a large oval diamond drop to the brooch. Her diamond pear-shaped ring is the ninth Cullinan chip (page 74).* OPPOSITE, BELOW LEFT: *Queen Elizabeth the Queen Mother wore the brooch at her Coronation in 1937, and here in 1946 at the re-opening of the Royal Opera House Covent Garden after the war. Her diamond tiara of interconnecting circles originally belonged to Princess Mary Adelaide, Duchess of Teck, Queen Mary's mother, who wore it also as a necklace, as did Queen Elizabeth the Queen Mother (page 88). It now belongs to Princess Margaret, who only wears it as a necklace.* OPPOSITE, BELOW RIGHT: *The Queen in 1957 leading in her filly Carrozza after it won the Oaks.*

# THE CULLINAN

Captain Frederick Wells, Superintendent of the Premier Mine, one of South Africa's most
productive, which lies three hundred miles northeast of Kimberley in the Transvaal,
was making his daily inspection on 25 January 1905, when he saw a flash of reflected light
from the setting sun on the shaft wall. As he got closer to the spot, he detected a
partially exposed crystal, which at first he thought must be a piece of broken glass planted
there as a joke by one of the workers. Using his pocket-knife he finally dug out a rock
that weighed 1⅓ lb and was 3⅞ inches long, 2¼ inches wide and 2⅝ inches high.
Although it was twice the size of any diamond ever discovered and, so he believed,
must surely be worthless, Wells was a professional and automatically sent his find to be
analysed. His discovery turned out to be a diamond weighing 3,106 carats, and,
because one side was smooth, the experts suggested that it was only part of a much larger
stone that had been broken up by natural forces. Perfectly clear and colourless, it was
immediately named after Sir Thomas M. Cullinan, Chairman of the Premier Diamond
Company, who had discovered the mine in 1902 after a long period of fruitless
prospecting in the area.

Captain Wells received a £3,500 reward for his find, and the Transvaal Government
bought the stone for £150,000, although it was insured for ten times that amount.
Understandably its discovery caused a world-wide sensation. The diamond's greatest
value lay in the number of smaller gems that could be cut from it, and Prime Minister Botha
proposed that the Cullinan be given to King Edward VII as a 'token of the loyalty
and attachment of the people of Transvaal to his throne and person'. In the aftermath of the
bitter Boer War, the diamond nearly became a political football when Parliament
voted only forty-two to nineteen in favour of the presentation, oddly enough the Boers being
for and the English settlers voting against. Sir Henry Campbell-Bannerman, the
British Prime Minister, indecisively told the King that it must be his own decision as to
whether he accepted or not after such a divided vote; but after persistent urging by
Winston Churchill he finally agreed to accept, and the Transvaal Government presented
Churchill with a model of the diamond in gratitude, which he delighted in showing off
to his friends, sometimes displaying it on a silver salver.

The last obstacle to be surmounted was that of safely transporting the stone to
England. Detectives guarded the gem, insurance was arranged, and then it was packed up
and sent off by ordinary parcel post while a fake stone was taken aboard a steamer
under police escort and ceremoniously deposited in the Captain's safe, where it was guarded
by detectives for the duration of the voyage. In England, on 9 November 1907, the
King's sixty-sixth birthday, Sir Francis Hopwood and Mr Richard Solomon, Agent-General
for the Transvaal in London, carrying the genuine stone with them, travelled by train
to Sandringham in Norfolk, guarded by two senior Scotland Yard policemen. They reached
the house safely, despite rumours of a planned robbery attempt. The presentation was
made to the King while members of the large house party looked on, including the Queen of
Spain, the Queen of Norway, Lord Revelstoke and Bendor Westminster. At lunch the
conversation centred on how the stone ought to be cut so that it could be inserted in the
Crown, and afterwards the King presented Solomon with the KCVO. The King
announced, through the Secretary of State for the Colonies, Lord Elgin, that he accepted this
magnificent gift 'for myself and successors' and said that he would arrange that 'this
great and unique diamond be kept and preserved among the historic jewels which form the
heirlooms of the Crown'.

King Edward took a great personal interest in the cutting of the Cullinan and the
famous Dutch firm of Messrs I. J. Asscher of Amsterdam were entrusted with the task. They
studied the stone for three months and then on 10 February 1908 at 2.45 pm, Joseph
Asscher prepared to undertake the most momentous professional gamble he would ever make.
He inserted his steel cleaving blade at the precise point they had agreed upon, and

with his heavy hammer gave one decisive blow. The stone didn't move, but the blade
snapped. Mr Asscher calmly inserted a new blade and struck again. This time
everything went according to plan and the diamond split in two, one piece weighing 1,977.5
carats, and the other, 1,040 carats. Amid the jubilation Mr Asscher slid quietly to the
floor in a dead faint. Further cleaving produced nine major stones, known as the 'chips',
ninety-six small brilliants and nearly 10 carats of unpolished 'ends'. The total weight
amounted to 1,063 carats, which meant there had been a loss in cutting of 65 per cent.
Later that year, Joseph Asscher and his brother, Louis, travelled to England and gave
the King the two principal stones. It had been previously agreed that all the rest would stay
with the Asschers as their fee for the job, but King Edward now purchased the sixth
Cullinan 'chip', an 11.5-carat marquise-cut stone and gave it to Queen Alexandra as a
present. The King called the four largest stones the Stars of Africa. The Cullinan I, a
530.2-carat pear-shaped stone, 2⅛ inches long, 1¾ inches wide and one inch thick at its
deepest point, and the Cullinan II, an oblong of 317.4 carats, were sent to the Tower
of London to be displayed with the rest of the Crown Jewels, as well as the hammer and
cleaver with which Joseph Asscher had shaped them. They are the two largest cut
stones in the world. A brooch and pendant setting were produced so that Queen Alexandra
could wear them pinned to her Garter sash for the annual Opening of Parliament, but
otherwise they remained on public display. Garrard, the crown jeweller, was instructed to use
the Cullinan I and II for the Coronation of King George V on 22 June 1911.

*Cullinan I, now always called the Greater Star of Africa, was set in the head of the Sceptre with the Cross, and Cullinan II was mounted at the front of the brow band of the Imperial State Crown.*

*In 1910 Prime Minister Botha insisted that all the other stones cut from the Cullinan be purchased by the South African Government from Asschers as he feared they might be bought by private individuals. They were to be given to Queen Mary, then the Princess of Wales, during a visit she was to make that year with her husband to open the South African Parliament. However, their tour was cancelled because of King Edward VII's death and, instead, they were presented to her at Marlborough House on 28 June 1910 by Sir Richard Solomon, then High Commissioner of the Union of South Africa – the same man who had given the uncut stone to King Edward three years earlier.*

*PAGE 73: The Cullinan III and Cullinan IV, known as the Lesser Stars of Africa, were set as a brooch by Queen Mary in 1910. It is the single most valuable item owned by the Queen, who inherited the pieces of jewellery made from the Cullinan cleavings on the death of her grandmother in 1953. The pear-drop (III) of 94.4 carats hangs from (IV) a square-cut stone of 63.6 carats. ABOVE: Queen Mary set the ninth Cullinan chip, a 4.4-carat pear-shaped stone, in a ring with a claw setting. (She is seen wearing it in the photograph on page 66.) OPPOSITE, LEFT: Queen Mary on 6 February 1911. Dressed in full mourning for King Edward VII, King George V had opened Parliament for the first time, and he and the Queen posed for the first official photographs of their reign. The Queen is wearing Queen Victoria's Koh-I-Noor diadem, earrings and her two large bow brooches in addition to the Crown collet necklace, from which she has removed the drop and substituted the Lesser Stars of Africa as a pendant. Pinned to her Garter sash are the Crown Jewels, Cullinans I and II, worn as a brooch, and she is wearing seven rows of diamonds as a collar. Queen Mary wore the Lesser Stars of Africa brooch on all important occasions, including the marriages of four of her children and the wedding of Princess Elizabeth in 1947. She would also hang the Cullinan I as a pendant from*

# THE LESSER STARS OF AFRICA BROOCH AND THE CULLINAN IX RING

*the Koh-I-Noor brooch. For her Coronation in 1911, she had Cullinan III placed in the surmounting cross of her new crown, and Cullinan IV was set on the circlet; this is the only occasion when they appeared as part of the Crown Regalia.* ABOVE, RIGHT: *In comparison to Cullinans I and II, it is perhaps understandable that Queen Mary used to refer to her Lesser Stars of Africa as the 'chips', and from this comes one of the most misapplied quotations of the present Queen's reign. On 25 March 1958, while on a State visit to Holland, the Queen and Prince Philip made a tour of the Asscher diamond works, and, in talking about the cutting of the Cullinan diamond fifty years earlier, she referred to the Cullinans III and IV, which were pinned to her lapel, as 'Granny's Chips'. It is these two stones alone that are so nicknamed. This was the first occasion on which the Queen had ever worn the brooch, and during the afternoon she unpinned it and handed it to Louis Asscher who had been a witness as his brother cleaved the stone. The elderly man, nearly blind, was deeply moved that Her Majesty had brought the Cullinans with her, knowing how much it would mean to him to see them again after all these years. The Queen has worn the brooch perhaps no more than six times during her reign, but she wore it for this 1985 portrait as well as the ring made from the Cullinan IX chip.*

# THE CULLINAN V HEART BROOCH

ABOVE, RIGHT: *At the time Queen Mary was given the 102 Cullinan cleavings in 1910, she had no idea that she was about to acquire the Cambridge emeralds, which came into her possession later that same year. This brooch, made to show off the Cullinan V, an 18.8-carat heart-shaped stone, then became the centre of a massive diamond and emerald stomacher, the pieces coming apart to be worn as separate brooches (page 92, above left). The heart-shaped platinum setting and the positioning of the collets in the brooch were all expressly designed to accentuate the shape of the stone. Queen Mary wore the brooch alone in 1911 pinned to the simple daytime dresses she wore aboard ship as she and the King travelled to India for the Delhi Durbar. It was on her toque hat during the 1935 Silver Jubilee service held in St Paul's Cathedral, and for the Coronation of her son King George VI in 1937 she wore the circlet portion of her own 1911 crown with this brooch inserted as the centrepiece of the front cross pattée. ABOVE: In 1926 Queen Mary wore the heart-shaped Cullinan V and attached to it the brooch made from the Cullinan VII and Cullinan VIII chips. RIGHT: Of all the Queen's jewellery, this is probably the brooch she wears most often, as here on a trip to Australia in 1963.*

# THE CULLINAN VII AND CULLINAN VIII BROOCH

ABOVE: *Queen Mary used the Cullinan VII, an 8.8-carat marquise-cut stone, as a pendant to the Cullinan VIII, a 6.8-carat oblong brilliant, to form a second brooch, made at the same time as the Cullinan heart brooch and very similar in design.* ABOVE, RIGHT: *Queen Mary photographed with her only daughter, Princess Mary, the Princess Royal, in VAD uniform, at Buckingham Palace in 1919. Queen Mary's platinum and diamond pendant and chain has some of the ninety-six smaller Cullinan cleavings in it, and was inherited by the Queen in 1953. She has never worn it in public, complaining that 'it gets in the soup'.* RIGHT: *The Queen and Prince Philip on their 1961 trip to Sierra Leone. Notice how Queen Mary always wore her brooches dead centre, while the Queen invariably pins her brooches on her left shoulder.*

# QUEEN VICTORIA'S WHEAT EAR BROOCHES

ABOVE: *In 1830 the new King William IV ordered six brooches that could also be worn as hair ornaments. They were made from diamonds that had belonged to his father, King George III, and were replicas of wheat ears, a popular motif of the period. In her will Queen Victoria designated them as Crown jewellery.*
ABOVE, RIGHT: *Queen Victoria in an unusual 1896 hand-tinted photograph when she was seventy-seven years old. She is wearing three of the brooches pinned along the curve of her neckline. In addition to her diamond tiara, she has a number of small brooches pinned to the crown of her lace veil.* RIGHT: *The Queen at the Royal Opera House in 1974 wearing two of the ears as hair slides. Other royal ladies such as Princess Anne, the Duchess of York, the Duchess of Kent, the Duchess of Gloucester and Princess Michael of Kent also often enhance an evening hairstyle with sparkling combs and slides.*

# THE SWISS FEDERAL REPUBLIC'S WATCH

ABOVE: *The Swiss Federal Republic presented this specially designed platinum watch to the Queen in 1947 as a wedding gift. It was made at Vacheron & Constantin, the world's oldest watch factory, founded in Geneva in 1785. The diamond-encircled round watch face is joined to the diamond-set strap with loops of diamonds.* ABOVE, RIGHT: *The Queen wore the watch to a reception in 1975.* RIGHT: *In 1981 the Queen gave the watch to the Princess of Wales as a wedding gift. She wears it here in 1983, leaving a film premiere with Prince Charles. Her engagement ring is a large oval sapphire surrounded by fourteen round diamonds and set in 18-carat white gold.*

# THE KING WILLIAM IV BUCKLE BRACELETS

On King George V's accession to the Throne in 1910, Queen Mary had two blue enamel buckle mounts set as the centrepieces of matching four-row diamond bracelets, one of which was made in 1838 and left to the Crown by Queen Victoria; the other, which had formerly had a large portrait medallion of Prince Albert, was worn by Queen Victoria every day of her life following her marriage. The buckles had originally belonged to King William IV, and are surrounded by two rows of brilliant-cut diamonds with his cypher of WR surmounted by a crown on one, and that of Queen Adelaide on the other.

RIGHT: *Queen Mary wore them at her Coronation in 1911, and here in 1914. She is also wearing the circlet part of her crown with the 106-carat Koh-I-Noor diamond set above Cullinan IV. Cullinans I and II are worn as a brooch, and Cullinan III as a pendant from Queen Victoria's collet necklace.* ABOVE, LEFT: *In 1937 Queen Mary gave the bracelets to Queen Elizabeth and she too wore them at her Coronation. She wears them here in 1947, at a reception at County Hall. They became the property of the Queen in 1952.* ABOVE, RIGHT: *The Queen wore them at a 1953 reception to celebrate her Coronation, also at County Hall.*

THE FIRST NATURAL-COLOUR PHOTOGRAPH OF THE QUEEN PUBLISHED IN THE "ILLUSTRATED LONDON NEWS" BY SPECIAL PERMISSION: HER MAJESTY.

# Queen Mary's Link Bracelet

ABOVE, LEFT: *In 1929 Queen Mary purchased from the estate of the Dowager Empress Marie Feodorovna of Russia this diamond tiara with a large sapphire mounted in the front scallop, sapphire and diamond cluster earrings, the diamond chain-link choker necklace, and the brooch of a square-cut sapphire surrounded by two rows of diamonds. She is wearing them for her official sixty-ninth birthday photograph in 1936. The sapphire surrounded by brilliant-cut diamonds in the tiara was removable and either a diamond flower matching the side motifs or a pink beryl could be worn in its place. Queen Mary gave the sapphire to Princess Margaret to be worn as a brooch, and the tiara to her daughter-in-law, Princess Alice, Duchess of Gloucester, who now shares it with her daughter-in-law, the present Duchess. The brooch was left to the Queen, but is not used. The earrings were left to Princess Marina, who left them to the Duchess of Kent.* ABOVE, RIGHT: *The diamond chain-link necklace could be divided into two bracelets, which is how Queen Mary wore it for her official birthday photograph in 1938. The Koh-I-Noor diamond, which is Crown property, had been removed from the front cross pattée of the diamond circlet, and given to Queen Elizabeth to wear in the new crown made for her Coronation in 1937, and Queen Mary has replaced it with the Cullinan V heart brooch.* LEFT: *The Queen wearing the bracelet which she inherited from Queen Mary in 1953. On her left wrist is a diamond evening watch with an oblong face and bracelet strap that she has had since the late 1940s.*

OPPOSITE: *Queen Mary first went to India as Princess of Wales in 1905 and instantly fell in love with the country. 'Lovely India, beautiful India', she said repeatedly. In 1907 the Maharajah of Bikaner presented her with these typically Indian twin diamond-studded bangles, which can either be worn separately or, when a hidden hinge is snapped, as one.* ABOVE, LEFT: *Queen Mary in 1911 wearing the bracelets on her left wrist.* ABOVE, RIGHT: *In 1947 Queen Mary gave them as a wedding gift to Princess Elizabeth, who wore them in 1951 to a dinner given by King Haakon of Norway who was in London on a State visit.*
*Her diamond bandeau tiara was made by Cartier, Paris, in a wreath design of English roses and foliage, a style typical of the early nineteenth century. The central large rose and the two slightly smaller side ones were detachable and could be worn independently as brooches. The piece was a wedding gift from the Nizam of Hyderabad and Berar, who himself possessed one of the world's most valuable jewellery collections. Although the Queen continues to wear the brooches – the large rose on its own, the smaller two together – the tiara was broken up and the diamonds used for the new ruby and diamond tiara she had made in 1973 (page 68). The diamond flower-petal earrings were a twenty-first-birthday present from the Diplomatic Corps.*

# QUEEN MARY'S INDIAN
## BANGLE BRACELETS

# THE QUEEN'S MODERN BAGUETTES
## AND BRILLIANTS BRACELET

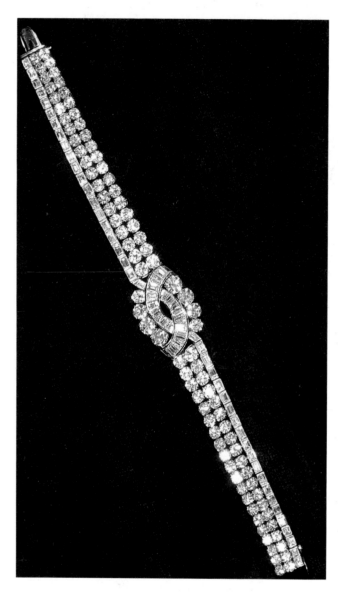

ABOVE: *A line of baguette diamonds runs alongside a double row of brilliants, meeting and criss-crossing in the centre.* ABOVE, RIGHT: *The Queen wore the bracelet on her State visit to Sri Lanka in 1982.* RIGHT: *In 1983 Her Majesty loaned the bracelet to the Princess of Wales for her first visit to Australia.*

# THE QUEEN'S ENGAGEMENT RING AND THE PRINCE PHILIP WEDDING BRACELET

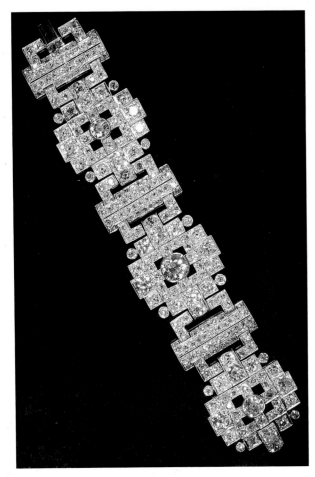

ABOVE, LEFT: *The diamonds in the Queen's engagement ring and her wedding present from Prince Philip, a bracelet, all came from a tiara that belonged to his mother, Princess Andrew of Greece. Her brother, Earl Mountbatten of Burma, loved to design jewellery for his wife and he had often used the London firm of Philip Antrobus Ltd, which was founded in Birmingham in 1815. He recommended them to his nephew, who also had very strong views on design and knew what he wanted done. Antrobus dismantled the tiara, and the platinum ring was set with eleven diamonds, a central solitaire stone of 3 carats with five smaller stones set in each shoulder. The ring was made by George Taubl, and the stones set by Harry Marchant. Prince Philip formally asked the King's permission to marry his daughter on 8 July 1947, he then produced the ring, but unfortunately it was discovered to be slightly too big and had to be sent back to Antrobus to be made smaller. However, the ring was returned in time for the Princess to wear it on 10 July, after the engagement was formally announced and the couple posed for photographers. That afternoon at a Buckingham Palace garden party the guests crowded around to get their first look at the ring. To this day, if the Queen is annoyed about anything, she will start to twist the ring round and round, a sign that her staff recognizes immediately. ABOVE: Prince Philip was also deeply involved with the design of the wide diamond and platinum bracelet that he gave to the Queen as his wedding gift. She wears it often at night or when in full ceremonial dress for a public event such as the Opening of Parliament. LEFT: The Queen in 1948.*

# Emeralds

THE QUEEN'S MAGNIFICENT collection of royal emeralds, as represented by the Cambridge and Delhi Durbar parure, has been seen and photographed countless times (pages 88 – 93). But the mere mention of the word emeralds in connection with the royal family raises a hornet's nest of speculation and hearsay as to the source of the emeralds given by the Duke of Windsor to his wife. Ever since the mid-1930s stories have circulated that when Princess Alexandra of Denmark arrived in England in February 1863 to marry the Prince of Wales, the future King Edward VII, she brought with her a valuable collection of uncut emeralds as a gift from the Danish people. In fact this story is a total fabrication, as can be confirmed by checking the meticulous records made of all the wedding gifts the couple were given.

The few small emeralds that the Princess of Wales did acquire at the time of her marriage were given to her in different pieces of jewellery. There was a wide diamond and emerald bracelet from the 'Ladies of South Wales'. The design is of leeks, the Welsh national emblem, entwined with a scroll bearing the motto in Welsh, 'May God preserve our own Princess'. The leaves and buds of the leeks are emeralds, the bulbs are of pearls and the roots of gold, in which are set tiny brilliants. This bracelet is currently worn by Queen Elizabeth the Queen Mother.

From the 'Ladies of North Wales' there was a large emerald and diamond oval brooch also depicting a leek, with a cabochon emerald drop. Queen Elizabeth the Queen Mother owns this, too, and wore it at Prince Charles's investiture as Prince of Wales in 1969.

Another of Princess Alexandra's wedding gifts, this from the 'Ladies of Bristol', was an oval diamond pendant with the three feathers' motif of the Prince of Wales, and a cabochon emerald drop. It was this pendant, kept in storage for many years, that Queen Elizabeth the Queen Mother gave to Lady Diana Spencer as an engagement present in 1981. The Princess often wears it on a diamond chain necklace, sometimes with or without the detachable emerald drop.

In 1875 King Edward VII, then Prince of Wales, made an extended tour of India and returned laden with valuable gifts. These included some magnificent pieces of jewellery for his wife, Princess Alexandra, and his mother, Queen Victoria. Over the next twenty-five years the Princess of Wales reset many of the gems from these pieces in new designs that more suited her ethereal style.

From 1901 to 1910, her years as Queen, she increased her personal collection of jewels through gifts and purchases, and also wore those jewels that were designated in Queen Victoria's will as being held in trust for all future Queens of England. When King Edward VII died in 1910, she handed these over to her daughter-in-law, Queen Mary. Queen Alexandra died intestate in 1925. On Saturday 9 January 1926 three of her surviving children, Queen Maud of Norway, Princess Victoria of Wales and King George V, with his wife, Queen Mary, gathered at Sandringham House, where Queen Alexandra had spent her last years, to divide into equal shares her jewels and other possessions.

It is quite clear that King George and Queen Mary included in their portion any jewellery that Queen Alexandra had inherited from Queen Victoria or that she had received as wedding gifts from the Prince of Wales and various civic bodies in 1863. The King and Queen established the precedent that although personal property these pieces were indivisible from the monarchy, and in December 1936, when the Duke of York became King George VI, Queen Mary handed them on to Queen Elizabeth.

Nearly ten years after Queen Alexandra's death, her grandson, the then Prince of Wales, began his relationship with Mrs Wallis Simpson, and the value of the jewellery he gave her caused nearly as much comment as did their association. It was then that the rumours began to spread in society circles that he had inherited these splendid jewels from Queen Alexandra. After the King's abdication in December 1936, the stories that he had left

England with jewels properly belonging to the new King, or that the jewellery worn by Mrs Simpson had originally belonged to the royal family reached such a crescendo that Mrs Simpson, living in France while she waited for her divorce decree to become final, issued two public denials. In an interview with writer and barrister Helena Normanton she flatly denied that she had ever been given any jewellery that had belonged to Queen Alexandra or any other member of the royal family. She added to this the information that the Duke of Windsor had never at any time inherited any jewellery from any member of the royal family. She also authorized her cousin Newbold Noyes in America to make a formal denial that the Duke had given her Crown jewellery that she had later been forced to return to the royal family.

Until his death in 1972 the Duke stated emphatically that he had never given his wife any jewels that were royal property. Buckingham Palace when questioned said that they knew of no royal jewels owned by the Duke and Duchess of Windsor, and in Paris the Windsors' lawyer, Maître Blum, repeatedly said that she had the receipts for the Duchess's jewellery, all of which had been purchased from jewellers such as Cartier, Harry Winston, David Webb, Van Cleef & Arpels and Boucheron. However, even after the Duchess died in 1986 the stories about 'Alexandra's emeralds' continued. To the gossips the fact that the Duke had bought his wife's jewellery was much less interesting than the myth that the Duchess had stolen a country's precious national heirlooms as well as its King.

The Queen's other pieces of emerald jewellery include a ring, a square emerald with a brilliant-cut diamond on either side that she once loaned to the Princess of Wales. The Princess wore it while watching polo at Smith's Lawn, Windsor, and when journalists noticed it there was much excited speculation in the press that Prince Charles had given it to her as an anniversary gift. Other emeralds in the Queen's collection are large detachable pendant drops that can be substituted for pear-shaped diamond drops in a pair of long diamond scallop-frame earrings with ribbon-bow studs that the Queen has worn with the Godman necklace (page 95). She was also given an emerald and diamond necklace as a wedding present by the city of Victoria, British Columbia, in the shape of dogwood flowers, the province's emblem, but the Queen has never worn this in public.

Queen Elizabeth the Queen Mother has a magnificent eighteenth-century emerald and diamond necklace said to have belonged to Queen Marie Antoinette of France, which she inherited from a close friend of the royal family, Mrs Ronnie Greville, in 1942. Queen Elizabeth had spent her honeymoon in 1923 at the immensely rich Mrs Greville's house, Polesden Lacey, in Surrey, which now belongs to the National Trust. She also owns pendant emerald earrings, diamond and emerald bracelets and two large emerald and diamond brooches.

Among the many gifts Queen Mary and King George V gave to Lady Alice Montagu-Douglas-Scott when she married the Duke of Gloucester in 1935 was a suite of emerald, pearl and diamond jewellery. Two necklaces of Indian pearl and emerald beads had been made from the seven-row collar that Queen Victoria gave the Princess of Wales as a wedding gift in 1863, and Queen Mary added a detachable oval cabochon emerald drop to hang from each (centre, page 92). Two wide diamond and emerald bracelets of different design were also included. Princess Alice used to wear them side by side, but the present Duchess of Gloucester wears only one.

As well, there was a large diamond corsage brooch with a horizontal scroll and filigree design with a round cabochon emerald set in the centre and three detachable emerald drops. Originally it had three long diamond tassels from which the emeralds were suspended, but Princess Alice replaced the two outer tassels and pendants with the two cabochon drops from the necklaces and hooked these directly onto the brooch on either side of the central emerald pendant. The diamond and emerald tassels were made into a new pair of pendant earrings.

Princess Alice later acquired a nineteenth-century diamond festoon necklace set with square-cut emeralds and matching earrings of square-cut emeralds set in clusters of diamonds. In 1953 Queen Mary bequeathed to Princess Alice another corsage brooch to add to the emerald demi-parure. This was V-shaped and made of diamonds, with two emeralds set one above the other in the centre and a pendant emerald drop. The brooch has been worn by the present Duchess. She also has an unusual sapphire ring that is very similar to an emerald one that Queen Alexandra wore in the 1890s. The ring has a cross-over design with two high cabochon stones set at angles to each other. Queen Alexandra wore hers next to her gold wedding band, which was set with six tiny gems – a beryl, an emerald, a ruby, a turquoise, a jacinth and a second emerald – spelling 'Bertie', the name by which King Edward VII was always known to his family.

This, the most magnificent parure of jewellery in the Queen's possession, was created by Queen Mary, using stones from four different sources, and endures as a tribute to her taste and majestic sense of style. The story begins in 1818, when King George III's seventh and favourite son, Adolphus, Duke of Cambridge, married Princess Augusta of Hesse, who was twenty-one to his forty-four. While they were visiting Frankfurt, a State lottery was held in aid of charity; the Duchess bought some tickets and won a small box containing some forty graduated cabochon emeralds. Back in England she used some of them to make a pair of drop earrings and a necklace with five pendant stones.

RIGHT: At her death in 1889 at York House, St James's Palace, the earrings, necklace and remaining emeralds became the property of her younger daughter, Princess Mary Adelaide, Duchess of Teck. She is photographed wearing the earrings and necklace around 1893. The Duchess had previously bought her diamond stomacher from Garrard, and set another of the emeralds in it, surrounding the emerald with two rows of diamonds. A second emerald was set in a diamond leaf mount and hung as a pendant from the bottom of the stomacher. When the Duchess died intestate in 1897, her jewellery was divided among her four children. Her daughter, Queen Mary, then the Duchess of York and living in her grandmother's old home, York House, took this striking diamond tiara with its design of crescents and stars, and large diamond necklace of interconnecting circles. The Duchess of Teck had worn both of these

pieces at her daughter's wedding in 1893 at the Chapel Royal, St James's Palace. In the 1930s Queen Mary gave the tiara to her daughter-in-law Queen Elizabeth, after removing the bottom two rows of diamonds so that it sat much lower on the head; she also gave the diamond necklace to Queen Elizabeth, who later passed it on to Princess Margaret.

The Duchess of Teck's second son, the unmarried Prince Francis, got the emeralds, including the centrepiece and pendant from the stomacher, which itself went to the youngest son, Prince Alexander. When Prince Alexander married Princess Alice of Albany, Queen Victoria's granddaughter, in 1904, he had a new detachable centre portion set with sapphires made for the stomacher and gave it to his bride. As Princess Alice, the Countess of Athlone, she remembered, in old age, wearing it at three Coronations: King George V's, King George VI's and the Queen's. On 28 June 1910, Queen Mary was given the cleavings from the Cullinan by the Union of South Africa: six large stones and ninety-six small brilliants. Less than six months later, on 22 October, her brother Francis died suddenly at the age of forty. He had given his mother's emeralds to his mistress, but within days of his funeral Queen Mary bravely sent an emissary to the lady asking her to return the jewels, which she did. Now the Queen had the Cambridge emeralds and the 102 Cullinan cleavings with which to make a completely new set of jewellery as she prepared for her Coronation, on 22 June 1911, and the Delhi Durbar, on 12 December, when she would be acclaimed Empress of India. The Indian word 'durbar' means both a gathering of chieftains to make administrative decisions and a purely ceremonial gathering at which they paid homage to their ruler.

# THE CAMBRIDGE AND DELHI DURBAR PARURE

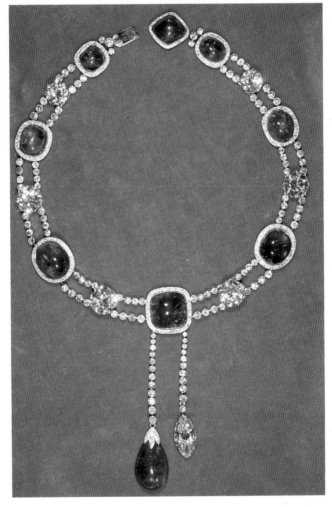

Queen Mary had a new diamond crown made for the Coronation, but an Act of Parliament
dating from the time of King Edward III, who tried to pawn the Crown Jewels in
Flanders to finance a war with France, prevents the Regalia from being taken out of the
United Kingdom, and so King George V had commissioned an Indian Crown
especially for the Delhi ceremony. Even though Queen Mary's crown was her personal
property she decided not to take it either, but to design a new diadem for the occasion.
While the jewellers were working on her new parure, Queen Mary was informed that the
'Ladies of India' wished to make her a gift of jewellery to mark the occasion of the
Durbar. She suggested that the gift should be Indian emeralds to add to the new set and so a
second necklace and a brooch were made to co-ordinate with the other pieces and sent
ahead to Delhi for the formal presentation. In June 1911, the Queen wore her mother's
original necklace, the Cambridge emerald earrings and brooch made from the two
emerald parts of the stomacher (page 88, above), for her son David's Investiture as Prince of
Wales at Carnarvon Castle, so the new pieces were actually made between then and
November.

PAGE 88: *Queen Mary photographed in 1912 after returning from India, wearing the
complete parure. Her new high scroll-and-festoon diamond tiara surmounted by five of the
Cambridge emeralds was described by King George V in a letter about the Durbar to
his mother, Queen Alexandra, as 'May's best tiara'. The emerald and diamond cluster
earrings matched the diamond chain bracelet with its three cluster plaques on her right
wrist. The delicate emerald choker with its connecting rosettes of small brilliants was also
made from the Cambridge stones; but the larger necklace and negligé pendant below
it was the gift from the 'Ladies of India', as was the ancient engraved square emerald brooch
pinned on the right of her bodice. In Delhi, on 9 December, the Queen received the
Maharani of Patiala and some of the ladies from her committee, who ceremoniously
presented her with the necklace and brooch she had planned so carefully back in
London. In her personally written thank-you speech she said:*

'The jewel you have given me will ever be very precious in my
eyes, and, whenever I wear it, though thousands of miles of land and sea
separate us, my thoughts will fly to the homes of India, and
create again and again this happy meeting and recall the tender love

*your hearts have yielded me. Your jewel shall pass to future
generations as an imperial heirloom, and shall always stand as a token
of the first meeting of an English Queen with the ladies of India.'*

Three days later, dressed in her heavily embroidered Coronation gown, she wore the complete
parure at the Durbar. When Queen Mary sent photographs of the splendid occasion
to her aunt, the Grand Duchess of Mecklenburg-Strelitz, she wrote back:

*'Mama's Emeralds appearing there amused and pleased me.
What would she have said to her Grandchild's Imperial glory? in which
I so rejoice!'*

PAGE 89, ABOVE: *The Cambridge earrings, oval cabochon emeralds, each set
in a cluster of eleven brilliant-cut diamonds.* PAGE 89, BELOW: *The
'Ladies of India' necklace has eight cabochon emeralds surrounded by
diamonds, set in two chains of small diamonds, with a single
large diamond between each emerald. Typically Edwardian was the
removable negligé pendant of two drops of unequal length; the
large pear-shaped emerald was part of the Indian gift, but the 11.5-
carat marquise-cut diamond was the Cullinan VI, which King
Edward had bought from Asscher in 1907 and given to Queen
Alexandra as a gift. After his death she gave it to Queen Mary,
who added it to the necklace. For certain ceremonial occasions, such as
the Opening of
Parliament in 1913,
however, she
suspended the 94.4-carat
Cullinan III
diamond as the pendant
drop instead.*

OPPOSITE: *In 1921 Queen
Mary bought from
Princess Nicholas of
Greece the diamond
and pearl tiara she had inherited on the death of
her mother, the Grand Duchess Vladimir
of Russia (page 116). Over the following years
the refugee Princess Nicholas sold a
number of pieces of jewellery in order to help
support her family and worthy Russian
charities. The Queen still had fifteen of the
Cambridge cabochon emeralds left, and
these were now put in pavé-set diamond mounts,
and the tiara adapted so that it could be
worn with either the pearl or the emerald drops.
ABOVE: Queen Mary wearing the tiara in
1937, together with the 'Ladies of India'
necklace from which she had removed the
negligé pendant. The 'Ladies of India' carved
emerald brooch pinned to her Garter
sash was left to the Queen, but she has never
worn it.* LEFT: *The Queen inherited the
parure on her grandmother's death in 1953 and
wears it here in 1957.*

OPPOSITE, ABOVE LEFT: *The stomacher of Cambridge emeralds and small Cullinan chips, which was designed in 1911, comes apart, so that it can be worn as separate brooches. In the centre is the 18.8-carat heart-shaped Cullinan V (page 76). From the 6.8-carat oblong Cullinan VIII hangs an emerald drop (page 77).* OPPOSITE, ABOVE CENTRE: *The cabochon emerald brooch surrounded by two circles of diamonds and with an emerald drop, pinned at the bottom of the stomacher, was made by simply putting together the two Victorian pieces removed from the Duchess of Teck's stomacher in 1897 (page 88).*

OPPOSITE, ABOVE RIGHT: *Queen Mary wearing the brooch in 1925. Following her brother Francis's death in 1910, she wore it at the Prince of Wales's Investiture in June 1911.* OPPOSITE, BELOW LEFT: *One of the Queen's favourite brooches, she wears it here in 1979.* OPPOSITE, BELOW CENTRE: *This diamond scroll brooch with a central lozenge-shaped emerald was made by taking the main portion from the centre of the stomacher and hanging the emerald drop from Cullinan VIII from it. It is possible to see where the two parts are connected.* OPPOSITE, BELOW RIGHT: *The Queen arriving for the 1967 Derby. She is also wearing a unique pair of pearl button earrings that have a small diamond on both the top and bottom.* LEFT: *By 1927, Queen Mary had had the delicate choker of Cambridge emeralds, made in 1911, redesigned in the fashionable Art Deco style. The diamond-encircled cabochon stones are now divided by geometric diamond plaques, each with a small emerald centre. The bangle bracelet set with two oval emeralds on her right wrist was part of the original parure. The Art Deco choker was left to the Queen, but she has never worn it. In 1981 she took it out of storage and gave it to the Princess of Wales as a wedding gift. That December, the Princess had the fourteen-inch-long necklace mounted on a band of dark green Velcro, so that she could wear it as a headband at a private party during the Christmas holidays.* RIGHT: *Instead of a tiara, she wore the necklace across her forehead as a bandeau, for the first time in public, at a charity dance on her visit to Australia in 1984. Her long pendant diamond earrings with an oval emerald drop, and a diamond Art Deco bracelet with zigzag bands of emeralds (not seen here), were bought by Prince Charles as a wedding gift at Wartski Ltd in 1981.*

# QUEEN MARY'S ART DECO BRACELET

LEFT: *Queen Mary later added this wide diamond bracelet set with two square emeralds to the parure, and wore it for her Silver Jubilee portrait in 1935.*
BELOW: *The Queen and Prince Philip arriving at Royal Ascot in 1967.*

# Queen Victoria's Fringe Earrings and The Godman Necklace

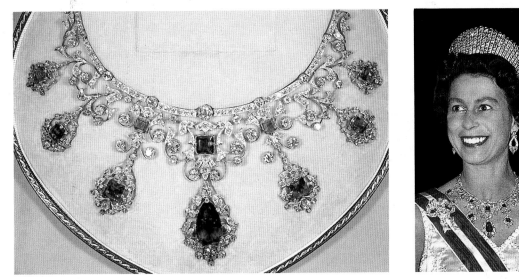

LEFT: *In April of 1850, Queen Victoria purchased a pair of diamond earrings whose emerald drops were framed by a swinging diamond fringe. In her will she left them to the Crown. For King Edward VII's Coronation, on 9 August 1902, Queen Alexandra literally covered her Medici collar and dress of embroidered Indian net with jewels. From her diamond fringe girdle she hung a hem-length double chain, which was caught up in swags by an assortment of brooches. From the bottom two of Queen Victoria's three bow brooches she suspended the emerald fringe earrings as pendants. Her new four-arched crown was made of platinum instead of the traditional gold. Entirely covered with brilliants, the 106-carat Koh-I-Noor diamond is set in the front cross pattée. This is the first occasion on which it was worn at a Coronation, but it is now a tradition that the stone is set in the Queen Consort's crown. The crown is on display in the Jewel House at the Tower of London.*
RIGHT: *In 1969 the Queen wore the earrings and the Godman diamond and emerald necklace to a reception at the Schönbrunn Palace in Vienna.* CENTRE: *The Godman necklace, which was thought to have a royal provenance, had been bought by Frederick DuCann Godman, the noted naturalist, expert on the zoology of Central America and a British Museum Trustee, while on holiday in Bavaria in the 1890s. He gave it to his two daughters, and in 1965, long after his death, the elderly spinster sisters wrote to the Lord Chamberlain saying that they believed they owned a piece of jewellery that had once belonged to the Empress Joséphine of France and that this might be of interest to Her Majesty. Sir Francis Watson, Surveyor of the Queen's Works of Art, met them at their bank and inspected the necklace, where it was stored in a vault. Disappointingly, it didn't match the detailed description of an emerald necklace in the inventory of the Empress's jewels, and further investigation in Bavaria, where her son by her first marriage, Eugène de Beauharnais, who married the Princess Amalie Auguste of Bavaria, had retired in 1814 after the overthrow of his stepfather, the Emperor Napoleon, proved that he had never inherited it from his mother. Despite the lack of a royal connection, the Misses Godman said that they would like to present the necklace to the Queen, only requesting that she wear it occasionally. Although it is very rare for a member of the royal family to accept a personal gift from someone they do not know, this was felt to be a special occasion and the Queen, greatly touched by such a generous gesture, was delighted to add the necklace to her collection. Now came the question of how to say thank you; the Godmans might be uncomfortable at a grand lunch or dinner, a large reception or garden party would be too impersonal, and so they were invited to meet the Queen at Buckingham Palace for a private audience.*

# QUEEN ALEXANDRA'S INDIAN
# NECKLACE

ABOVE, CENTRE: *In 1863, one of Princess Alexandra of Denmark's wedding gifts from Queen Victoria was a suite of Indian ornaments, comprising a collar, armlet and two bracelets, made from uncut emeralds, diamonds and pearls. The seven-row collar of pearl and emerald beads was hung with a multitude of diamond pendants with emerald or pearl drops.* ABOVE, LEFT: *Queen Alexandra, then Princess of Wales, on 2 July 1897, at the Duchess of Devonshire's costume ball to celebrate Queen Victoria's Diamond Jubilee. The Indian necklace lies just below her dog-collar.* BELOW, LEFT: *In the 1920s Queen Mary broke up the piece. She made a rope of the pearl and emerald beads, which she wore before giving them to her daughter-in-law, Princess Alice, Duchess of Gloucester, as a wedding gift in 1935, and she gave one of the diamond pendants, with a pearl drop, on a thin gold chain to her first granddaughter, Princess Elizabeth, who wears it here in 1931 for her official fifth-birthday photograph.* RIGHT: *In 1960 ten-year-old Princess Anne was photographed with her month-old baby brother, Prince Andrew, wearing her mother's necklace.* ABOVE, RIGHT: *An identical necklace was given to the Queen's niece, Lady Sarah Armstrong-Jones, who is photographed with her mother, Princess Margaret, and her brother, Viscount Linley.*

# Gold

THE QUEEN HAS NEVER SHOWN any great liking for plain gold jewellery, except for watches, one of which was an official present from Canada in 1951, and her wedding ring. The nugget of 22-carat Welsh yellow gold from which the Queen's simple narrow band was made was actually produced before the First World War and presented to the Duke of York in 1923 to fashion a wedding ring for Lady Elizabeth Bowes-Lyon. The nugget was taken from the Clogau St David's mine in Bontddu, Gwynedd, and was big enough to make Princess Elizabeth's ring in 1947, Princess Margaret's in 1960, Princess Anne's in 1973 and the Princess of Wales's in 1981. In 1981 a new bar of 22-carat Clogau St David's gold was presented to the Queen by the British Legion, and the first ring made from this was for Sarah Ferguson when she married Prince Andrew in July 1986. The tradition of using Welsh gold goes back to the wedding of Princess May of Teck in 1893, and it has been used for every royal wedding ring since then.

Prince Albert, King Edward VII and King George V all wore wedding rings on the fourth finger of their left hand, but since 1923 a tradition has been established by the male members of the royal family of wearing a narrow wedding band next to the crested gold signet ring on the little finger of their left hand. The only exception to this is Prince Michael of Kent who wears a wide gold band on his wedding-ring finger.

Unlike the Queen, the younger ladies in the royal family often wear gold, especially Princess Anne who always wears gold chain necklaces if she is not wearing the more traditional pearls. A ring worn by the Princess of Wales, the Duchess of York, the Duchess of Gloucester and Princess Anne is the Cartier rolling ring, first designed by French jeweller Louis Cartier in 1923 and consisting of three interlaced bands of yellow, pink and white gold in the style of a traditional Russian wedding ring.

Queen Victoria gave each of her grandchildren a gold watch on their tenth birthday, adding to her good wishes the hope that the gift would teach them to be punctual as well as punctilious in all their duties. Today the Princess of Wales wears a round-faced 18-carat gold watch that she received as an engagement present, Princess Anne has a gold Rolex and the Duchess of York was given two of Cartier's gold Panther watches as wedding gifts.

Another style emulated by Queen Victoria's descendants is that of the heavily laden gold charm bracelet. Queen Victoria's was usually hung with miniatures of her husband and children; Princess Marina, Duchess of Kent, wore Russian Easter eggs made from different precious stones on one of hers; Princess Alexandra wears charms which have sentimental meaning; and both Princess Margaret and Princess Anne had charm bracelets when they were teenagers.

The Princess of Wales had a gold link bracelet long before her marriage and Prince Charles gives her an appropriate charm for her birthday every July. One of the most successful of these came in 1983 just after the couple returned from Australia on their first official overseas tour together. They had taken the one-year-old Prince William with them and during the tour his father revealed he had been nicknamed 'Wombat' long before they had left home. When they returned to England Prince Charles had Collingwood design a gold wombat charm for his wife.

A gold necklace owned by the Princess follows an even older fashion trend and demonstrates how some things never change. A sixteenth-birthday present from a member of her family was a gold 'D' on a short chain, strikingly similar to a gold pendant 'B' that Anne Boleyn, King Henry VIII's second wife, wore in the sixteenth century.

Another birthday gift in a similar vein was given to the Princess by her husband two years after their marriage. This was on a narrow twisted gold hoop necklace, commonly called a torque in ancient Britain, from which hung a gold disc with 'William' written on it in the Prince's handwriting. The present Duke of Gloucester has also designed a personalized gift for his wife: a large gold brooch in the shape of an interlocked 'R' and 'B', representing their names, Richard and Birgitte.

# *Pearls*

ALTHOUGH DIAMONDS without a doubt are the most regal of all gemstones, it is pearls that seem to be inextricably linked with royal ladies. This is not just an English phenomenon either; looking at portraits and photographs of royalty, pearls are inescapable, an integral component of the royal uniform.

It was during the Tudor era and particularly the reign of Queen Elizabeth I that pearls really ruled supreme. The Queen inherited her father King Henry VIII's passionate love of fine jewels, but above anything else she preferred pearls, perhaps because they were said to represent virtue and chastity and she revelled in being her people's Virgin Queen.

Queen Elizabeth I wore ropes of pearls as necklaces, literally yards of them hanging down as far as her knees, while more pearls were threaded through her auburn wigs, and her crowns and lace ruffs were studded with them. Her dresses, made of the most sumptuous and costly materials, were heavily embroidered in intricate patterns with hundreds of pearls. Some of these were fakes, however, produced by putting an iridescent paste made from the scales of a fish called the bleak into thin glass beads.

Disappointingly, one of the most famous royal pearls never belonged to Queen Elizabeth. This was the pear-shaped *La Peregrina* (the incomparable). Discovered in the Gulf of Panama, it was sold to King Philip II of Spain who presented it to his wife, Mary Tudor, a month before their marriage in 1554. When Queen Elizabeth succeeded her half-sister, Mary, the pearl was sent back to Spain.

With each succeeding reign pearls were added to the Crown collection and worn by every royal lady. Princess Victoria of Kent, the future Queen, wore her first string of pearls at the age of two and attended her first Buckingham Palace Drawing Room, on 24 February 1831, dressed very simply in white with just a single-row pearl necklace and a diamond ornament tucked in her hair. By the time she was sixteen she was wearing four rows of pearls as a necklace and a four-row pearl bracelet, adding heavy pendant pearl earrings to complete the set.

When she succeeded her uncle King William IV on 20 June 1837, she inherited the jewels that had been accumulating in the royal coffers, including pearls that had belonged to Mary Queen of Scots, Queen Anne and Queen Caroline (page 104).

The most valuable part of the royal collection consisted of a number of exceptionally fine pearls that had originally been given to Catherine de Medici by her uncle Pope Clement VII when she married the future King Henry II of France. In turn, Queen Catherine had given the pearls as a wedding gift in 1559 to her eldest son's bride, Mary Stuart, Queen of Scots. After Queen Mary's execution in February 1587 six necklaces and twenty-five loose pearls, some described as being as big as nutmegs, were bought by Queen Elizabeth I for about £4,000. It was four of these loose pearls that were set in Queen Victoria's new Imperial State Crown in 1838 (page 167).

Queen Elizabeth had left all Queen Mary's pearls to her successor, King James I, ironically, Queen Mary's son. He gave them to his daughter, Elizabeth, Queen of Bohemia, who left them to her youngest daughter, the Electress Sophia of Hanover. The Electress Sophia's son came to England as King George I when the Stuart line ended with the death of Queen Anne in August 1714, bringing with him the Hanoverian pearls, which included those of Mary, Queen of Scots. Queen Victoria wore the pearls – which Prince Albert held were the finest in Europe – for the duration of her reign and left them to the Crown in her will.

Queen Victoria's daughter-in-law, the Princess of Wales, the future Queen Alexandra, made the tight, neck-covering, multistranded pearl dog-collar her personal trademark. In fact, chokers, which were an eighteenth-century fashion, were reintroduced in Paris in the 1860s, with black velvet chokers being much favoured by ballet dancers, as can be seen in the paintings of Edgar Degas.

When in 1862 Queen Victoria began searching for a suitable bride for her eldest son, the Prince of Wales, her daughter Princess Vicky, Crown Princess of Prussia, thought that of all the likely candidates the best was Princess Alexandra of Denmark, but the one question mark hanging over her suitability was a small scar on the side of her neck. If, as malicious gossip had it, the scar was a result of an attack of scrofula (tuberculosis of the lymphatic glands), which could have left her barren, marriage to the heir to the throne would be impossible. After investigating the matter, however, the Crown Princess was able to reassure her mother that there was no truth in the rumours; the scar was caused by nothing more sinister than a normal childhood illness. So Princess Alexandra was introduced to the Prince of Wales at a carefully contrived meeting and they were married on 10 March 1863.

As a young girl the Princess's dark brown ringlets covered the scar, but as a married woman convention dictated that she should wear her hair up. During the day the high collars of the period covered her neck, and at night she wore wide black velvet chokers to which she pinned different brooches or the diamond rivière necklace she had received as a wedding gift from the City of London Corporation. Before long, however, she was wearing strings of pearls to create the same effect, sometimes as many as eleven rows, kept in place by diamond-studded upright bars called spacers, and over the years these became an integral part of her public image. Coincidentally, four hundred years earlier Queen Anne Boleyn, King Henry VIII's second wife, had also worn high pearl chokers, in that case to hide a large mole on her neck.

Queen Alexandra's daughter-in-law, the future Queen Mary, also wore pearl chokers, but it was not until 1981 and the marriage of Lady Diana Spencer to the Prince of Wales that they again became fashionable. Pearls, says the Princess of Wales, are her favourite gem, and she started a craze for them that swept through every age group and was reflected at every price level.

The Princess's influence as a fashion pacesetter in the early days of her marriage had a rocketing effect on pearl sales. By wearing hers with even the simplest of sportswear she took them out of the 'dressing-up' category and made them part of fashion, rather than an accessory to fashion.

The Princess's first pearl choker was a family gift when she was eighteen, and was seen constantly. It consisted of three rows with a turquoise and pearl cluster clasp, the clasp showing when it matched the colour of her outfit, hidden at the back when it did not. She has now altered the clasp to be all pearls. When she left Buckingham Palace in a horse-drawn carriage after her wedding reception, the Princess was wearing a five-strand pearl choker with a large pearl and diamond clasp with a pearl-drop pendant, borrowed from her eldest sister, Lady Sarah McCorquodale. Also borrowed during 1982 was a six-row choker with a large oval diamond-studded centrepiece. The single string of pearls she had before her engagement is still seen often; so is another longer row of much larger pearls with a diamond and sapphire clasp, which she received as a wedding gift. Prince Charles bought his wife a striking version of the classic string of pearls from Leo de Vroomen, made from large dark grey and natural pearls. Another favourite necklace is two twisted rows of pearls with a pearl cluster clasp.

As the Princess rarely wears brooches, she cleverly converted her wedding gift from Queen Elizabeth the Queen Mother, a gigantic oval sapphire surrounded by diamonds – very similar to the Queen's 'Prince Albert Brooch' – so that it could also be worn as the centrepiece of a seven-row pearl necklace. However, her two-row choker with a small 'sapphire' and 'diamond' clasp is a blatant fake from the international chain of Ken Lane jewellery shops; the Duchess of Kent bought an identical one. And when the Princess appeared in a burgundy crushed-velvet evening dress, deeply plunged at the back, with a long rope of pearls knotted to swing against her spine, it too was a no-nonsense fake. So are some of her favourite earrings – large round button pearls set in circles of 'diamond' chips and a jaunty pair of mother-of-pearl hearts swinging from silver bows. Both came from the costume jewellery shop, Butler & Wilson.

Interestingly enough, it is neither the Queen nor Queen Elizabeth the Queen Mother – both of whom wear pearls on even the most informal occasions, including fishing for salmon or a summer picnic – who demonstrate the versatility of pearls, but some of the younger royal ladies. As a young woman Princess Alexandra converted a rectangular pearl and diamond brooch into the clasp of a three-row choker, which she continues to wear twenty-five years later. She also owns a magnificent cabochon emerald brooch with a detachable emerald drop, which can be worn either as a brooch or as the centrepiece of a three- or four-row pearl choker. She inherited this from her mother, Princess Marina, Duchess of Kent, who had received it from her mother, Princess Nicholas of Greece. In 1942, when she was six, Princess Alexandra posed with her parents at her brother Prince Michael's christening wearing a brooch of two square rubies surrounded by small diamonds, which today is the clasp of a pearl bracelet.

Her sister-in-law, the Duchess of Kent, has been equally clever in adapting pieces of jewellery. An oval sapphire brooch set in diamonds that she had before her marriage twenty-six years ago, is today worn as the front clasp of a three-row pearl choker. And a large diamond flower brooch that she inherited from Princess Marina can now also be worn as the centrepiece of the same necklace, as can Princess Marina's black pearl and diamond pendant brooch. Although the best of her necklaces are fine heirloom pearls, the Duchess is far too unpretentious to judge things by their value and looks just as elegant in a single row of walnut-sized fake pearl beads that she found while out window-shopping.

Almost all the jewellery owned by Princess Michael of Kent originally belonged to Princess Marina, who died in 1968. She has also adapted her brooches to wear as front clasps or pendants on her multirowed or twisted pearl necklaces, or on a diamond collet chain. Although on their own the brooches are not of any great size or excessive value, set against a backdrop of rows of pearls, large earrings and a multitude of bracelets and rings, they contribute to a glittering array. One five-row pearl choker with diamond motifs and a matching bracelet were made in 1934 from 374 fine oriental pearls that originally belonged to Queen Mary, and were given by her son, the Duke of Kent, to Princess Marina as a wedding gift.

Queen Mary took enormous pleasure in her magnificent ropes of matchless pearls, some of them as large as cherries. During the day one or two rows would cascade down the bodices of her timeless, high-necked, long-sleeved, ankle-length dresses, and at night, dressed in splendid lace or brocade, she often added a typically Edwardian eleven-row dog-collar with two diamond floral plaques (page 114). She left this to her daughter-in-law Princess Alice, Duchess of Gloucester, who today shares it with her daughter-in-law, the present Duchess.

During the Second World War Queen Mary went to live with her niece, the Duchess of Beaufort, at historic Badminton House in Gloucestershire. Despite wartime austerity, Queen Mary dressed for dinner every night, and in an evening gown and ropes of pearls kept court for her depleted staff as if she were still in Buckingham Palace. If there were air-raid warnings during the night, the entire Household would seek the sanctuary of the reinforced shelter in the cellars, arriving there to find the Dowager Queen, then in her seventies, sitting 'upright like an image', as she herself wrote to her sister-in-law Princess Alice, Countess of Athlone. Although she admitted she was terrified, she was immaculately dressed and coiffured, still wearing her pearls and prepared for any eventuality. Her maid sat on one side, her lady-in-waiting on the other, each struggling to stay awake and zealously guarding two leather suitcases carefully packed with their mistress's priceless collection of jewellery.

But if there is any royal lady who has had a life-long love affair with pearls it is Queen Elizabeth the Queen Mother. As a nine-year-old she was photographed wearing a two-row necklace of seed pearls and carrying an armful of wild flowers. At a dance at Glamis Castle, her family's Scottish ancestral home, she wore a rose brocade 'Van Dyke' dress with pearls threaded through her hair. For her wedding in 1923 to the Duke of York her ivory chiffon dress was embroidered with silver and pearls, and she wore a two-row necklace of pearls around her neck. During the sixty years and more since then her characteristic ropes of pearls have been her trademark; it is inconceivable even to imagine her without them.

One of the Queen Mother's most impressive two-row pearl necklaces has been made from 222 pearls with a clasp of two magnificent rubies surrounded by diamonds that had originally belonged to the ruler of the Punjab, Ranjit Singh. After Britain annexed the Punjab in 1849, the pearls were presented to Queen Victoria by the East India Company. Queen Elizabeth inherited more magnificent pearls from Mrs Ronnie Greville in 1942. Throughout the war as she and the King toured bomb sites and factories, worker's cooperatives and army installations, the Queen wore beautifully tailored outfits in pale dusky shades that would not show the bomb dust, her customary pearls and a glittering brooch. When she was once asked if perhaps it would be advisable to leave off her jewellery and look more austere, she replied that it certainly would not, that if the people came to see her they wore their best clothes, and she didn't intend to act any differently when she went to see them.

The Queen, like her mother, always wears pearls during the day, usually a three-row necklace, of which she has three. One is of graduated pearls from the family collection, which the Queen had made up with a diamond clasp soon after her accession. The second triple-row necklace was a Coronation present to the Queen in 1953 from the Amir of Qatar. It too has a clasp of brilliant-cut diamonds. The third was a gift from King George to celebrate his Silver Jubilee (page 103).

The most interesting pearls Princess Margaret owns are a pair of matching bracelets left to her by Queen Mary in 1953. Originally the property of King William IV's wife, Queen Adelaide, and later worn by Queen Victoria, the seven rows of pearls are each fastened with a large square blue enamel clasp emblazoned with Queen Adelaide's cypher in diamonds.

In many cases the multiple-strand necklaces worn by the royal ladies are not one necklace at all, but two or three different ones worn together to create the desired effect, and it doesn't seem to matter if the strands are of different sized beads or if the colours of the different strings do not match exactly. It is also no modern fad that they are happy to wear imitation pearls. Queen Alexandra, more than eighty years ago, used to have her friend Lady de Grey bring her back ropes of imitation pearls from Paris. Queen Alexandra once delayed the Opening of Parliament because a string of her pearls broke on the way there; she wouldn't descend from her carriage until a footman had gathered up every stray bead, fake though they were.

# THE QUEEN'S FIRST PEARL NECKLACE

Queen Victoria started a family tradition by giving each of her five
daughters two fine pearls a year from birth, so that when they
were grown-up they would have enough for a necklace. However, by
1866, when she was also buying pearls for a growing number
of granddaughters, Queen Victoria asked her eldest daughter, Vicky,
married to the Prussian Crown Prince, to explain to her
sisters that with the price of a pearl having risen to between £30 and
£40 she had to cut back and could only provide one a year
for their daughters, since she was still making up the necklaces of her
own two youngest daughters, Louise and Beatrice.

BELOW: *King George VI followed his great-grandmother's example
and gave the Queen a thin platinum chain to which he added
two pearls on each birthday. She wears it here, aged three, in 1929.*

RIGHT: *Princess Anne wore the necklace at her mother's
Coronation, and here in 1954, when she was four years old. The
Queen's diamond and drop-pearl earrings were a wedding
present from the Sheikh of Bahrain. Her two rows of large pearls,
which fasten with an oval diamond-cluster clasp, had
originally been part of the Hanoverian collection. They are Crown
property and passed to the Queen when Queen Mary died in
1953. The Queen wore the necklace at Prince Andrew's wedding in*

*1986, with the clasp showing on the side, and no brooch, a
nearly unprecedented break in her personal style.*

*Her brooch in this picture is the one she had designed by
Frederick A. Mew of Cartier as a setting for the 54.5-carat rare
pink diamond she had been given by John T. Williamson as
a wedding gift in 1947. Dr Williamson was an eccentric Canadian,
who had discovered a diamond mine in Mwadui, Tanganyika,
in 1940, when he was only thirty-three. He developed it into the
richest diamond-bearing mine in the world, giving him an
annual income of £2,000,000. In October 1947, the year he sold
out to De Beers, the mine yielded the finest pink diamond
ever seen, and Dr Williamson, a fanatical monarchist, sent it to
Princess Elizabeth. In March 1948, accompanied by Queen
Mary, the Princess went to the Clerkenwell factory of Briefel &
Lemer, in East London, to watch the diamond being cut into
a 23.6-carat brilliant. Dr Williamson supplied a number of small
white diamonds to be used in the platinum setting, but because
he had hoped to find more pink diamonds to add to his original gift,
work on the brooch was postponed until 1952. Then the
'Williamson Pink' became the centre of a jonquil-shaped flower with
curved petals of noisette-cut diamonds, a stem of baguette
diamonds and two large noisette-cut diamonds as leaves. The brooch
is 4½ inches long.*

# THE KING GEORGE V JUBILEE NECKLACE

ABOVE: *When King George V celebrated his Silver Jubilee, on 6 May 1935, he gave his two
granddaughters their first serious jewellery: pearl necklaces. Princess Elizabeth was
given three perfectly matched rows, and Princess Margaret, being four years younger, two
rows. The Princesses, who wore their pearls for their parents' Coronation two years
later, are seen here with them in 1938.*

# THE QUEEN ANNE AND THE QUEEN CAROLINE NECKLACES

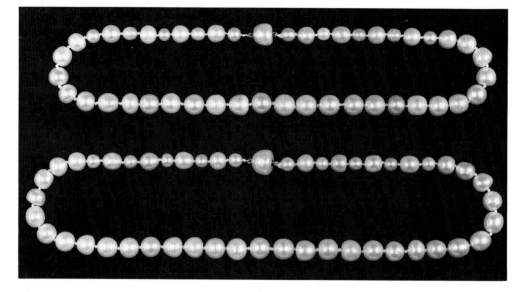

ABOVE: *These two rows of large, lustrous, graduated pearls, with pearl clasps, are always worn together and were left to the Crown by Queen Victoria. The top row, of forty-six pearls, weighs 1,045 grammes and is said to have belonged to Queen Anne, the last of the Stuart monarchs. Horace Walpole wrote in his diary:*

*'Queen Anne had but few jewels and those indifferent, except one pearl necklace given her by Prince George.'*

*Queen Caroline, the wife of King George II, had a great deal of valuable jewellery, including four very fine pearl necklaces. After wearing all of them at her Coronation, the fifty best pearls were made into a single necklace – the bottom row of the pair – which weighs 1,429.2 grammes. In 1947 both necklaces were given to Princess Elizabeth as a wedding present by her father King George VI.* BELOW: *Princess Elizabeth was married to Prince Philip on 20 November 1947. John Colville had recently been appointed her Private Secretary, and was to travel to Westminster Abbey in her carriage procession. Half an hour before they were scheduled to leave Buckingham Palace he was summoned to her second-floor sitting room. The two-row pearl necklace her father had given her had been left on display with all the other wedding gifts at St James's Palace and she particularly wanted to wear them. Could Colville get to St James's and bring them back? He rushed down the seemingly endless red-carpeted corridor, hurtled down the Grand Staircase, and ended up in the quadrangle, where he commandeered King Haakon VII of Norway's large Daimler. Although traffic had been stopped since early morning,*

# THE QUEEN'S FOUR ROW CHOKER

the crowds were so deeply packed across Marlborough Gate, that the car, even flying its royal flag, had to halt while he fought his way through on foot. When he arrived at the Friary Court entrance to the State Apartments there was only an elderly janitor to listen to his odd story, but he finally allowed Colville upstairs to explain his mission to the CID men who were guarding the thousands of presents. Their dilemma was: if they accepted his story and he turned out to be a clever jewel thief who had made off with the Crown pearls, they were in trouble; but if they refused to let him have the necklace and it all turned out to be true, they were equally in trouble. There was no one to consult; time was running out, and only after they had found his name in the wedding programme as one of the Household officials in attendance on the Princess did they allow him to remove the pearls. This portrait was taken in the Music Room of Buckingham Palace after the ceremony.

RIGHT: The Queen had this four-row choker made from pearls in her collection. The large, conical, diamond-studded clasp is deep enough for her to add another two rows of pearls, if she desires. LEFT: In 1982 the Queen loaned the necklace to the Princess of Wales to wear at a banquet at Hampton Court Palace, given by Queen Beatrix and Prince Claus of the Netherlands, who were in England on a State visit.

LEFT: *The Empress Marie Feodorovna, Queen Alexandra's younger sister, had one of the world's most valuable collections of jewellery, but her favourite jewels were her pearls. Interspersed in this four-row choker of 164 pearls are twenty diamond-studded vertical bars, between every two pearls at the front, and between every three pearls at the back. The necklace is made to convert into two bracelets, and the octagonal clasp is a large sapphire surrounded by two rows of diamonds. Following her death in exile in Denmark in 1928, after the Russian Revolution, her jewels were sold in England by Hennell and Sons.* RIGHT: *Queen Mary bought the necklace as well as a number of other pieces of jewellery, and she wore it here in 1931. Her small V-shaped tiara with a large centre sapphire had also belonged to the Empress. Queen Mary left the tiara to Queen Elizabeth the Queen Mother, who has never worn it in public, but loaned it to Princess Margaret for a number of years.* BELOW, LEFT: *The Queen inherited the necklace in 1953. She wore it with the clasp in front at the Horse of the Year Show in 1956.* BELOW, RIGHT: *In 1960 she wore it to an Order of the British Empire Service at St Paul's Cathedral, turned around with the clasp at the back.* OPPOSITE: *The Queen has loaned the necklace to Princess Anne, and she wears it here in 1974 on a visit to Toronto. Her diamond tiara was presented to her by the World Wide Shipping Group after she launched their tanker World Unicorn in 1973.*

# THE EMPRESS MARIE FEODOROVNA
## OF RUSSIA'S NECKLACE

# QUEEN ALEXANDRA'S BRACELET

ABOVE: *For her Coronation on 9 August 1902, Queen Alexandra wore on her left wrist a four-row pearl bracelet with a large sapphire and diamond clasp. The pearls may have been the eighty-eight that were made into a bracelet by Queen Victoria in 1838, and left to the Crown. This photograph is of particular historical interest because, compared with most other pictures of Queen Alexandra, it was never retouched, and so gives us the rare opportunity of seeing exactly what she looked like at the age of fifty-eight.* RIGHT: *The Queen wearing the bracelet on a visit to New Zealand in 1954.*

# QUEEN MARY'S BRACELET

ABOVE: *For her official 1935 Silver Jubilee photograph, Queen Mary wore on her right wrist a five-row pearl bracelet that has a large, oval, diamond-cluster clasp.*
LEFT: *The Queen inherited the bracelet in 1953 and wears it here in 1956.*

# Pearls and Diamonds

THE COMBINATION OF PEARLS and diamonds has a special appeal, for the luminescence of pearls – their depth and lustre enhanced by constant proximity to human skin – is further heightened by the hard-edged brilliance of diamonds. Yet as 'white jewels' they retain an innate innocence that belies their monetary value.

To many people the combination of pearls and diamonds is a symbol of royal mourning. In Victorian England they could be worn during the period of half-mourning when it was permissible to lighten the unrelieved black of the previous six months of full mourning, during which only onyx, black enamel or jet were allowed. In 1910 when her husband, King George V, succeeded his father, King Edward VII, Queen Mary began the custom of 'white' jewellery for the entire mourning period, which continues to this day. Mourning now lasts for a much shorter time, decided on by the monarch, but black clothes, stockings, veils and accessories are still de rigueur.

However, aside from this one sombre association pearl and diamond jewellery has been a perennial favourite of royal ladies for the last six generations. One of Queen Elizabeth the Queen Mother's most frequently worn brooches is a festoon design of diamonds with a pearl centre and a pearl drop hanging from a looped chain of diamond collets. It was a gift to Queen Victoria in 1897 from 'The Ladies and Gentlemen of Her Majesty's Household' in celebration of her Diamond Jubilee. She left it to the Crown in 1901 and it came to Queen Elizabeth in 1936. Another brooch that Queen Victoria left to the Crown was a large diamond-shaped design set with numerous diamonds, eight pearls and three pendant pearl drops. Queen Elizabeth the Queen Mother wore this a great deal in the 1950s but it has not been seen for many years.

A pair of earrings that Queen Elizabeth the Queen Mother has worn constantly since the early days of her marriage are pearl drops, each suspended from two brilliant-cut diamonds (page 46). On an official visit to New Zealand many years ago she took time off to go fishing, one of her favourite pastimes, and despite wearing all the proper gear, including high waders, she kept on her pearl necklace and pendant earrings. Around 1940 Queen Elizabeth put away her sapphire engagement ring and since then has worn a large oriental pearl surrounded by a cluster of diamonds. This ring is very similar to one worn by Queen Mary until her death in 1953.

A tiara Queen Elizabeth the Queen Mother had as the Duchess of York in the late 1920s was of graduated diamond fan-shaped festoons given height by pearls and collet diamonds set on upright spikes. She wore it in the style of the day, low on her forehead covering her fringe. In the late 1950s she gave it to her younger daughter, Princess Margaret, who has always worn it in the more usual manner on the crown of her head (page 141).

When Queen Mary died in 1953 she left Princess Margaret one of her favourite necklaces, a simple chain set alternately with large pearls and fine collet diamonds. The Princess has added to it a large detachable baroque pearl pendant that had been her mother's, and wears the necklace with a striking pair of earrings – large round pearls suspended from upside-down diamond Vs.

Since the cult of courtly love in the fifteenth century heart motifs have appeared constantly in jewellery design and were much favoured by the royal family. Queen Alexandra, when Princess of Wales in the 1880s, had a wonderful festoon necklace of four rows of pearls caught up in loops by graduated heart charms set with diamonds. Almost exactly a hundred years later, the present Princess of Wales bought herself an Italian-made necklace from Collingwood with money from a legacy she had been left. The two rows of small cultured pearls, with a gold spacer bar between every two pearls, has a large central heart pavé-set with diamonds.

Queen Alexandra also had a number of small brooches in the shape of hearts as did the future Queen Mary. For her twenty-first birthday on 26 May 1888, Princess May's mother, the Duchess of Teck, her uncle the Duke of Cambridge and her aunt the Grand Duchess of Mecklenburg-Strelitz gave her a pearl and diamond heart-shaped brooch. When she married the Duke of York in 1893 one of his wedding gifts to her was a heart-shaped brooch – a double row of diamonds surrounding two pearls and surmounted by a diamond-set ribbon bow. The ribbon bow was later removed. Queen Mary gave this brooch to her daughter-in-law Princess Alice, Duchess of Gloucester.

Queen Mary gave Princess Alice two more pieces of pearl and diamond jewellery as a wedding gift in November 1935, part of a seven-piece suite she assembled from different items already in the royal collection. There was a brooch with an enormous oval baroque pearl set in a frame of brilliant-cut diamonds, which had been worn by Queen Alexandra and Queen Mary (page 135), and a pair of diamond stud earrings with small pendant pearl drops, which are worn today by the present Duchess. Other jewels in the suite included a long diamond rivière, two diamond rings and a large corsage brooch set with clusters of diamonds and with three detachable oval diamond drops hanging from diamond chains. This had also belonged to Queen Alexandra (page 59, top left).

In 1953 Queen Mary left to Princess Alice a long bar brooch of eight collet diamonds with a pearl at each end and a large pearl and diamond cluster in the centre. Queen Mary had a distinctive way of wearing brooches: she would pin one at the centre of her collar and a second – often a horizontal bar design – about twelve inches below it at breast level.

Princess Marina had a number of pieces of pearl and diamond jewellery, many of which are worn by her daughter and two daughters-in-law. A tiara, a delicate design of high diamond festoons set on a band of either cultured pearls or diamond collets and with a pearl surmounting each festoon motif, was worn for a period in the 1960s first by Princess Alexandra and then by the present Duchess of Kent. Today it belongs to Princess Michael of Kent. One of Princess Marina's wedding gifts in 1934 was a tiara that had belonged to her mother, Princess Nicholas of Greece, the former Grand Duchess Helen of Russia, only daughter of the Grand Duchess Vladimir. It consisted of fifteen linked diamond circles with a pearl set in the centre of each. Her own daughter, Princess Alexandra, also wore it, but it appears to have been sold after Princess Marina's death in 1968 in order to pay death duties. When she died in 1957, Princess Nicholas left Princess Marina a pair of pearl button earrings set with single diamonds, which is owned today by Princess Alexandra. Princess Michael has another pair of Princess Marina's earrings, long pendant oriental pearls set in diamond-studded mounts, each suspended from three diamonds. Princess Marina's favourite earrings, large pearl buttons set in clusters of diamonds and suspended from diamond studs, were inherited by the present Duchess of Kent.

Princess Marina often wore a pair of pearl and diamond brooches: a large black pearl framed by two rows of diamonds with a detachable pendant pearl drop hanging from a collet diamond; the other identical but set with natural pearls. Today the Duchess of Kent wears the black-pearl brooch, with or without the detachable pearl pendant, either as a brooch or as the centrepiece of a three-strand pearl necklace. Princess Michael wears the brooch set with natural pearls pinned on her shoulder or on a black velvet choker, again with or without its detachable pearl drop. It also appears as the centrepiece of either a two- or a three-row pearl necklace and as a pendant on a longer three-row pearl necklace or on a single row of diamond collets, which had also belonged to Princess Marina. Princess Marina's five-row pearl bracelet with a wide diamond clasp was inherited by the Duchess of Kent, and a ring, a large pearl with a cluster of three brilliant-cut diamonds on either side, now belongs to Princess Michael.

A fascinating example of how jewellery can be redesigned is displayed by a tiara that Princess Alexandra has had for nearly thirty years. As a young woman she had seven diamond flowers each with five petals and a pearl in the centre set on a plain circlet, which when worn was hidden by her hair. At the time of her engagement to the Hon.

Angus Ogilvy in 1962, Collingwood used the seven flowers as the basis for a more impressive tiara that she first wore at the pre-wedding ball the Queen gave in the couple's honour at Windsor Castle in April 1963. Set on a diamond bandeau base, the flowers were now connected by large diamond ribbon bows, the central flower rising above two additional small flowers and a bow. To make up a suite, Mr Ogilvy gave Princess Alexandra as a wedding gift a pearl and diamond trefoil necklace identical to Queen Victoria's Golden Jubilee necklace (page 118), and both tiara and necklace were adapted so that turquoises could be substituted for the pearls. There was also a pair of earrings to match each set. When Princess Alexandra acquired a diamond and sapphire necklace some years later sapphires were also bought for the tiara, and a pair of antique diamond pendant earrings were adapted so that their central diamonds could be replaced by sapphire drops. There are few better examples of versatility among the royal jewels.

Most of Princess Anne's jewellery is gold, but in 1973 while on a trip to the Far East she was given two very large round pearls and these were set as earrings each in a circle of diamonds. A second pair of earrings, an oval pearl surmounted by a cockade of five small diamonds, was a gift from Madame Imelda Marcos during a visit the Princess made to the Philippines. Another pair, designed by English jeweller Andrew Grima, consists of cultured pearls and diamonds set in double gold scroll frames, the bottom frames being detachable. These earrings were a gift to the Princess from the Esso Petroleum Company when she launched their ship *Esso Northumbria* at the Swan Hunter Shipyard in 1969. She wore them for many of her official pre-wedding photographs taken with Captain Mark Phillips at Windsor Castle in 1973. At the same launch Swan Hunter gave Princess Anne a beautiful brooch that she often wears – a diamond rose spray set in gold with a pearl centre.

There are essentially three different designs for pearl and diamond earrings, of which one at least is owned by every royal lady and all three by the Queen: a simple pearl button with a single diamond (page 125); a pearl set in a cluster of diamonds (page 122); and a pendant pearl suspended from a diamond stud (page 121).

Queen Mary left the Queen a ring set with a single pearl and a brilliant-cut diamond and with diamond shoulders that was a wedding gift to her in 1893 from her three brothers, the Princes Adolphus, Francis and Alexander of Teck; but she has never worn this in public. In addition to all the family jewellery she owns, the Queen possesses a number of other pearl and diamond pieces. These include two pairs of earrings – pendant pearls suspended from five tiers of collet and baguette-cut diamonds which have never been seen in public, and small oval pearl drops suspended from diamond studs, which she occasionally wears at night. She also has three different brooches: a floral spray looped around an enormous pearl; an unusual long narrow diamond triangle with two pearls and a canary yellow diamond set in the middle; and the third, first seen in the mid-1980s and which the Queen now wears quite often, a large diamond quatrefoil set with pearls having a pearl and diamond cluster in the centre.

The French have a saying that 'the rarest things in the world, next to a spirit of discernment, are diamonds and pearls' and generations of British royal ladies may have proved its truth.

# THE CAMBRIDGE LOVER'S KNOT TIARA

One of the most charming tributes that Queen Mary ever paid to the maternal side of her
family was the tiara that she had made by Garrard in 1914 to her own design and
from pearls and diamonds already in her possession. It was a copy of one owned by her
grandmother, Princess Augusta of Hesse, who married the first Duke of Cambridge,
seventh son of King George III, in 1818. She had been given it by her family prior to her
marriage. There was a strong French influence in its neo-classical design of nineteen
openwork diamond arches, each enclosing an oriental pearl drop from a diamond lover's knot
bow, and surmounted by single diamonds and upright oval pearl spikes. Princess
Augusta's tiara was set on a circular band of perfectly matched pearls, but Queen Mary
chose a base of diamonds for hers. In the nineteenth century it was a popular design
and there are five known versions still in existence. When the Duchess of Cambridge's eldest
daughter, and namesake, Augusta, married the Grand Duke of Mecklenburg-Strelitz
in 1843, she gave her the tiara as a wedding present. The Grand Duchess, in turn, became
godmother, and ultimately closest confidante, to her niece, the future Queen Mary,
who saw her annually and knew the tiara well. In 1912 she wrote to her aunt:

'If you have a dinner to celebrate yr birthday you must wear on
yr 90th birthday the pearl & diamond diadem & yr English orders, do
please do so for my sake. Think how beautiful you will look with
yr white hair and still lovely neck.'

PAGE 113: *Queen Mary's tiara as seen today with the upright pearl spikes removed.* OPPOSITE, ABOVE LEFT: *The Duchess of Cambridge wearing her tiara at the time of her marriage in 1818.* OPPOSITE, ABOVE RIGHT: *The Grand Duchess of Mecklenburg-Strelitz in the 1890s. She is also wearing the necklace from the 'Cambridge sapphires' parure (page 64, below left).* OPPOSITE, BELOW LEFT: *Queen Mary in 1926, wearing the tiara as originally made.* OPPOSITE, BELOW RIGHT: *By 1935 she had removed the upright pearls and is wearing four of them as pendants on her ropes of pearls. She gave her pearl and diamond dog-collar to Princess Alice, Duchess of Gloucester, who has now passed it on to her daughter-in-law, the present Duchess.* RIGHT: *In her will, Queen Mary left the tiara to the Queen, who wears it in 1955. In 1981 the Queen gave it to the Princess of Wales as a wedding present, who wore it for the first time at the State Opening of Parliament that November.* BELOW: *In 1985 the Princess wore the tiara and pearl and diamond drop earrings, which had been a wedding gift from the jewellers Collingwood, on her official visit to Washington.*

# THE GRAND DUCHESS VLADIMIR
# OF RUSSIA'S TIARA

*Marie*

*St. Petersbourg 1904*
*le 1: Décembre*

At the beginning of the twentieth century the Grand Duke Vladimir Alexandrovitch, son of Tsar Alexander II, brother of Tsar Alexander III and uncle of Tsar Nicholas II, was the richest and most influential aristocrat in Russia. Artistic and clever, in 1874 he had married the twenty-year-old German Princess Marie von Mecklenburg-Schwerin, who bore the Russian name of Marie Pavlovna, although she was known as 'Miechen' because there were so many other Grand Duchess Maries in the family. The Empress Alexandra was agonizingly shy, uninterested in society and totally engrossed in her family, so the Grand Duchess Vladimir became the leading hostess in St Petersburg and set up an alternative Court in her magnificent Vladimir Palace on the Neva river. Her collection of jewels nearly equalled that of the Dowager Empress Marie Feodorovna, and in the Russian style they were displayed to her guests. When the Duchess of Marlborough, American-born Consuelo Vanderbilt, visited St Petersburg in 1902, she wrote in her diary:

'After dinner the Grand Duchess showed me her jewels set out in glass cases in her dressing-room. There were endless parures of diamonds, emeralds, rubies and pearls, to say nothing of semi-precious stones such as turquoises, tourmalines, cat's eyes and aquamarines.'

ABOVE: *Around 1890, the Grand Duchess commissioned a Russian jeweller to make her a diamond tiara of fifteen interlaced circles, with a swinging oriental pearl suspended in each. She spent a fortune at the Paris firm of Cartier and under her patronage they held a number of exhibitions in St Petersburg. In 1911 she left the tiara in Cartier's Paris workroom for cleaning, and while this was being done they took the opportunity of making at least three copies, which later led to the mistaken assumption that Cartier had designed the original as well.*

*The Grand Duke had died in 1908, and at the time of the Russian Revolution, in 1917, the Grand Duchess moved with her retinue of servants and ladies-in-waiting to Kislovodsk in the Caucasus, which was still in the hands of loyal Cossack troops. Towards the end of 1919 she made her escape by horse-drawn carriage and train, finally settling in Zurich. She had taken a case of jewels with her when she left St Petersburg, but the bulk of her collection had been left walled up in a hidden safe in the Vladimir Palace. Before the war one of her protégés had been a young Englishman called Stopford, who appears to have been attached to the British Embassy in some unofficial capacity and who managed to stay in touch with her in Kislovodsk. Once she was safely abroad, he enlisted the help of one of her loyal elderly retainers to get him into the sacked Palace at night. The looters had not discovered the secret safe and he was able to remove the jewels, dividing them into the smallest possible pieces before wrapping them in newspapers and packing them into two shabby leather Gladstone bags.*

According to the Countess of Airlie, Queen Mary's lady-in-waiting and closest
confidante, Stopford actually disguised himself as an old woman and hid this tiara in the
lining of his black bonnet, cramming the fifteen pearl drops into cherries that were
sewn on as trimming. Whether this part of the story is true or not most certainly Stopford
managed to get all the jewels out of Russia, possibly using diplomatic channels to do
so. On 6 September 1920 the Grand Duchess died while staying in the French spa of
Contrexéville. Her jewels were divided among her four children: the emeralds went to
Grand Duke Boris, the pearls to Grand Duke Cyril, the rubies to Grand Duke Andrei, and
the diamonds to her only daughter, the Grand Duchess Helen, who in 1902 had
married Prince Nicholas of Greece, the third son of King George I and Queen Olga.
OPPOSITE, BELOW: *In 1921, Queen Mary bought the tiara from Princess Nicholas who
had settled in Paris with her husband and three daughters, one of whom was Princess
Marina, the future Duchess of Kent. Queen Mary had the last fifteen of the
Cambridge emeralds mounted as drops so that they could be interchanged with the pearls
(page 91).* ABOVE: *The Queen inherited the tiara in 1953. She is photographed in
1959 on the Grand Staircase of Buckingham Palace. Her pearl studs were made in 1951.*

# QUEEN VICTORIA'S GOLDEN JUBILEE NECKLACE AND QUEEN MARY'S PENDANT EARRINGS

OPPOSITE, BELOW: *In 1887 the 'Women of the British Empire' each gave between a penny and a pound to provide a celebratory memorial for the Queen's fifty years on the throne. Part of the money raised was used to commission a large equestrian statue of Prince Albert, the Prince Consort (not for the Albert Memorial in London, which has often been said erroneously), which the Queen unveiled on Smith's Lawn, Windsor, on 12 May 1890, and the remainder was spent on this necklace, which was presented to Queen Victoria on 24 June 1887. The design is of graduated diamond trefoils, each with a pearl centre. The centrepiece is a quatrefoil of diamonds with a pearl centre and drop pendant. Surmounting it is a pearl and diamond crown. It is possible to detach the centrepiece and wear it as a pendant, but no one has ever done so. Queen Victoria left the necklace to the Crown in 1901. It is interesting that there are at least three necklaces of this design in existence. Princess Alexandra, the Hon. Mrs Angus Ogilvy, was given one as a wedding gift by her husband in April 1963, and it only lacks a crown on top of the quatrefoil to be indistinguishable from the Queen's.* OPPOSITE, ABOVE LEFT: *Queen Victoria's official Diamond Jubilee photograph in 1897. She is wearing the necklace as well as the matching diamond trefoil and pearl earrings, which have been worn by Queen Elizabeth the Queen Mother since 1937. The Queen Mother also has the round pearl and diamond cluster brooch.* OPPOSITE, ABOVE CENTRE: *These earrings were converted by Queen Mary from a pendant necklace. Each has an oval pearl suspended from a collet diamond hanging in an ornate frame of scroll design, set with diamonds.* OPPOSITE, ABOVE RIGHT: *Queen Mary, then the Princess of Wales, in about 1902, wearing the pendants on a narrow chain.* ABOVE: *The Queen in Nepal on a State visit in 1986.*

# THE DUCHESS OF TECK'S EARRINGS

# QUEEN VICTORIA'S DROP EARRINGS

OPPOSITE, ABOVE LEFT: *These perfectly matched pearl earrings are each surrounded by eight diamonds. They were a twentieth-birthday present to the Queen from her grandmother, Queen Mary, who had inherited them in 1897 on the death of her mother, Princess Mary Adelaide, Duchess of Teck. The Queen wore them for her wedding, and when she had her ears pierced and could wear the many others she owned, they were seen constantly, and have been seen as recently as 1984 when she visited Canada.* OPPOSITE, BELOW LEFT: *Princess Mary Adelaide, Duchess of Teck in 1883.* OPPOSITE, ABOVE RIGHT: *Queen Mary in 1910. She is also wearing one of the black enamel and diamond mourning brooches made to observe the death of King Edward VII. Queen Alexandra had an identical brooch. Both Queen Mary and her mother had pierced ears, but clip-on backs were added to the earrings when they were given to the Queen.* OPPOSITE, BELOW RIGHT: *The Queen and Prince Philip four days after their wedding in 1947. In addition to the earrings, she is wearing a double string of pearls, which her parents had given her during the war, and a platinum-set chrysanthemum brooch with sapphire stamens and diamond petals and stem, which had been a gift from Sir John Laing and Sons Ltd and the Anglo-Iranian Oil Company Ltd when she launched the oil tanker British Princess at Sunderland in 1946.*

ABOVE, LEFT: *In 1838, when she was nineteen, Queen Victoria was drawn by Richard James Lane, wearing a pair of pearl drop earrings. In 1847, Prince Albert gave her another, similar pair, but with larger pear-shaped pearls, each hung from a diamond stud from the royal collection. When she died she left them to the Crown.* ABOVE, RIGHT: *The Queen is wearing them for the annual Garter ceremony at St George's Chapel, Windsor, in 1954.*

# QUEEN ALEXANDRA'S CLUSTER EARRINGS

ABOVE, TOP: *These large pearl earrings, each surrounded by ten diamonds in a cluster shape, were designed by Garrard in 1863 for the Prince of Wales to give to his bride, Princess Alexandra of Denmark, as part of his wedding gift (page 129). The design had been a popular one since the early 1850s.* ABOVE, LEFT: *Queen Alexandra wearing them at her Coronation on 9 August 1902.* ABOVE, RIGHT: *Queen Mary arriving at the ballet in 1950.* OPPOSITE: *The Queen inherited them from Queen Mary in 1953. Since Queen Elizabeth the Queen Mother has continued to wear the similar trefoil earrings that match the Golden Jubilee necklace, the Queen wears the cluster earrings with it instead.*

# QUEEN MARY'S BUTTON EARRINGS

In 1893 a fund was opened by Lady Elizabeth Biddulph to raise money for a wedding present for Princess May of Teck. A pearl and diamond necklace, which could be converted into a tiara, was designed and made by the jewellers Hunt and Roskell (page 38). The presentation was made on behalf of 650 'Ladies of England', and a subsidiary committee, chaired by Lady Clinton, had raised enough money from the 'Ladies of Devonshire' to add a matching pair of pearl button earrings, each with a small diamond on top. In her thank-you letter to Lady Elizabeth, Princess May wrote:

*'I shall always value their presents as a token of affection for me and mine, and ever remember their great kindness.'*

ABOVE: *Queen Mary, wearing the Devon earrings, at her desk in Buckingham Palace in 1922. She gave the earrings to the Queen in 1947 as a wedding present.* OPPOSITE, ABOVE RIGHT: *The Queen in 1965 at the Presentation of Colours to the 1st Battalion Welsh Guards, of which she is Colonel-in-Chief. Her diamond and platinum brooch is the Regiment's emblem.* OPPOSITE, ABOVE LEFT: *Queen Mary also had a larger pair of earrings in the same style. She wears them here in 1939.* OPPOSITE, BELOW: *The Queen inherited them in 1953. In 1968 she wore them to the Royal Air Force Club. On her left wrist is the diamond and platinum Cartier watch with the smallest face in the world, $5/16$ inch in diameter, given to her by the President of the French Republic on her State visit to France in 1957. On her right wrist is a bracelet of diamond links and circles, set with alternate large black and natural pearls.*

# QUEEN ALEXANDRA'S DAGMAR NECKLACE

OPPOSITE, BELOW: *In 1863 Princess Alexandra of Schleswig-Holstein-Sonderburg-Glücksburg's father was the elected heir to the childless King Frederick VII of Denmark. For her marriage to the Prince of Wales that same year, the King had the crown jeweller in Copenhagen, Jules Didrichsen, design a necklace in the Byzantine style. It had 118 pearls and 2,000 diamonds. Festoons connecting gold medallions, with a large diamond in the middle of each, surround a centrepiece of diamond-set scrollwork. The two large pear-shaped pendant pearls on either side were so valuable they had been exhibited at the Great Exhibition at the Crystal Palace in 1851. This is its original case.*
*Hanging on a gold loop from the centrepiece is a cloisonné enamel facsimile of the eleventh-century gold Dagmar Cross, in which was set a fragment reputed to belong to the True Cross and a piece of silk taken from the grave of King Canute. Queen Dagmar had been the benevolent and much loved wife of King Waldemar the Victorious. When she died in 1212, she was buried with this pectoral cross upon her breast, and when her tomb was opened centuries later the cross was removed as a precious relic and put on display in the Museum of Northern Antiquities in Copenhagen. It became a tradition that Danish princesses were given a copy of the cross when they married. The central figure is the head of Christ, with St Basil, St John Chrysostom, St Mary and St John on the four arms.* OPPOSITE, ABOVE LEFT: *Queen Alexandra, when Princess of Wales, wearing the Dagmar Cross hung on a string of pearls.* OPPOSITE, ABOVE RIGHT: *Queen Alexandra at her Coronation on 9 August 1902. She has pinned the Dagmar necklace across her bodice and it can just be seen under the swags of pearls. Queen Victoria's enormous diamond stomacher pinned above it divides into three sections. Queen Mary also wore it at her Coronation in 1911 (page 55), but as an arc; Queen Elizabeth the Queen Mother wore only the centre portion for her Coronation in 1937. Queen Alexandra's diamond fringe girdle had belonged to Queen Victoria, who wore it as a bordure framing the neckline of her dress (page 55).* ABOVE: *The Queen attending a dinner at the German Embassy in London in 1958. She has removed the cross and the two large pearl drops from the Dagmar necklace.*

ABOVE: *Photographed in its original velvet case, this is the suite of jewellery made by Garrard and given to Princess Alexandra by the Prince of Wales as a wedding present in 1863, and which she wore on her wedding day. The necklace has eight circular clusters of diamonds with a large pearl in the centre of each, connected by festoons of diamonds. From each of the three front clusters hangs a pear-shaped pearl. The matching earrings are owned by the Queen today (page 122), but the oblong diamond brooch, set with three pearls and with three detachable pendant pearls suspended from single large diamonds, and the necklace have belonged to Queen Elizabeth the Queen Mother since the accession of King George VI in 1936.* OPPOSITE, ABOVE LEFT: *Princess Alexandra wearing the brooch, around 1896. Her diamond tiara, consisting of a three-row circlet surmounted by scroll ornaments (which could be connected by Greek devices, but not seen here), was also a wedding gift from the Prince of Wales, and could be dismantled and worn as a number of different ornaments. The bottom diamond necklace also comes apart, and is the one that was strung in separate sections from Queen Victoria's bow brooches down the length of her skirt (page 59).* OPPOSITE, ABOVE RIGHT: *Queen Mary wore the oblong brooch, without the pearl pendants, pinned on the side of her bodice in 1938. The round pearl surrounded by a circle of diamonds pinned above her stomacher is the brooch Queen Victoria wore with her Golden Jubilee necklace (page 118).* OPPOSITE, BELOW LEFT: *Queen Mary arriving at St Paul's Cathedral on 26 April 1948 for the service to celebrate the Silver Wedding of King George VI and Queen Elizabeth. She is wearing the brooch complete with its pendant drops.* OPPOSITE, BELOW RIGHT: *In 1972 the Queen wore the brooch at an official reception during her State visit to France. This is the only time she has ever worn it.*

# QUEEN MARY'S 'WOMEN OF HAMPSHIRE' PENDANT BROOCH

ABOVE: *In 1893, the 'Women of Hampshire' committee, led by the Duchess of Wellington, collected £775 to buy a wedding gift for Princess May of Teck. The Duchess assembled a number of items at her London home, Apsley House, and a representative group travelled up from Hampshire to make their choice. They selected a fine diamond pendant with a pear-shaped pearl drop. In her thank-you letter dated 4 July 1893, Princess May asked the Duchess to 'please tell them how grateful I am for the beautiful diamond and pearl pendant, which I shall often wear.' By 1911 the pendant had been converted into a brooch.* ABOVE, LEFT: *Queen Mary wearing the brooch in 1948.* ABOVE, RIGHT: *The Queen inherited the brooch in 1953 and wears it here on a visit to Guernsey in 1957.*

# QUEEN MARY'S BAR BROOCH

*Queen Mary owned this unusual brooch, a large round pearl crossed by a curved diamond bar that ends in two three-leaf clovers, as early as 1931 when she posed for a formal photograph with the five-year-old Princess Elizabeth.* ABOVE, LEFT: *Queen Mary wearing the brooch in 1948. The jewelled enamel buckle clasp on her coat and her parasol handle were both made by Fabergé.* ABOVE, RIGHT: *The Queen inherited the brooch in 1953, but wore it for the first time in public at the 1985 Windsor Horse Show.*

PEARLS AND DIAMONDS

# THE DUCHESS OF TECK'S CORSAGE BROOCH

ABOVE, RIGHT: *This corsage jewel is typically Victorian in execution, designed to be big and impressive, but less grand than a stomacher. The brooch consists of a large pearl set in a circle of diamonds enclosed in a diamond-plaited scroll frame with twelve further collet stones set around the edge. A U-shaped chain of larger collet diamonds ends in three pendant pearl drops.* ABOVE, LEFT: *Princess Mary Adelaide, Duchess of Teck, wearing the brooch, around 1895. It was inherited in 1897 by her daughter, the future Queen Mary, who gave it to the Queen as a wedding gift in 1947.* LEFT: *The Queen wore the brooch as she arrived in Nepal in 1961.*

# The Duchess of Cambridge's Pendant Brooch

RIGHT: *A baroque pearl in a diamond-set mount hangs from a diamond pendant below a large round pearl framed by fourteen brilliant-cut diamonds.* BELOW, LEFT: *The brooch belonged to Queen Mary's grandmother, Princess Augusta, Duchess of Cambridge, who was painted wearing it by Heinrich von Angeli, in 1877. When she died at the age of ninety-one, on 6 April 1889, at York House, St James's Palace, the brooch was inherited by her younger daughter, Princess Mary Adelaide, Duchess of Teck. She died intestate in 1897 and her jewellery was divided among her four children, this brooch being part of Queen Mary's portion.* BELOW, CENTRE: *It was one of her favourite brooches and she wore it constantly for the rest of her life. With her passion for family history, it must have pleased Queen Mary to wear her grandmother's brooch at the christening of her great-grandson, and godson, Prince Charles, in the Music Room at Buckingham Palace on 15 December 1948. She had also worn it for his mother's christening, the present Queen, in 1926.* BELOW, RIGHT: *The Queen inherited it in 1953 and wore it at Windsor Castle on her forty-eighth birthday on 21 April 1974. Despite the deceptive simplicity of its design, at a Buckingham Palace garden party in 1985, the brooch, pinned to the left shoulder of Her Majesty's pale blue silk long-sleeved dress, was so large that it was easily picked out as the Queen moved slowly through the crowd of eight thousand people.*

# Queen Mary's Kensington Bow Brooch and Warwick Sun Brooch

ABOVE: *In July 1893, the committee of the Kensington Wedding-Gift Fund, representing the inhabitants of Kensington, visited Princess May of Teck's home at White Lodge, Richmond, to present her with this bow-shaped diamond brooch with a large oriental pearl drop. It was made by Collingwood and Company. She wore the brooch at King Edward VII's Coronation in 1902, and at her own in 1911, as an appropriate symbol of her childhood at Kensington Palace.* LEFT: *A line drawing of the Warwick sun brooch given to Princess May as a wedding present by the Earl of Warwick's family.* OPPOSITE, ABOVE LEFT: *The Duke and Duchess of York at the Duchess of Devonshire's Costume Ball on 2 July 1897, to celebrate Queen Victoria's Diamond Jubilee. Dressed in sky-blue satin, the Duchess has attached the Warwick sun brooch as a pendant to her five-row pearl necklace. Framing the neckline of her bodice is the pearl and diamond necklace that was a wedding gift from the 'Ladies of England' (page 38). Below that is the Kensington bow brooch, and pinned below the diamond stomacher is the Dorset bow brooch. The enormous baroque pearl brooch pinned at the corner of her bodice originally belonged to Queen Alexandra, and was given to Princess Alice, Duchess of Gloucester, as a wedding gift by Queen Mary in 1935.* OPPOSITE, ABOVE RIGHT: *The Queen inherited the Kensington and Warwick brooches in 1953. She wore the Warwick sun brooch pinned to her Garter sash to open the New South Wales Parliament, in Sydney, Australia, in 1954, the only time she has worn it in public.* OPPOSITE, BELOW: *She wore the Kensington bow brooch in July 1986 when she attended a dinner given by the President of West Germany during his State visit to Great Britain. Her six-row pearl necklace set with different-sized diamond plaques and the matching earrings were a gift to the Queen from the Amir of Qatar on her 1979 visit to the Gulf States.*

# QUEEN ELIZABETH THE QUEEN MOTHER'S FLOWER BROOCH

LEFT: *In the late 1930s, Queen Elizabeth wore this five-petalled flower brooch with a cluster centre. She is seen here with her two daughters in 1936.* BELOW: *The Queen, then Princess Elizabeth, borrowed the brooch from her mother on a number of occasions and wore it at the International Horse Trials, at Badminton, in 1953. Princess Margaret is pictured on her left.*

# PRINCESS
# MARIE LOUISE'S
# BRACELET

ABOVE: *Princess Marie Louise was the younger daughter of Queen Victoria's third daughter, Princess Helena, and Prince Christian of Schleswig-Holstein. She was born in 1872 and died in 1956 at the age of eighty-four. Known to the Queen as 'Cousin Louie', she was an endless source of family anecdotes, and it was her idea to create Queen Mary's Dolls' House, now on display at Windsor Castle. She left one of the two pearl and diamond honeycomb bracelets on her left wrist to the Queen and the diamond brooch on her bodice to Queen Elizabeth the Queen Mother. She is photographed here two years before her death.* LEFT: *The Queen wearing the bracelet at a banquet given by King Faisal of Saudi Arabia at the Dorchester Hotel in 1967. The King had given Her Majesty her diamond necklace two days earlier (page 56).*

# Rubies

A LOVE AND APPRECIATION of fine rubies has run through the royal family since King Henry VIII, who customarily wore a chain of magnificent rubies slung around his shoulders as a collar. Queen Victoria began her collection of rubies with a half-hoop ring that was a wedding gift in 1840 from her uncle the Duke of Sussex. In 1849 Prince Albert had a demi-parure of necklace, earrings and brooch made for Queen Victoria out of rubies and diamonds already in the royal collection, and in 1853 she bought herself another ruby necklace. In 1855 when she and Prince Albert paid an official visit to the Emperor Napoleon III and the Empress Eugénie in Paris, General Canrobert, who sat next to the Queen at a banquet, noticed that among the rings she wore on every finger was one set with a superb blood-red ruby that he described as being of a 'prodigious size'.

Today Queen Elizabeth the Queen Mother wears seven of Queen Victoria's most beautiful pieces of jewellery, which are set with rubies and brilliant-cut diamonds. These include an oriental-inspired tiara with a design of flowers, leaves and arches, a cluster-and-drop necklace, a pair of pendant earrings and four brooches. Queen Victoria left these jewels to the Crown in 1901. Interestingly, these pieces – some of which were designed by Prince Albert – were originally set with opals. Prince Albert was especially fond of opals and in addition to those he gave his wife, Queen Victoria and he gave a suite of opal-set jewellery to their eldest child, Victoria, the Princess Royal, when she married the Crown Prince of Prussia in 1858. After Prince Albert's death in 1861, the Queen continued the tradition and in 1863, in both her name and his, a somewhat macabre gesture, she gave Princess Alexandra of Denmark a suite of opal and diamond jewellery on her marriage to the Prince of Wales, consisting of a pendant, earrings and three brooches.

Queen Alexandra seems to have believed the old adage that opals bring bad luck, and after Queen Victoria died she replaced the opals in the tiara, the cluster-and-drop necklace and the pendant earrings with blood-red Burmese rubies, stones that she and Queen Victoria had been given in princely gifts from the fabulously rich rulers of the Indian states. Queen Mary chose not to wear these pieces, perhaps because her first fiancé, the Duke of Clarence, the Duke of York's elder brother, had given her a half-hoop ruby engagement ring before his untimely death shortly before they were to be married. Queen Elizabeth the Queen Mother has worn these ruby pieces ever since King George VI acceded to the throne in 1936. Two of Queen Victoria's opal brooches that had been reset with rubies are often pinned on her Garter Riband. Presiding over her first Court at Buckingham Palace as Queen on 5 June 1937, she dazzled everyone wearing her ruby parure with a gold brocade gown embroidered with diamanté. In 1948 she and the King posed in profile for a special-issue postage stamp to mark their Silver Wedding anniversary. The Queen was wearing her ruby parure, which a friend described as 'incomparable', saying: 'They look good enough to eat.'

Over the years more ruby-set brooches and bracelets have been added to her collection. One brooch, from the people of Australia, is a 3½-inch-long, three-dimensional hibiscus flower set with 346 flawless diamonds and thirty-four Burmese rubies. When Her Majesty was given the brooch in Canberra she immediately pinned it on, saying, 'How beautiful, how very beautiful'.

Since her marriage in 1947 the Queen has been given six brooches of varying design set with rubies and diamonds. She wore one of these, a modern gold free-form shape, set with seven carved rubies, for her 1986 Christmas television broadcast to the Commonwealth. In the early 1960s she acquired a new cluster-and-drop necklace (page 68) and a pair of pendant earrings with detachable pear-shaped ruby drops in diamond collet frames. The rubies can be exchanged for diamond drops. A most unusual ring was made at the same time, which the Queen occasionally wears at evening events when she knows she won't have to shake many hands. The design of the ring is of a large oval ruby set in a cluster of seventeen closely set diamonds with seventeen small collet rubies set at intervals round the outside edge. As recently as 1985, on a State visit to England, the Amir of Qatar presented the Queen with a diamond swag necklace with a centrepiece of two large rubies.

One of the most intriguing jewels the Queen owns and which she herself is fascinated by, although she has never worn it, is a magical 352.5-carat spinel ruby carved in Arabic with the names of previous owners. Known as the Timur ruby or *Khiraj-i-alam* ('tribute to the world'), it belonged to Tamerlane who was born in Samarkand more than six hundred years ago and conquered Persia, Afghanistan and India. He wore the ruby set in his headdress. Subsequent owners were shahs of Persia and Mogul emperors of India. The last, Shuja Shah, was given sanctuary in Lahore in 1833 by Ranjit Singh, the 'Lion of the Punjab', and forced to forfeit all his jewels, including the Timur ruby.

When the Punjab was annexed by the British East India Company in 1849, all the State jewels came under the jurisdiction of a Board of Administration, who displayed the Timur ruby in London at the Great Exhibition of 1851. The East India Company then presented it to Queen Victoria, along with the 222 pearls with a ruby clasp presently worn by Queen Elizabeth the Queen Mother and an emerald girdle, which is part of the Indian collection at Buckingham Palace.

Another Arabic inscription carved on the stone, dated 1740, declares:

'This is the ruby among the twenty-five thousand jewels of the King of Kings, the Sultan Sahib
Qiran, which in the year 1153 from the collection of jewels of Hindustan reached this place.'

Today the Timur ruby is set in a necklace of diamond trident-shaped links, between two other large Indian-cut rubies. Although the Queen has said the necklace is so lovely she should have a dress specially designed to wear with it, she has never done so. The Timur ruby was left to the Crown by Queen Victoria in 1901.

Mr Antony Armstrong-Jones gave Princess Margaret a flower-shaped ruby and diamond engagement ring set in gold when they became engaged in 1960. It was bought from a jeweller although fanciful journalists delighted in speculating that the artistic bridegroom had designed it himself. The Princess's first rubies were set in the gold Cartier flower clip that she was given by her parents in 1942, a twin to Princess Elizabeth's clip set with sapphires (page 154). Another ruby and diamond flower brooch was received as a gift in 1948 when she launched the oil tanker *British Mariner* at the Govan Shipyard in Glasgow. Her most historically important necklace, which she wears often, is a neo-classical design by Federico Giuliano. This gold enamelled fringe necklace is set with cabochon rubies and moonstones, and with it Princess Margaret very often wears antique diamond and ruby girandole pendant earrings.

Twenty-five years after Princess Margaret showed off her engagement ring, Sarah Ferguson displayed a similar one when she and Prince Andrew announced their engagement. The ring – an oval ruby surrounded by ten spiky diamond drops, set in 18-carat white and yellow gold – was designed by Prince Andrew, a talent he has inherited from his father, Prince Philip. Miss Ferguson said that she thought the ring was 'stunning', with 'a lovely stone', and that it seemed especially appropriate in view of her red hair.

There was a great deal of conjecture as to what the Queen and Prince Philip would give the new Duchess of York as a wedding gift and it was suggested that it might be ruby jewellery to match her engagement ring. But instead the Queen chose a modern cluster-design diamond suite of earrings, necklace and bracelet. However, there were rubies set in the round clasp of another wedding gift, a string of pearls.

Princess Alexandra owns wonderful rubies, including a stunning bracelet of oval rubies and baguette diamonds with an ornate diamond and ruby clasp, which she wore for the formal photographs taken at the time of her engagement to the Hon. Angus Ogilvy in 1962. The bracelet had been a gift to her mother, Princess Marina, from her father, the Duke of Kent, in 1936. Princess Alexandra has a striking pair of large ruby and diamond five-petalled flower brooches that had also belonged to Princess Marina.

Princess Alexandra's great-grandmother, Queen Olga of Greece, had a nineteenth-century diamond floral wreath tiara set with rubies. After her death in 1926 it was inherited by her daughter-in-law, Princess Nicholas of Greece, who loaned it to her daughter, Princess Marina, to wear for the Opening of Parliament in 1937, the first of King George VI's reign. On that occasion she also wore the ruby bracelet Princess Alexandra has now, and a ruby and diamond *sautoir* necklace and earrings that had been among the Duke of Kent's wedding gifts to her.

Considering the fabulous rubies owned by members of the royal family, perhaps there is truth in the ancient tradition that rubies smooth tempers, protect against seduction and help the possessor to acquire lands and titles.

# QUEEN MARY'S CLUSTER EARRINGS AND THE KING GEORGE VI AND QUEEN ELIZABETH BANDEAU NECKLACE

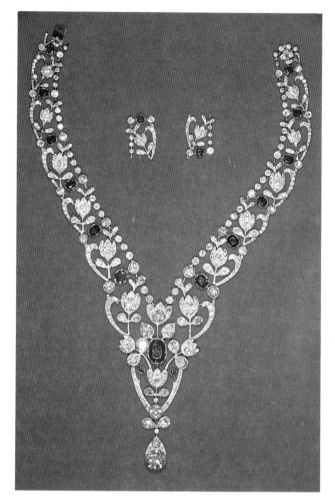

ABOVE, LEFT: *For her fifty-ninth birthday, on 26 May 1926, King George V presented Queen Mary with these earrings – large oval rubies each set in a cluster of nine brilliant-cut diamonds. Later that year, the Queen officially added them to the other pieces of ruby jewellery left to the Crown by Queen Victoria and King Edward VII. Many of these pieces are presently worn by Queen Elizabeth the Queen Mother. Queen Mary's earrings were given to the Queen by her parents in 1947.* ABOVE: *This V-shaped diamond and ruby floral bandeau collar ending in a drop diamond pendant is of Victorian workmanship and was bought by the Queen's parents as a wedding gift.*
LEFT: *The Queen arriving at Claridges for a State banquet given by the Greek royal family in 1963. Her wide Art Deco diamond bracelet is formed of eight oblong plaques studded with small rubies.*

# Queen Elizabeth the Queen Mother's Quartet of Bracelets

ABOVE: *These four matching Cartier diamond-strip bracelets have different baguette centres: sapphire, emerald, ruby and diamond.* ABOVE, RIGHT: *The Duke of York, later King George VI, bought them separately as gifts for his wife in 1924 and 1925. The Duchess of York, now Queen Elizabeth the Queen Mother, wearing all four in 1929. Her diamond fan-motif tiara, worn in the style of the day across her forehead, now belongs to Princess Margaret. Her Victorian turquoise and diamond brooch, and the matching earrings worn as pendant drops on her ropes of pearls, were part of a suite she received as a wedding gift from King George V in 1923, and which now also belong to Princess Margaret.* RIGHT: *The Queen wearing the diamond and ruby bracelets at a Variety Performance in Windsor for her Silver Jubilee in 1977.*

# QUEEN MARY'S ROSE OF YORK BRACELET

OPPOSITE: *When she married the Duke of York in 1893 Princess May of Teck was given a number of jewels in the shape of the Rose of York. One such, from the Duke of York himself, was a ruby and diamond pendant with a square ruby centre. Queen Mary gave it to Princess Elizabeth in 1947 as a wedding present, set as the centrepiece of a gold cuff bracelet with bands of ruby and diamond leaves on either side.* ABOVE, LEFT: *In 1898 Queen Mary, then Duchess of York, had removed the diamond-studded pendant loop, and wore it as a brooch on her high stiff collar when photographed here with her two oldest sons, the future Kings Edward VIII and George VI.* ABOVE, RIGHT: *In May 1953, shortly before her Coronation, the Queen wore the bracelet together with another wedding gift, a Cartier platinum and diamond necklace and pendant designed to represent English roses and foliage, given to her by the Nizam of Hyderabad and Berar.*

# The Queen's Fifth Wedding Anniversary Bracelet

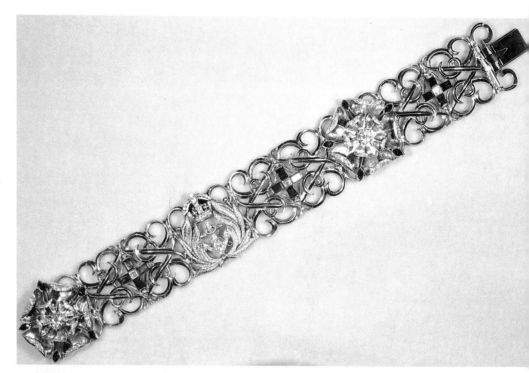

ABOVE: *Over the years, Prince Philip has designed a number of gifts for the Queen. This bracelet, made by Boucheron, was to celebrate their fifth wedding anniversary in 1952. It has gold links in the shape of interlocked E's and P's, and the centre medallion is Prince Philip's naval badge set in diamonds. There are two sapphire baguette crosses, a ruby cross, and two ruby and diamond studded flowers with fluted petals.*
LEFT: *The Queen wearing the bracelet, as she and Prince Philip arrived at Royal Ascot, in 1954.*

# Sapphires

IT IS SAID THAT SAPPHIRES are the symbol of love and purity, and it is fascinating to discover how many royal brides have chosen a sapphire engagement ring. In 1923 Queen Elizabeth the Queen Mother, or Lady Elizabeth Bowes-Lyon as she was then, chose a platinum ring set with a large Kashmir sapphire and diamonds; she told a reporter from the *Daily Mail* that the sapphire was her favourite stone. When her brother-in-law the Duke of Kent married Princess Marina of Greece in 1934, the Princess's engagement ring was a square 7-carat Kashmir sapphire with a baguette diamond on either side set in platinum. The following year the Duke of Gloucester became engaged to Lady Alice Montagu-Douglas-Scott and her ring also had a square sapphire.

As Princess Marina was a Greek Princess, after the Anglican wedding ceremony in Westminster Abbey she and the Duke of Kent had a Greek Orthodox service in the private chapel at Buckingham Palace – later destroyed by German bombs during the Second World War. Following her own church's tradition Princess Marina then moved her wedding ring to her right hand and kept it there for her lifetime.

In the next generation, Princess Alexandra chose a platinum ring with a large oval sapphire flanked on either side by a large diamond. She usually wears her engagement ring on the fourth finger of her right hand, together with two eternity rings – ruby and diamond, and emerald and diamond. With her wedding ring on her left hand she wears a ring with an oval star sapphire that she inherited from her mother, Princess Marina.

The present Duchess of Kent also has a sapphire and diamond engagement ring as does her sister-in-law Princess Michael of Kent, whose ring is set with a round sapphire and a round diamond that were left to Prince Michael by his mother, Princess Marina.

Princess Anne was given a sapphire and diamond ring by Captain Mark Phillips when they became engaged in 1973; her ring has a round sapphire with a round diamond on either side. In 1981 Prince Charles gave Lady Diana Spencer a large oval sapphire set in a cluster of fourteen brilliant-cut diamonds (page 79). On the evening of Sunday 22 February the Prince and Lady Diana had dined with the Queen at Windsor Castle and afterwards they looked at a large tray of more than a dozen rings that had been sent down from London. Without a minute's hesitation Lady Diana chose her favourite, which she says 'wasn't the largest by far!' It had to be quickly altered to fit her finger so that she could wear it for the official engagement photographs taken in the garden of Buckingham Palace on the following Tuesday.

The royal love of sapphires dates back to Prince Albert's wedding gift to Queen Victoria of a large oval sapphire and diamond brooch on 9 February 1840 (page 150). For her birthday on 24 May 1845, he gave her a slightly smaller sapphire and diamond brooch that was almost identical to his wedding gift, and which was later set as the pendant on a new sapphire and diamond cluster necklace. For her portrait painted by Winterhalter in 1846, Queen Victoria wore a narrow bandeau tiara of sapphires and diamonds, surmounted by fifteen cabochon sapphires. Twenty years later on 6 February 1866, after opening Parliament for the first time since Prince Albert's death, she noted in her diary that she had worn an ordinary evening dress, her widow's cap with a flowing tulle veil and this 'small diamond and sapphire coronet'.

In February 1922 Princess Mary, the Princess Royal, only daughter of King George V and Queen Mary, married Viscount Lascelles, later the sixth Earl of Harewood. Her father's wedding gift was a parure, consisting of Queen Victoria's sapphire bandeau tiara but with the upright cabochon stones removed, her sapphire and diamond cluster necklace with Prince Albert's 1845 brooch as a detachable oval pendant and a matching cluster bracelet. The King and Queen attended the Harewoods' first dinner party and dance at their London residence, Chesterfield House, after which the King wrote in his diary: 'Dear Mary looked charming and wore my sapphires.' The Princess Royal wore the necklace at the present Queen's Coronation in 1953. After her death in 1965 many of her jewels were auctioned at Christie's to pay death duties. Among the pieces sold was the sapphire necklace, which was bought by the American jeweller Harry Winston. Queen Victoria's bandeau tiara is still owned by her son, the seventh Earl.

The most magnificent antique sapphire and diamond parure in the royal family originally belonged to Queen Mary's maternal grandmother, Princess Augusta of Hesse, who married Prince Adolphus, Duke of Cambridge, seventh son of King George III and Queen Charlotte. The original pieces in the parure date from around 1800 and were a tiara set with seven high upright motifs, a short cluster necklace with a number of cluster pendant drops and a V-shaped stomacher, which could be worn as three separate brooches. When the Duchess's eldest daughter, Augusta, married the Grand Duke of Mecklenburg-Strelitz her mother gave her the 'Cambridge sapphires' as a wedding gift. The Grand Duchess was intensely proud of being a British princess and was godmother to her younger sister's only daughter, Princess May of Teck. When Princess May grew up, aunt and niece had an extremely close relationship and after Princess May became Queen Mary the Grand Duchess remained her closest confidante until her death in 1916, even though the Grand Duchess's country of birth and her country by marriage fought bitterly on opposite sides during the First World War. The Grand Duchess left the Cambridge sapphires to her niece and Queen Mary subsequently redesigned a number of pieces and added others to make a parure (pages 64 and 114).

In 1934 she gave the parure as a wedding gift to her goddaughter Princess Marina of Greece, when she married her son the Duke of Kent. There were the tiara, cluster earrings with detachable pendant drops, a long ornate cluster necklace with a detachable pendant drop, a plainer choker necklace with pendant drops, the stomacher and two bracelets. When Princess Marina died in 1968 the parure was inherited by the present Duchess of Kent, but in the early 1980s she decided that the Cambridge tiara and long cluster necklace were too grandiose to wear comfortably, so she fashioned a new tiara of five sapphires set in diamond clusters on a narrow diamond band. She wears it in addition to the choker necklace, two pairs of earrings and one of the original brooches.

Princess Marina's husband, the Duke of Kent, had inherited Queen Mary's love and appreciation of beautiful things. He was responsible for the decoration and running of their houses in Belgrave Square and Buckinghamshire, and helped choose Princess Marina's clothes and bought her exquisite jewellery, much of it from Cartier. He was especially fond of sapphires. Two striking crescent sapphire and diamond clips that he bought are owned today by Princess Michael, as is a large platinum pansy-shaped brooch set with sapphires, emeralds and diamonds. This last was a gift to Princess Marina on the birth of Prince Michael, and she wore it at his christening.

Princess Michael also has another brooch of Princess Marina's, a sapphire surrounded by diamonds with a detachable pendant pearl drop, which she sometimes wears as the centrepiece of a twisted pearl choker or of two long rows of haematite beads. A bar brooch that Princess Marina inherited from Queen Mary in 1953 – a square sapphire flanked by two brilliant-cut diamonds – is now used by Princess Michael as the clasp of a four-row pearl choker.

Other pieces of Princess Marina's sapphire jewellery are worn by the present Duchess of Kent. One is an unusual brooch of an oblong cabochon sapphire with diamond at each corner; another is a large rectangular stone with triangular clusters of small diamonds set on each side. The Duchess also inherited a sapphire and diamond bracelet, originally fastened with a velvet ribbon tied in a bow so that it could be worn alternatively as a choker necklace. Princess Marina gave a triangular clip of baguette sapphires and diamonds as a christening present to her first granddaughter, Lady Helen Windsor, the Duke and Duchess of Kent's only daughter.

In 1923 Queen Mary had also assembled a suite of sapphire and diamond jewellery for her first daughter-in-law, the Duchess of York, later Queen Elizabeth. This comprised an unusual necklace of sapphire and diamond clusters, from which fell thirteen long drops of collet diamonds interspersed with small sapphire and diamond clusters; a diamond and sapphire scroll corsage brooch with a negligé pendant; a narrow bracelet whose central motif matched that of the brooch; a half-hoop ring of three collet diamonds; an all-diamond brooch in the shape of the Rose of York, which had been a wedding gift in 1893 to Queen Mary from the 'Officers of the West Yorkshire Regiment'; and a cluster brooch with an oval sapphire surrounded by diamonds. The Queen Mother often wears the corsage brooch, but she has never worn the necklace in public and has given the other two brooches to Princess Margaret.

King George VI, who loved sapphires and had a connoisseur's appreciation of the stones, purchased many pieces of sapphire jewellery from Cartier as gifts for Queen Elizabeth and for his daughter Princess Elizabeth. One of Queen Elizabeth's most loved brooches, a large sapphire six-petalled flower with a central cluster of diamonds, was an anniversary gift from King George VI; she very often wears it at the races.

Since the 'Prince Albert Brooch' is Crown property, Queen Elizabeth the Queen Mother relinquished it to the Queen after King George VI's death in 1952, but she often wears an almost identical one, as does Princess Anne.

The Queen has many pieces of sapphire jewellery, either inherited or given as gifts by her family. In addition, she was presented with a magnificent suite of a necklace, earrings and ring by Sheikh Rashid when she visited Dubai in 1979. Made by Asprey, the perfectly matched sapphires are so large and the looped design of the diamond necklace with its sapphire cluster pendants is so ornate that the Queen is reported to have exclaimed in amazement when she saw it. She has only worn it once in public. The Queen has another necklace that she wears only on private occasions. Made around the turn of the century by the Revivalist jewellers Carlo and Arthur Giuliano, this long openwork gold necklace is set with multicoloured sapphires and zircons and decorated with green enamel leaves.

Other pieces of sapphire jewellery owned by the Queen include three brooches: a Cartier floral spray set with sapphires, rubies, diamonds and an aquamarine, which her parents gave her in 1943; a cabochon sapphire bumblebee with diamond wings; and a filigree Maltese cross set with five large sapphires and a number of small diamonds. She also has two sapphire and diamond tiaras that she has never worn in public and a ring – an oval sapphire set in a cluster of diamonds – that she occasionally wears with the necklace and earrings her father gave her as a wedding gift in 1947.

The Princess of Wales's most magnificent wedding gift was a sapphire and diamond suite from the Crown Prince of Saudi Arabia. Made by Asprey, it consists of an enormous Burmese sapphire pendant set in a jagged sunray fringe of baguette diamonds and hung on a thin diamond necklace; a matching pair of earrings and ring; a two-row bracelet of brilliant-cut diamonds with a smaller version of the sapphire pendant as a centrepiece; and a wristwatch, the face set in the same diamond sunray fringe and the strap consisting of seven oval sapphires set in clusters of diamonds. The suite came in a green case with the Saudi Arabian crest embossed on top. The Prince of Wales was given a green malachite casket with gold jewel-studded leaves and with a jewelled butterfly on each corner. Set in the centre of the lid was a gold palm tree with crossed swords, the Saudi Arabian national symbol. According to the Princess, when she first saw the Saudi Arabian suite she exclaimed, 'Gosh, and I don't even know this man!'

The Princess often wears the necklace and earrings, and occasionally the bracelet, but she has used the stones from the watch and ring to make completely new pieces of jewellery. Four of the sapphire and diamond clusters from the watch strap were made into a pair of earrings, with two of the clusters as detachable pendant drops. The oval sapphire from the ring was set in the diamond sunray frame of the watch and is now the centrepiece of a wide choker of midnight-blue velvet backed with Velcro. On either side of the sapphire is a chain of small diamonds, three deep, which runs halfway round the choker. The Princess wore the choker as a headband on her official visit to Japan in 1986, at a State banquet hosted by the Emperor.

Another wedding gift to the Princess of Wales from Queen Elizabeth the Queen Mother was a massive Sri Lankan oval sapphire set as a brooch in a double row of diamonds. The Princess thought it was beautiful but as she does not often wear brooches, the year after her marriage she had it adapted so that it could be worn as the centrepiece of a seven-row pearl choker. She was photographed wearing it for the first time in public in 1985 at her brother Lord Althorp's twenty-first-birthday dance at Spencer House in London.

The Princess also owns a diamond and sapphire watch, which was presented to her at the 1983 International Spring Fair in Birmingham. She has three pairs of sapphire earrings: double half-hoops, one of sapphires and the other of diamonds; tiny sapphire studs; and double oval clusters of sapphires surrounded by diamonds. However, some of the sapphire jewellery that the Princess wears in public is in fact fake, such as four favourite pairs of earrings. First she had tiny 'diamond' flower-shaped studs from which could be suspended 'sapphire', 'ruby' or 'diamond' pendants; then she acquired small oval 'sapphire' drops to hang from the flower studs; 'sapphire' chips set in oval gold pendants; and long oval 'sapphire' drops hanging from four 'diamonds' set in a square.

It may seem extraordinary that the future Queen of the United Kingdom, heiress to the world's most fabulous jewellery collection, should choose to bedeck herself in costume jewellery that is available to any girl in the country, but perhaps it is just because of the role that lies ahead that she chooses to do so now. She explains that 'it's more sensible for someone who's only twenty-five to do so', and that she enjoys mixing the real with the fake.

# THE KING GEORGE VI VICTORIAN SUITE

In 1947 King George gave Princess Elizabeth a long necklace of oblong sapphires
surrounded by round diamonds and separated by diamond collets as a wedding gift.
To match it there was a pair of free-swinging, square-shaped sapphire earrings, bordered with
diamonds and hanging from three collet stones. The suite was made around 1850.
The colour of the stones exactly matched the blue of the Garter Riband, although this choice
may have been a coincidence on the part of the King. In 1952 the Queen had the
necklace shortened by removing the largest stone, plus one of the smaller sapphires, and in
1959 a pendant was made using the big stone.
OPPOSITE, ABOVE: *The King George VI sapphire suite in its velvet case, including the extra link
that was removed.* OPPOSITE, BELOW: *Princess Elizabeth photographed in her drawing
room at Clarence House before leaving for an official visit to Kenya in 1952. King George
VI died while she was there, and this picture was withheld from distribution until after
the end of Court mourning on 1 June 1952. The necklace is its original length.* When Noel
Coward saw her wearing the suite at the 1954 Royal Command Performance at the
Palladium, he wrote:

'After the show we lined up and were presented to the Queen,
Prince Philip and Princess Margaret. The Queen looked luminously
lovely and was wearing the largest sapphires I have ever seen.'

ABOVE: *In 1963 a new sapphire and diamond tiara and bracelet were made to match the
original pieces. The Queen wore the complete parure when she and Prince Philip
attended a charity concert in 1969.*

# THE PRINCE ALBERT BROOCH

ABOVE: *This magnificent brooch, a large oblong sapphire surrounded by twelve round diamonds, was given to Queen Victoria by Prince Albert of Saxe-Coburg-Gotha on Sunday, 9 February 1840, at Buckingham Palace. It was the day before their wedding and she noted in her diary that, after a religious service in the Bow Room, 'dearest Albert' came upstairs to her sitting room and gave her four fans and a 'beautiful sapphire and diamond brooch'. For their wedding in the Chapel Royal, St James's Palace, she wore it with her Turkish diamond necklace and earrings.* OPPOSITE, ABOVE LEFT: *While Prince Albert was alive the Queen wore it constantly, as here in an 1843 lithograph – which in 1851 she arranged to have produced cheaply enough so that even the poorer of her subjects could afford to buy it. During her forty years of widowhood, however, she was rarely seen wearing the brooch. In her will she instructed that it was to be considered a Crown piece of jewellery and held in trust for all future Queens of Great Britain. Her two bar brooches were remade as the double bar brooch (page 65).* OPPOSITE, ABOVE RIGHT: *Queen Alexandra wore the Prince Albert brooch pinned on the right of her bodice for her Coronation in 1902.* OPPOSITE, BELOW LEFT: *Queen Mary often wore it in the daytime, as seen here in 1927, with matching earrings.* OPPOSITE, CENTRE: *Queen Elizabeth the Queen Mother, who wore the brooch only occasionally during the war years, did so at the 1942 christening of Prince William of Gloucester. It came to the Queen on her accession.* OPPOSITE, BELOW RIGHT: *The Queen in July 1972, at the launch of a RNLI lifeboat.*

# The Empress Marie Feodorovna
# of Russia's Brooch

<small>ABOVE:</small> *A cabochon sapphire brooch surrounded by two rows of diamonds with a pearl drop hanging from a collet diamond. The brooch was a wedding gift in 1866 to Princess Dagmar of Denmark, on her marriage to the Tsarevich Alexander, from her sister and brother-in-law the Prince and Princess of Wales.* <small>OPPOSITE, ABOVE LEFT:</small> *Queen Alexandra, Empress Marie and their youngest sister, Thyra, the Duchess of Cumberland, playing cards with their father, King Christian IX, at the Palace in Copenhagen in April 1905. The Empress, who is seated on King Christian's right, is wearing the brooch pinned on her bodice.* <small>OPPOSITE, ABOVE RIGHT:</small> *Queen Mary purchased the brooch from the Dowager Empress Marie's estate in 1929. She wears it here in 1938.* <small>OPPOSITE, BELOW:</small> *The Queen inherited the brooch in 1953, and wears it while visiting the Solomon Islands in 1982.*

# QUEEN ELIZABETH THE QUEEN MOTHER'S LEAF BROOCH

ABOVE: *Framed in diamond baguettes, this Cartier leaf-shaped brooch has a pavé-set diamond vein down the centre, and is set with irregularly shaped Indian-cut Ceylonese cabochon sapphires, and small round emeralds, amethysts and a ruby. The Duke of York bought it for his wife in 1928.* ABOVE, RIGHT: *Queen Elizabeth the Queen Mother, then Duchess of York, wore it pinned to her velvet cloche hat in 1930.* RIGHT: *She gave it to her daughter as a wartime birthday gift, and twenty-year-old Princess Elizabeth wore it on her lapel during a visit to Nottingham in 1946.*

# THE QUEEN'S FLOWER SPRAY BROOCH

# THE QUEEN'S SET OF FLOWER CLIPS

ABOVE, LEFT: *A Cartier gold spray brooch with one flower of all blue sapphires and another of pink sapphires and cushion-cut rubies. Both have square-cut diamond centres and one of the three leaves is set with pavé-set diamonds. It was a birthday gift to the Queen from her parents in 1945 together with a matching pair of earrings in the shape of miniature flowers on tiny stems.*
LEFT: *For her twenty-third birthday, on 21 April 1949, the first photograph was released of the Duke and Duchess of Edinburgh with Prince Charles.*

ABOVE: *The Queen's Cartier gold flower clips, with clusters of cushion-shaped sapphires and brilliant-cut diamonds in their centres, were bought separately in 1942 and 1945 by King George and Queen Elizabeth. Princess Margaret was given an identical set, but with ruby clusters. She sold hers some years ago at Christie's.* RIGHT: *Princess Elizabeth on her first visit to Washington in 1951.*

# QUEEN MARY'S RUSSIAN BROOCH

# THE QUEEN'S EIGHTEENTH BIRTHDAY BRACELET

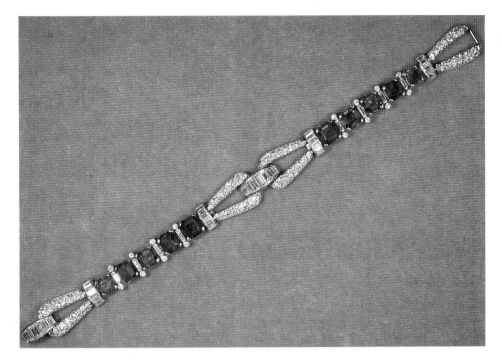

OPPOSITE, ABOVE: *Queen Alexandra's sister, the Empress Marie Feodorovna of Russia, gave Princess May of Teck this unusual brooch of a large square-cut diamond and a square cabochon sapphire set in a scroll frame of round diamonds as a wedding present in 1893. The Empress and her husband, Tsar Alexander III, later added sapphire and diamond bracelets to the gift.* OPPOSITE, BELOW RIGHT: *In 1925 Queen Mary pinned the brooch horizontally on her collar.* OPPOSITE, BELOW LEFT: *In 1974 the Queen, who had inherited the brooch in 1953, wore it pinned vertically on her shoulder.* ABOVE: *For her eighteenth birthday, in 1944, the King gave Princess Elizabeth this unusual Cartier linked bracelet of square-cut sapphires interspersed with baguette diamonds and ending in diamond loops joined by arcs of baguette diamonds.* RIGHT: *The Queen and Prince Philip leaving the theatre in 1955.*

# Turquoises

DESPITE THE NUMBER OF PIECES of antique turquoise jewellery in the royal family the Queen owns only one modern set – a cluster-and-drop necklace and matching earrings of turquoises, with diamonds and sapphires, that she was given by the King of Jordan when he paid a State visit to England in 1966. The Queen had never worn it in public until she paid a return visit to King Hussein and Queen Noor in 1984; she wore it then at the State banquet they gave in her honour.

Turquoises had a sentimental meaning for Queen Victoria and Prince Albert. The Prince's parents, the Duke and Duchess of Saxe-Coburg-Gotha, were unhappily married and when the Duchess sought her freedom, due to her husband's cruelty, she was forced to give up custody of her two small sons. The youngest, Albert, was only four. She died of cancer at 31 without ever seeing her children again. When Prince Albert and Queen Victoria became engaged he gave her a little turquoise brooch that had been his mother's, and after their wedding, on 10 February 1840, the Queen and Prince Albert presented each of her twelve bridesmaids with a turquoise and pearl brooch designed in the shape of his crest, the Coburg Eagle.

Queen Victoria already owned a number of pieces of turquoise jewellery that had been birthday or Christmas gifts: from her mother, the Duchess of Kent, she had a gold chain with a turquoise clasp; from her uncle King Leopold of the Belgians a turquoise ring; from her aunt Queen Adelaide a necklace and matching earrings of turquoise and pearls; and from two of her uncles, the Dukes of Sussex and Cambridge, she had two turquoise bracelets. Three years after her marriage in 1843, Prince Albert designed and had made a complete turquoise parure for the Queen, which she said was in his usual excellent taste.

By the early 1900s turquoises were considered the height of fashion and the two turquoise parures in the royal family today, one worn by Princess Margaret and the other by the Duchess of Gloucester, were both assembled by Queen Mary. Princess Margaret had been given a string of turquoise and pearl beads as a baby – the companion string to her sister's of coral and pearls (page 25) – which she later gave to her own daughter, Lady Sarah Armstrong-Jones. For Princess Margaret's twenty-first birthday in August 1951, her mother, Queen Elizabeth, gave her the magnificent antique parure of pale Persian turquoises set in diamonds that she had been given as a wedding gift in 1923 by her father-in-law, King George V. It consisted of a long necklace with a number of graduated pendant drops, matching pendant earrings, hair ornaments, a large square brooch and a high oval tiara (page 141). Princess Margaret wore the brooch at Prince Andrew's wedding in July 1986. A bow brooch and a ring were subsequently added to the set.

The second parure was given by Queen Mary in 1935 to Lady Alice Montagu-Douglas-Scott on her marriage to the Queen's third son, Prince Henry, Duke of Gloucester. There is a V-shaped, scroll-design tiara, a long chain necklace of twenty-six turquoise and diamond oval clusters, matching cluster earrings and ring, two bow brooches, a bow-shaped corsage brooch with a tassel, a bangle bracelet and two four-row turquoise bead bracelets. The three brooches had originally been a confirmation present in December 1850 to Queen Mary's mother, the seventeen-year-old Princess Mary Adelaide, later Duchess of Teck. She had worn the two bow brooches as part of her feathered headdress and the corsage brooch pinned to her bodice when she attended her first Buckingham Palace Drawing Room as a débutante.

In 1893 the Duke and Duchess of Teck had given the three 1850 turquoise brooches, a tiara, a necklace and earrings to their daughter, Princess May, when she married the Duke of York. These six pieces are part of the Gloucester parure, and over the years another drop necklace was added and the Teck earrings worn as detachable pendant drops on the oval cluster earrings.

# THE PRESIDENT AYUB KHAN OF PAKISTAN NECKLACE

ABOVE: *In 1966 the President of Pakistan, Field-Marshal Mohammed Ayub Khan, made a State visit to Britain and gave the Queen a two-row pearl necklace hung with graduated turquoise pendants ending in seed pearl drops. Her Majesty wears it at a dinner during the visit. When Princess Anne was a teenager the necklace was divided into two. Six small pendants from the lower row were removed and added to the shorter strand so that it now has pendants all the way around. A pair of earrings was made from two rosettes out of the extra centrepiece, with the last two small pendants being suspended as drops. LEFT: Princess Anne wore the set to a dinner at the Royal Academy in June 1986.*

# The Crown Regalia

THE ITEMS THAT COMPRISE THE CROWN REGALIA are not just decorative objects but the visible proof of royalty; they are symbols of the power and authority handed down from generation to generation. Their antecedents can be traced back to the Coronation in 828 of the first English king, Egbert, although the various items had to be remade for King Charles II in 1660 when the monarchy was restored after the Protectorate.

The Crown Regalia belongs to the State and is displayed to the public in the Jewel House of the Tower of London. It attracts nearly two million people a year – a larger number of visitors than any other public exhibition in Great Britain. Although William the Conqueror began work on the Tower of London in 1066, he travelled around the country a great deal and kept the Crown Jewels under his bed when staying at the ancient palace at Winchester. During King Henry III's reign (1216–72), he established the first royal storeroom in the Tower and in 1303 his successor and son, King Edward I, had the Regalia moved there from Westminster Abbey. The Regalia has been on public show since the seventeenth century. Since 1782 it has been under the jurisdiction of the Lord Chamberlain, who is responsible for its security and for seeing that the items are cleaned and kept in perfect repair.

The crowning of a new monarch is the most impressive and awe-inspiring event in British pageantry. In 1307 the Abbot of Westminster wrote down the ritual governing the crowning and anointing of a new king in the *Liber Regalis*. Historically it was important that links should be established between each new king or change in dynasty and the previous reign. The ritual and the Regalia emphasized this continuity of the monarchy. The new king was usually crowned at Westminster Abbey about eighteen months after his accession, the time needed to make the necessary arrangements. Traditionally, a Coronation crown was set with jewels rented from the crown jeweller – for about 4 per cent of the value of the stones. After the ceremony these jewels were replaced by paste substitutes and then the crown was put on display. This system persisted until Queen Victoria's Coronation in 1838.

On 27 March 1605 King James I issued a royal decree declaring that the Crown Regalia and a number of other ornaments and jewels were indivisible from the Kingdom, thereby attempting to preserve them for posterity. But his successor, his son King Charles I, was so short of funds when he acceded to the throne in 1625 that he was forced to sell some of the royal jewels and gold plate. At the start of the Civil War his French-born wife, Queen Henrietta Maria, sailed to the Netherlands on 23 February 1642 in order to dispose of a large quantity of plate and jewels. With the money she raised she sent her husband powder and carbines, and coins with which to pay his troops. When the King left London for York on 3 March he lost control of the Jewel House. The Queen returned to England a year later, but in 1644 fled to exile in France taking with her as many of the royal jewels as she could lay her hands on, including many famous diamonds. She was forced to pawn or sell the jewels one by one for ridiculously low sums, many to her own nephew King Louis XIV. She sent most of the funds she raised back to her husband's supporters, living herself in miserable poverty. But all her efforts were in vain, for King Charles I was captured, put on trial and beheaded in Whitehall on 29 January 1649.

Britain was now governed by Oliver Cromwell and a Commonwealth Parliament who in that August ordered:

> 'that those gentlemen who were appointed by this House to have the custody of the regalia, to deliver them over unto the trustees for sale of the goods of the late King, who are to cause the same to be totally broken, and that they melt down all the gold and silver, and sell the jewels to the best advantage of the Commonwealth.'

The Commission spent three days making an inventory of everything in the Jewel House and valuing each item. The total value of the Regalia came to £2,647 18s 4d. Much of the metal was converted into coin, while individual gems and some other items were sold for as much at they would fetch. The Regalia was regarded as symbolic of the 'detestable rule of kings', but the Puritans also believed that the work of goldsmiths represented immoral vanity. Cromwell himself called them 'worthless churche stuffe'.

When King Charles II was restored to the throne in 1660 a new set of Coronation Regalia had to be made. This included two crowns, three sceptres, an orb, a ring, a pair of spurs, swords and various other items. The different pieces signify dignity, justice, mercy and courage, and during the Coronation ceremony the monarch swears to maintain all such virtues. The royal goldsmith, Sir Robert Vyner, completed all the new pieces in only eleven months at a cost of £31,978 9s 11d. A number of the stones that had been sold in 1649 were returned by Stuart sympathizers and set in the new Regalia.

Additions have been made to the Regalia since King Charles II's day. For example, a new crown has been created for each consort. In 1902 Queen Alexandra's crown was made by the jewellers Messrs Carrington of Regent Street (page 95). The frame was of platinum and it was set with 3,688 diamonds. In the centre of the front cross pattée was set the 106-carat Koh-I-Noor diamond. Queen Alexandra was the first Queen Consort to wear this stone in her crown. The crown weighed only twenty-two ounces, in stark contrast to St Edward's Crown, which weighs just under five pounds. Most of the jewels were hired. Until Queen Victoria only Queen Adelaide had insisted on having her own jewels set in her crown for her Coronation in 1831. On their Coronation day Queen Alexandra was so late that King Edward sent a footman with the message: 'If you don't come down at once you won't be crowned Queen.'

In 1911 Queen Mary had a crown made to her specifications by Garrard (page 55). In addition to the Koh-I-Noor diamond she also used Cullinans III and IV in the setting, the only time that these two stones – her personal property – have ever appeared as part of the Regalia. The crown belonged to Queen Mary not the State. She removed the detachable half arches that surmounted it and continued to wear it as an open circlet at Courts and on State occasions (page 80). In 1914 Queen Mary presented it to her husband, King George V, for the use of future Queen Consorts. However, on the accession of her son King George VI she decided to break with a tradition dating back to Plantagenet times that no Queen Dowager ever attended the crowning of her husband's successor. For the Coronation on 12 May 1937 she wore the circlet of her own crown, having removed the Koh-I-Noor diamond and given it to her daughter-in-law Queen Elizabeth.

The crown made for Queen Elizabeth in 1937 was only partially new (page 179). The circlet had been made for Queen Victoria in 1853 to display the Koh-I-Noor diamond. Among the many other diamonds set in the crown was one that had been in a stomacher presented to Queen Victoria by the Sultan of Turkey, and the detachable drop from Queen Victoria's collet necklace, which was set in the surmounting cross. Queen Elizabeth wore the circlet when she accompanied the King to State Openings of Parliament. She also wore it on 2 June 1953 when she followed the precedent set by her mother-in-law and attended the Coronation of her daughter the present Queen. The Koh-I-Noor diamond is still set in Queen Elizabeth the Queen Mother's crown, which is kept on show in the Jewel House.

On 12 December 1911 King George and Queen Mary, as Emperor and Empress of India, attended the Delhi Durbar witnessed by a crowd of eighty thousand spectators. When officials began planning the occasion they discovered that by law the Crown Jewels could not be taken out of Britain. This embargo dated back to King Edward III who had tried to pawn the Regalia in Flanders. A new crown was needed, hence the creation of the Imperial Crown of India. It has 6,170 diamonds, the biggest of which is 34 carats, four sapphires, four rubies and nine emeralds, one of which weighs 36 carats. The crown weighs 3½ lb. The King wrote in his diary after the Durbar:

> 'Today we held the Coronation Durbar, the most beautiful and wonderful sight I have ever seen & one I shall remember all my life. The weather was all that could be wished, hot sun, hardly any wind, no clouds. May and I were photographed before we started in our robes. I wore the same clothes and robes as at the Coronation with a new Crown made for India which cost £60,000 which the Indian Government is going to pay for.'

During the Second World War only four people in the country, including King George VI, knew where the Crown Regalia had been taken for safekeeping, and all four took the secret to their graves. However, there is an extraordinary tale found in the memoirs of Marion Crawford, the Princesses' governess. Undoubtedly apocryphal, the story bears repeating as the governess claims to have been witness to the unlikely event. Princess Elizabeth and Princess Margaret lived secretly at Windsor Castle during the war years, while the King and Queen remained at Buckingham Palace, visiting Windsor at the weekends. The two Princesses explored every corner of the ancient castle and Sir Owen Morshead, Librarian and Assistant Keeper of the King's Archives, was often their guide. One day he took the Princesses and Miss Crawford down to the very lowest level. The cold stone passage passed vaults that had once been dungeons but were now used as air-raid shelters. Many of them still had huge iron locks on the doors. Sir Owen unlocked one of these and they entered a room full of priceless paintings. In one corner there was a jumble of old furniture, broken chairs and tables waiting to be repaired. He moved everything aside revealing a wall cupboard, which when opened was found to be full of old cardboard boxes and yellowing newspapers. All these were removed until finally, at the very back, there remained a large, old-fashioned leather hat box. By now the Princesses were convulsed with giggles at all the trouble Sir Owen had taken to unearth a mouldy old hat box. But when he opened it they were silent, for it contained the Imperial State Crown, and even in that gloomy setting the diamonds sent out a thousand sparkling reflections. Other equally decrepit cases concealed the rest of the Crown Jewels.

Shakespeare wrote in *Henry VI*, 'How sweet a thing it is to wear a crown,' but there were sovereigns who disputed this. Frederick the Great described his crown as just a hat that let the rain in, and after forty-two years as Queen, Elizabeth I said:

> 'To be a King and wear a crown is a thing more glorious to them that see it than it is pleasant to them that bear it.'

But for the spectators, pageantry, processions and the Crown reinforce the links that bind them to the Monarch.

# THE KING GEORGE IV STATE DIADEM

In 1821 King George IV was busy acting as stage manager for his own Coronation and he
not only designed the fanciful Tudor costumes to be worn by Court officials, but also
a completely new crown for the ceremony, and a diamond diadem to encircle his velvet Cap
of Maintenance. He wanted his crown to have a floral design, but the Privy Council
ruled that this would be improper, as the Coronation crown had always had fleur-de-lys
motifs, even prior to Edward the Confessor. Instead he used the floral emblems for his
diadem and, following tradition, the jewels set into it were hired for the occasion; but in a
last-minute change of mind he never wore it. In 1838 the diadem was reset with
pearls and diamonds from the royal collection and worn for the first time by Queen Victoria
at her Coronation. For the next thirty years she wore it constantly: at her children's
christenings and weddings; at State banquets; even at a dinner at Cambridge University, of
which Prince Albert was Chancellor; and she is pictured wearing it on the world's first
postage stamp, issued in 1840, when it became familiar throughout the world. In her will she
left it to the Crown.

ABOVE: *The completely circular diadem has four crosses pattée set with diamonds, representing
St George, the front one with a rare honey-coloured diamond in the centre; and four
diamond bouquets incorporating roses, thistles and shamrocks, the emblems of the United
Kingdom. The diamond scrollwork band, remounted for Queen Alexandra in 1902, is
framed between two rows of pearls — eighty-one in the upper row and eighty-eight in the
lower.* PAGE 164, ABOVE LEFT: *The nineteen-year-old Queen Victoria, as painted by Sir
George Hayter in 1838, shown with the Crown and Sceptre of England placed on a table by*

her side and the Garter Collar worn around her shoulders, as was traditional in royal portraiture. BELOW, LEFT: *Queen Alexandra in 1905. Her large diamond corsage brooch is just the centre part of Queen Victoria's massive stomacher (page 126).* BELOW: *Queen Mary in May 1913, visiting Berlin for the wedding of the Kaiser's only daughter, Princess Viktoria Luise, to Prince Ernst August, Duke of Brunswick. It was commonly agreed by everyone present that in her heavily beaded gown, flowing lace veil and staggering collection of nine diamond necklaces, Cullinans III and IV worn as a*

*pendant, six diamond brooches, diamond earrings and two diamond bracelets she was the most dazzling woman there.* OPPOSITE: *The Queen inherited the diadem in 1952 on the death of her father, and wore it for this formal portrait taken in 1957. Because the Queen wears the diadem to and from the State Opening of Parliament each year, and is pictured with it on all United Kingdom postage stamps, the diadem is seen by more millions of people than any other item of royal jewellery.*

# The Imperial State Crown,
# The Sceptre and The Orb

An Imperial State Crown was made for King George IV's Coronation and set with hired
stones, as was traditional (the bill came to £6,525). It was also worn by his brother,
King William IV, but when Queen Victoria succeeded him in 1837 it was much too large
for the diminutive eighteen-year-old Queen to wear. The Lord Chamberlain in
1838 commissioned the crown jewellers, Messrs Rundell, Bridge and Rundell of Ludgate
Hill, to make a smaller but otherwise identical crown of gold and silver, set
with historic stones from the royal collection. The cost of the work – including new brilliants,
pearls and a fine sapphire, a purple velvet cap lined with white satin and with
an ermine border, and a morocco carrying case with a lock and key and engraved plate –
amounted to £1,000.
Queen Victoria's crown had to be slightly enlarged for King Edward VII to wear in 1902,
and in 1911 certain stones were reset for the Coronation of King George V.
In 1937 a new, duplicate frame was made for King George VI and it was his crown that
was remodelled in 1953 to fit the Queen. The first time she wore it was
following her Coronation (St Edward's Crown is used for the ceremony itself), and it is the
crown she uses for the annual Opening of Parliament.
The Opening of Parliament usually takes place at the beginning of November and before
this event the Imperial State Crown is taken to Buckingham Palace from the
Jewel House at the Tower of London. This gives the Queen the opportunity to try it on and
get used to the weight. Until 1962 it was conveyed to the Houses of
Parliament in a closed carriage, but in that year a new tradition was established when the
crown was removed from its leather carrying case and securely attached to a
small circular table set in the floor of Queen Alexandra's State Coach – an 1860s vintage
brougham that had been converted into a 'glass State Coach' for the Queen's
great-grandmother. The jewels glint and flash under concealed battery-operated spotlights as
the coach moves along the Mall from the Palace to Westminster, escorted by a
Regalia Escort of the Household Cavalry and four Royal Watermen. For the waiting crowds
it is a prelude to the symbolism and pageantry to come as the Queen carries
out her role as constitutional monarch; the Opening of Parliament is the only time when she
is seen sitting on her throne and wearing her crown.
Things were a lot more relaxed in Queen Victoria's day. In 1847, Warder Lunn, the
Gentleman Porter of the Tower, complained that the Lord Chamberlain's
Department was in the habit of sending an ordinary one-horse hackney cab to collect the
crown and, as there were three persons travelling with it, he was forced to sit on
top with the driver. As he pointed out to the Deputy Lieutenant of the Tower, aside from the
lack of ceremony, from his position he could not see what was happening inside
the carriage and would be unable to stop anyone passing the crown out of the window. Not
much notice was taken of his complaint, but at least a larger public vehicle was
hired so that he could travel inside with the rest of the party.
When the Regalia procession reaches the House of Lords the crown is carried
upstairs on a crimson velvet cushion to the Queen's Robing Room. When Her Majesty
arrives in the Irish State coach at 11.15 am, she is escorted there and at a
Georgian dressing table with a small mirror she removes the King George IV State Diadem
and puts on the Imperial Crown and the crimson velvet Robe of State with its
eighteen-foot train.
OPPOSITE: The Imperial State Crown is a copy of the one made for King
George IV's Coronation in 1821, and has an openwork frame thickly encrusted with
diamonds. The pattern of oak leaves and acorns on the arches symbolizes the
famous oak tree at Boscobel in which King Charles II hid from Cromwell's troops after his

defeat at Worcester. Although the frame is gold, the settings of the stones are
silver. The circumference is 23¾ inches, the height 12⅜ inches and it weighs 2 lb 13 oz.
It is set with 2,873 diamonds, 273 pearls, seventeen sapphires, eleven emeralds
and five rubies. The circlet base has alternate emeralds and sapphires surrounded by
diamonds; in the centre front is the 317.4-carat Cullinan II, the Second Star
of Africa, which was presented to King Edward VII by the Transvaal Government in 1907
and set in the crown by King George V in 1911. Above is a band of 109
pearls invisibly strung as a necklace, and below is another string of 128 pearls. Mounted on
the circlet are upright fleurs-de-lys and crosses pattée covered in diamonds, with
emeralds and rubies set alternately as the centre stones of each motif.
Just above Cullinan II, in a jewelled Maltese cross, is a giant irregularly
shaped ruby spinel known as the 'Black Prince's ruby'. Edward of Woodstock, Prince of
Wales, eldest son of King Edward III and Queen Philippa, got his nickname
posthumously when his tomb in Canterbury Cathedral was opened two hundred years after his
death in 1376 and it was discovered that he had been buried in a suit of black
armour. He was very fond of jewellery; in 1355 alone he had bought twenty-seven rings set
with rubies, diamonds or pearls. The uncut spinel, which had previously
belonged to Abu Said, one of the Arab rulers of Granada, was said to have been given to
the Prince as a gesture of appreciation by Abu Said's murderer, Pedro the
Cruel, King of Castile, after the battle of Najera in 1367. The Black Prince had helped
King Pedro to win the battle, thus restoring him to his throne, which he had
lost a year earlier to his illegitimate half-brothers. Legend has it that thereafter the Black
Prince wore the jewel in his breastplate, that King Henry V had it set in the
helmet he wore at the Battle of Agincourt in 1415 when he defeated the French army, and
that when King Richard III lost the Battle of Bosworth Field in 1485 and was
slain, the ruby was in his helmet.

*The stone was not mentioned again until it was recorded as being in Queen Henrietta
Maria's crown, but it does not seem to be among the jewels she took with her when she fled
to France in 1644 during the English Civil War. The jewel might well have been the
'ballas ruby' that was sold for £4 by Oliver Cromwell when he broke up and disposed of the
Regalia after the execution of King Charles I in 1649. At the Restoration in 1660, a
jeweller called William Gomerdon sold King Charles II what was described as 'a great
oriental ruby' and this was subsequently set in the State Crown of King James II. At
the Coronation of William and Mary the records referred to it as 'the King's great ruby',
and in Rundell, Bridge and Rundell's account for the Coronation of King George IV
it was listed as 'the large ruby'. In 1858 an official inventory of the Crown Jewels was
prepared, in which the tradition that the spinel had been given to the Black Prince by
King Pedro of Castile and that King Henry V wore it at Agincourt, was set down as fact,
the stone described as 'a ruby pierced through after the Eastern custom, the upper part
of the piercing being filled by a small ruby'.*

*The crown's four oak leaf-covered arches are set with rose-cut diamonds and oriental
pearl acorns. At the apex, below the diamond-set globe, hang four large pear-shaped pearl
drops. The drops were probably among a collection of pearls presented to Catherine
de Medici by her uncle, Pope Clement VII. She gave them to Mary, Queen of Scots, who
married Queen Catherine's son, the Dauphin of France. After Queen Mary's
execution, her magnificent collection of pearls was bought by Queen Elizabeth I for £4,000.
These became part of Queen Victoria's inheritance and the four pearls have been in
the crown since 1838.*

*Atop all is the diamond cross pattée with the most ancient gem in all the Regalia.
This is a square sapphire (½ inch across) that was said to have been set in the 1043
Coronation Ring of King Edward the Confessor, the last of the Saxon line. He died
in 1066, and in October 1163 his perfectly preserved body was moved to a new resting place
in Westminster Abbey. At this time the ring on his finger, with which he had been
buried, was removed as a holy relic, as well as his royal robes, which were kept by the monks
at the Abbey for use as vestments on special occasions. Numerous legends had already
sprung up about the sapphire, including one that it could cure cramp. Since that time it has
been part of the Crown Jewels, though there is no explanation of how it escaped being
sold during the Civil War. In the seventeenth century King Charles II had the stone
rose-cut.*

*When the Cullinan diamond was set in the crown for the 1911 Coronation of King
George V, it replaced a very large, oblong, partly pierced sapphire, 1¾ by 1¹⁄₁₆ inches and
an inch thick, which was then moved to a similar position at the back of the
browband. This is known as the 'Stuart sapphire' and was first recorded as being the property
of King Alexander II of Scotland in 1214. It was eventually set in the crown of King
Charles II, and when King James II fled to France in 1688 it was one of the valuables he
took with him. On his death it was inherited by his son, James, who in turn gave it to
his son, Charles Edward, the Young Pretender, who bequeathed it to his brother, Henry,
Cardinal York, who wore it in his mitre. There are several stories about what
happened to it then, but the most plausible is that just before he died in 1807 Cardinal York
sold the sapphire, then surrounded by sixteen diamonds, to an Italian named Arenberg.
It was bought back from him on behalf of the Prince Regent, later King George IV, in
1813, who paid £4,000 for its return. He gave it to his daughter, Princess Charlotte,
but when she died in childbirth in 1817 it was sent back to the King as Crown property. In
June 1821 the clerk of the Privy Council and diarist Charles Greville recorded that at
a dinner at Devonshire House the King's mistress, the Marchioness Conyngham, was wearing
the sapphire set in her headdress. However, when King William IV succeeded his
brother in 1830 he managed to get it back and in 1838 it was set in the new crown made
for Queen Victoria.*

ABOVE, LEFT: *Queen Victoria's Coronation portrait by Sir George Hayter. She wrote in her diary:*

'The Crown being placed on my head was, I must own, a most beautiful impressive moment: all the Peers and Peeresses put on their coronets at the same instant.'

*At the State banquet that night, when Lord Melbourne complained that he had found the Sword of State very heavy to carry, the Queen told him: 'So was the Crown. It hurt me a good deal.'* ABOVE, RIGHT: *The date of King Edward VII's Coronation in 1902 had to be postponed only days before the ceremony when he underwent an emergency operation for appendicitis. In order to avoid any extra physical strain, the heavy St Edward's Crown was only carried in the procession, while King Edward was crowned with his mother's lighter crown.* PAGE 170, ABOVE LEFT: *On 22 June 1911 King George V posed for this formal portrait after his Coronation. When he wore the crown for his first State Opening of Parliament, he wrote in his diary: 'I think [it] the most terrible ordeal I have ever gone through.' Of the 1924 State Opening he wrote:*

'My speech was, I think, the longest on record & took 20 minutes to read. The crown gave me an awful headache. I could not have borne it much longer.'

PAGE 170, ABOVE RIGHT: *Although twenty-six years separated these two photographs, the graven images of father and son are identical. King George VI used to practise his parliamentary speech sitting at his desk in Buckingham Palace with the Imperial State Crown upon his head, so that its weight wouldn't disconcert him during the ceremony.* PAGE 171: *The Queen sitting in front of a photographic backdrop of the interior of the Chapel of King Henry VII in Westminster Abbey, after returning to Buckingham Palace*

*from the Abbey on Coronation Day, 2 June 1953. Her Majesty is wearing the purple Coronation Robe trimmed with ermine, gold Garter Collar and dress of white satin with coloured beaded embroidery of the flower emblems of Great Britain and the Dominions, among them – the English Tudor rose, Scottish thistle, Irish shamrock, Welsh leek, Canadian maple leaf, Australian wattle and Indian lotus flower. Cecil Beaton was waiting to take the official photographs, and later wrote in his diary:*

*'The Queen looked extremely minute under her robes and Crown, her nose and hands chilled and her eyes tired. "Yes", in reply to my question, "The Crown does get rather heavy." She had been wearing it for nearly three hours.'*

*It had only been in January that the Lord Chamberlain, responsible for the Crown Jewels, had asked the Keeper of the Jewel House to move the Imperial State Crown to the crown jeweller's workshop for alterations. It was transported there in its usual carrying case, a large black leather box with a brass handle on the top, and a swing door on the side. Inside, the crown is protected by white satin.*

*The most important consideration was that the crown should fit the Queen properly and be as comfortable as possible. It was dismantled for a general overhaul and cleaning, and in order to make it look a little more feminine and graceful the height was lowered by an inch. This was done by altering the angle of the oak leaf arches without depressing them in the centre – which would have wrongly indicated that it was not an Imperial crown. The crown also had to fit over the Queen's purple velvet Cap of Maintenance, trimmed with minever, which literally does maintain the crown on the Sovereign's head. As seen in the portrait, in the Queen's right hand is the gold and enamel Sceptre with the Cross, which was handed to her at the Coronation by the Archbishop of Canterbury with the words:*

*'Receive the Royal Sceptre the Ensign of Kingly Power and
Justice.'*

It is one of the most ancient emblems of power, used since the days of the Roman
emperors and Saxon kings. The Sceptre is 36½ inches long, weighs 41.70 oz and is
set with 234 diamonds, thirty-two rubies, fifteen emeralds, eight sapphires and an amethyst. It
was made by Sir Robert Vyner for King Charles II's Coronation in 1660, at the
restoration of the Stuart line. It remained unchanged until 1911, when King George V
instructed that the 530-carat Greater Star of Africa, the largest part of the Cullinan
diamond, be added to it; it was then positioned at the top of the shaft. Above the diamond is
an enormous faceted amethyst set as an orb and girdled with a band of diamonds,
emeralds and rubies, which in turn is surmounted by a diamond-studded cross pattée with a
square emerald in the centre on one side, and a square-cut diamond on the other. The
setting of the Star of Africa is four gold clasps. This allows it to be detached and worn as a
brooch or pendant, which Queen Mary did until 1914.

On the morning of the Queen's Coronation, the Crown Jewels were set out on a long
table in the Annexe of the Abbey (a temporary structure built for the occasion) while the
various dignitaries were arriving and the different processions forming. Sir Winston

*Churchill was fascinated with the array; finally he picked up the Sceptre and, pointing out*
*the Cullinan diamond to Dr Malan, South Africa's Prime Minister, said:*

*'Your country has been generous to us in the past. I trust such generosity*
*in other ways may continue.'*

*In her left hand the Queen holds the Orb. First used by the early Christians, this emblem*
*was then adopted by the Roman emperors, who displayed it as the symbol of their*
*universal dominion, and subsequently it was inherited by the early Saxon kings. During the*
*Coronation ceremony it is given to the Sovereign by the Archbishop, who says:*

*'Receive this Orb set under the Cross, and remember that the whole*
*world is subject to the Power and Empire of Christ our*
*Redeemer.'*

*Made of polished gold, six inches in diameter and weighing nearly three pounds, the*
*Orb is surmounted by a cross, symbol of Christianity. Originally made by Sir Robert*
*Vyner in 1660, slightly altered for King James II, and reset and enlarged for King William*
*III, the Orb was not used again until the Coronation of King George IV in 1821.*
*At that point the old pearls were replaced by new ones and one new diamond and a rosette of*
*coloured stones were added. Queen Victoria had six more diamonds inserted in 1838.*
*The horizontal band of red and white enamel encircling the golden ball has sixteen clusters of*
*rubies, emeralds, sapphires and rose-cut diamonds, bordered by 266 pearls. The arch,*
*bordered with two rows of 138 pearls, has six more gem-set clusters. Altogether there are*
*fourteen rubies, eight emeralds, eight sapphires and 176 diamonds. At the apex of the*
*arch is a large faceted amethyst on which is placed a cross pattée set with 182 diamonds, an*
*emerald, a sapphire and seven pearls. There had been no rehearsal for Queen*

Victoria's Coronation and when Lord John Thynne, acting on behalf of the Dean of Westminster, approached her with the Orb, she said to him:

'What am I to do with it?'
'Your Majesty is to carry it if you please, in your hand.'
'Am I?' said the Queen, 'it is very heavy.'

Things were better organized on 2 June 1953, however: for the rainswept journey back to Buckingham Palace from Westminster Abbey in the gold, 4½-ton Royal State Coach, hidden brackets and ledges had been installed to bear the weight of the Orb and Sceptre, giving the appearance that the Queen was holding them.

OPPOSITE: *King George VI's funeral cortège passing through London in February 1952. Lying on the red, gold and blue Royal Standard that drapes the coffin are the Imperial State Crown on a purple velvet cushion, the Sceptre with the Cross and the Orb. The large wreath of white flowers were from King George's widow, Queen Elizabeth the Queen Mother, with a note inscribed, 'for my dear husband, a great and noble King'.*

After King George V died at Sandringham on Monday 20 January 1936, his body had lain for two days in the small estate church of St Mary Magdalene. It was brought up to London by train on 23 January, and at King's Cross Station the jewel-encrusted Imperial State Crown, which had been brought there from the Tower of London, was affixed to the lid of the coffin. A small procession escorted the hand-drawn, black-draped gun carriage on its way to Westminster Hall for the lying-in-state. King Edward VIII and his three brothers followed close behind on foot. In his memoirs, written more than twenty years later, the Duke of Windsor wrote:

'That simple family procession through London was, perhaps, more impressive than the State cortège on the day of the funeral, and I especially remember a curious incident that happened on the way and was seen by very few. In spite of the rubber-tyred wheels the jolting of the heavy vehicle must have caused the Maltese cross on top of the crown — set with a square sapphire, eight medium-sized diamonds, and one hundred and ninety-two smaller diamonds — to fall. For suddenly, out of the corner of my eye, I caught a flash of light dancing along the pavement.

My natural instinct was to bend down and retrieve the jewels, lest the equivalent of a King's ransom be lost forever. Then a sense of dignity restrained me, and I resolutely marched on. Fortunately, the Company Sergeant-Major bringing up the rear of the two files of Grenadiers flanking the gun-carriage had also seen the accident. Quick as a flash, with scarcely a missed step, he bent down, scooped up the cross with his hand, and dropped it into his pocket. It was one of the most quick-witted acts that I have ever witnessed. It seemed a strange thing to happen, and, although not superstitious, I wondered whether it was a bad omen.'

Oddly enough, despite his seemingly total recall of what had happened, it wasn't the Company Sergeant-Major who retrieved the Maltese cross, but Lieutenant Huntington, the Grenadier Guards officer in charge of the bearer party.

Two Members of Parliament, Walter Elliot and Robert Boothby, who were watching from the pavement, heard the King mutter, 'Christ! What will happen next?', and Elliot remarked to his companion: 'A fitting Motto for the coming reign.' Harold Nicolson wrote in his diary: 'A most terrible omen', perhaps remembering that at King George III's Coronation a jewel had fallen from his crown, later said to be a portent of the thirteen American colonies also lost to the Crown.

# St Edward's Crown

During the Commonwealth Oliver Cromwell disposed of the Regalia; the gold was melted down and sold for the sum of £238. When the monarchy was restored on 29 May 1660, new Regalia had to be made before there could be a Coronation. A committee was set up to oversee the work and Sir Gilbert Talbot, Master of the Jewel House, relayed their orders to Sir Robert Vyner, the court goldsmith. They instructed that one of the two crowns required was to be a replica of St Edward's Crown, traditionally used at the actual moment of crowning, but never worn again during a reign. The original heavy gold crown had been used since the Coronation of King Edward II; it was then known as King Alfred's Crown, and described as 'wyerworke set with slight stones and two little bells'. It may have been worn by King Edward the Confessor, later known as St Edward, the last Anglo-Saxon monarch, hence the name. However, William the Conqueror brought a similar one to England with him in 1066, and which one of the two survived, if either, is not known. By 1139 the monks of Westminster were officially recognized as the custodians of the Crown Jewels, and when the rest of the Regalia was moved from the Abbey to the Tower of London St Edward's Crown was allowed to remain there as a religious relic. It continued to be used at Coronations until the establishment of the Commonwealth. The new crown had to be made large enough to fit over King Charles II's enormous periwig – at 6 feet 2 inches he was immensely tall for his time. There is no record of any charge for the 4 lb 7 oz of gold used in the crown, and it is possible that it was either gold from an old crown or even an old crown that was refurbished. It was

set with jewels hired for the Coronation on 23 April 1661 at
a cost of £500. This crown was used by every monarch
until King George IV, who was instead crowned with the new
Imperial State Crown. His brother, King William IV,
his niece, Queen Victoria, and his great nephew, King
Edward VII, followed his example, but in 1911 King
George V decided to revert to the ancient tradition and had
the paste jewels and imitation pearls with which the
crown was set removed and real ones set in their place, which
are still there today. OPPOSITE: Entirely made of gold,
the arches of St Edward's Crown are dipped in the centre to
show that it is not a 'crown Imperial'. Two rows of
gold beads border the circlet and outline the arches. On the
band are sixteen diamond rosettes each surrounding a
semi-precious stone, which includes amethysts, green
tourmalines, a pink tourmaline, yellow topazes, a white
topaz and an aquamarine. Above the circlet are four jewelled
crosses pattée and four jewelled fleurs-de-lys. The
arches are also set with semiprecious stones alternating with
clusters of five rose-cut aquamarines and white topazes,
and at the apex is a golden orb girdled with diamonds. At the
very top is a jewel-set cross with two platinized-gold
drops hanging from the arms. Altogether there are about 475
stones including the sixteen large ones set in the circlet.
The crown is twelve inches high, and twenty-six inches in

circumference. The purple velvet Cap of Maintenance is edged with ermine.
ABOVE: *The climax of the Coronation – this is the only time in the Queen's reign that she will
ever officially wear St Edward's Crown. As the Archbishop of Canterbury held the
crown aloft, he used words dating back to 973:*

'God crown you with a crown of glory and righteousness, that
having a right faith and manifold fruit of good works, you may obtain
the crown of an everlasting kingdom by the gift of Him whose
kingdom endureth for ever.'

*Then, in the hushed silence, he placed it on her head, and her hand reached up to settle it
more firmly. Immediately the Peers and Peeresses put on their coronets, and the
Abbey was filled with the sound of trumpets and everyone shouting 'God save the Queen'. To
prepare for the five-pound weight the Queen had worn the crown during the preceding
weeks in Buckingham Palace, as well as at the long rehearsal at the Abbey on 27 May, and,
in order to avoid the confusion that occurred at her father's Coronation, two tiny gold
stars were positioned in the velvet lining so that the Archbishop would know which way to put
it on. King George VI always claimed that he was never sure he wore the crown the
right way around, and Cosmo Gordon Lang, Archbishop of Canterbury, confirmed the story:*

'The King was very anxious that the Crown should be placed on
his head with the right side to the front. Accordingly it was arranged
that a small thin line of red cotton should be inserted under one
of the principal jewels on the front. It was there when I saw the Crown
in the Annexe before the ceremony. But when the Dean brought
the Crown to me on its cushion from the Altar and I looked for my
little red line it was not there. So I had to turn the Crown round
to see if it was on the other side; but it was not. Some officious person
must have removed it.'

# THE ARMILLS
## AND
# THE CORONATION RING

BELOW: *The Queen on the balcony of Buckingham Palace, just after five o'clock on Coronation Day. The bracelets, or Armills, a sign of rank, were first mentioned in the Anselm Ordo around 1100, and were listed in the Coronation accounts of King Richard II, King Henry VIII, King Edward VI, Queen Mary and Queen Elizabeth I. Although the early Stuarts did not wear them, a pair of bracelets was destroyed in 1649 and so a new pair was made for the Regalia in 1660. From then on they were carried in the*

Coronation procession but not worn, and it was not until 1953 when the Queen received new Armills for her Coronation that they again became an integral part of the Regalia. At the suggestion of Prime Minister Menzies of Australia, the Armills were given by all the Governments of the Commonwealth as symbols of their bond of unity. Each bracelet weighs 4½ oz and is 1½ inches wide. They are made of pure gold, lined with red velvet, and are unadorned except for two narrow engraved bands and a Tudor rose marking the clasp. When Archbishop Geoffrey Fisher fastened them on the Queen's wrists, he said:

'Receive the Bracelets of sincerity and wisdom, both for tokens of the
Lord's protection embracing you on every side; and also for
symbols and pledges of that bond which unites you with your Peoples: to
that end that you may be strengthened in all your works and
defended against your enemies both bodily and ghostly, through Jesus
Christ our Lord. Amen.'

The Coronation Ring or 'wedding ring of England', as it is known, signifying the bond that unites the Sovereign and people, is placed on the fourth finger of the right hand in acknowledgment that the Sovereign is 'wedded' to the State. The Queen Consort is also given a ring. One superstition claims that the tighter the fit, the longer the reign.
Three rings still exist – the two that were made in 1821 for King William IV and Queen Adelaide, and the one that had to be made to fit Queen Victoria's tiny hand in 1838.
The traditional design of a cross of St George, patron saint of England, picked out in rubies on a sapphire base and surrounded by a cluster of diamonds dates back to King Henry V, although the earliest record of a ring being used is for the Coronation of King Edgar in 973. Of the three rings the Queen chose to wear King William IV's. The ruby cross is formed of four baguette stones with a square-cut one in the centre. Twelve brilliant-cut diamonds surround the square-cut sapphire and two more are set on the shank. As the Archbishop placed the ring on the Queen's finger, he said:

'Receive this Ring, the ensign of Kingly Dignity, and of Defence
of the Catholic Faith; and as you are this day solemnly invested in the
government of this earthly kingdom, so may you be sealed with
that Spirit of Promise, which is the earnest of an heavenly inheritance,
and reign with Him who is the blessed and only Potentate, to
whom be glory for ever and ever. Amen.'

Although this was the only occasion on which Her Majesty has ever worn the ring, the first Queen Elizabeth refused to remove hers from her finger for the forty-five years of her reign. As she lay dying in Richmond Palace in 1603 she finally agreed to take it off, but it was so tight on her swollen finger that it had to be cut off with a file. The childless Queen refused to name her chosen heir until the very last minute; when she finally did, a messenger galloped to Scotland with the ring to inform King James of his inheritance.
For some inexplicable reason Queen Victoria's ring, a gift from her mother, Victoria, Duchess of Kent, was made to fit the wrong finger by the crown jewellers, Rundell, Bridge and Rundell. Charles Greville, clerk of the Privy Council, observed what happened during the ceremony:

'The ruby ring was made for her little finger instead of the
fourth, on which the rubric prescribes that it should be put. When the
Archbishop was to put it on, she extended the former, but he said
it must be on the latter. She said it was too small, and she could not get
it on. He said it was right to put it there, and, as he insisted, she
yielded, but had first to take off her other rings, and then this was forced
on, but it hurt her very much, and as soon as the ceremony was over
she was obliged to bathe her finger in iced water in order to get it off.'

# THE SCOTTISH REGALIA

ABOVE: *The Scottish Crown, personal emblem of the Sovereign, the Sceptre, emblem of royal power, and the Sword, signifying justice, were presented to the Queen after a thanksgiving service in St Giles' Cathedral in Edinburgh, on 24 June 1953, during her Coronation visit to Scotland. The 'Honours of Scotland', as they are known, are kept in the Crown Room of Edinburgh Castle and by the Treaty of Union cannot be taken out of Scotland. The Sceptre and a gold rose were presented to King James IV by Pope Alexander VI in 1494, and the Sword of State was a gift from Pope Julius II in 1507. The 4½-lb gold crown, set with semiprecious stones and Scottish pearls, was remodelled for King James V in 1540, incorporating, he claimed, fragments of Robert Bruce's crown, made in 1307, seven years before he defeated the British at Bannockburn and won Scotland's independence.*

*The Regalia was last used for King Charles II's Scottish Coronation at Scone in 1651, nine years before his restoration to the English Throne. Securely hidden during the Commonwealth, despite all Oliver Cromwell's efforts to find them, the Scottish Crown Jewels survived his destruction of the rest of the British Regalia. They were later discovered in an oak chest. In 1818, the Prince Regent issued a royal warrant to Sir Walter Scott giving him permission to display the Regalia to the public in Edinburgh Castle, and when as King he visited Scotland four years later, the Scottish Crown, Sceptre and Sword were carried in procession before him during his stay in Edinburgh.*

# THE QUEEN'S 1937 CORONATION CORONET

The first great royal ceremony that Princess Elizabeth and Princess Margaret took part in was their parents' Coronation on 12 May 1937. Once it was agreed that the two little girls would attend, one aged eleven and the other nearly seven, elaborate coronets of gold, lined with crimson velvet and edged with ermine, were designed for them by the crown jeweller. Replicas were made and brought to Buckingham Palace for approval, but the King, Queen and Queen Mary, having examined them closely as the Princesses tried them on, decided that they were far too ornate and cumbersome to be appropriate. Queen Mary then suggested that they should have simple lightweight circlets of silver gilt with jewel-like chasing, fashioned in the form of miniature medieval crowns and ornamented with Maltese crosses and fleurs-de-lys. The end result was a triumph: pretty and delicate, they looked as if they had come from a child's dressing-up box. The Princesses also wore matching ankle-length white lace dresses with short puff sleeves and a row of small silver bows the length of the skirt. Their purple velvet robes, trimmed with ermine and gold tassels, were miniature versions of the one that their grandmother had worn when Princess of Wales for the Coronation of King Edward VII in 1902.

The two Princesses rode in the family procession to Westminster Abbey in a State Coach with their aunt the Princess Royal and her husband, the Earl of Harewood. At the moment their mother was crowned Queen, they too put on their coronets. Queen Mary had broken with the precedent that a Queen Dowager never attends the crowning of her successor and was beside them in the royal gallery over the tomb of Anne of Cleves, one of the wives of Henry VIII. As she later wrote in her diary:

'Lilibet and Margaret looked too sweet in their lace dresses and
robes, especially when they put on their coronets.'

Their governess Marion Crawford later noted in her memoirs that during the long procession back to Buckingham Palace they waved and smiled to the cheering crowds as they had practised in their school room, and Princess Margaret was so excited by all the people and noise that she bounced about on the high seat until her coronet tilted down over one ear, at which point Princess Elizabeth, very much the big sister in charge, barked, 'Be quiet, Margaret!' ABOVE: *The royal family on the balcony of Buckingham Palace after returning from Westminster Abbey on 12 May 1937.*

# THE ROYAL FAMILY ORDERS

A tradition of most royal families, Family Orders are in the personal gift of the Sovereign and are given to female members of the immediate family. In Great Britain this custom was introduced by King George I, the first of the Hanoverian monarchs. Until the end of Queen Victoria's reign the Order consisted of a cameo miniature set in diamonds, but King Edward VII introduced its present form of a portrait painted on ivory.

During the summer of 1826, King George IV invited the seven-year-old Princess Victoria, her elder half-sister, Princess Feodora, and their mother, the Duchess of Kent, to stay at Cumberland Lodge in Windsor Great Park. He himself was living at the nearby Royal Lodge with his mistress, Lady Conyngham, and her family. In 1872 Queen Victoria wrote in her recollections:

'When we arrived at the Royal Lodge the King took me by the hand, saying: "Give me your little paw." He was large and gouty but with a wonderful dignity and charm of manner. He wore the wig which was so much worn in those days. Then he said he would give me something for me to wear, and that was his picture set in diamonds, which was worn by the Princesses as an Order to a blue ribbon on the left shoulder. I was very proud of this, and Lady Conyngham pinned it on my shoulder.'

A new Family Order is established at the start of each reign; the list of those to whom it is given is never publicized. The first anyone knows of its presentation is when the recipient wears the Order in public. The eighteen-year-old Princess Anne was given the Order on 23 April 1969, and the Princess of Wales received it in November 1982, some sixteen months after her marriage. The Badge is worn with evening dress only, or on State occasions, on the left shoulder attached to a heavy moiré-silk square fringed *bow. The Queen herself wears the Orders of her grandfather, King George V, and her father, King George VI.*

OPPOSITE, LEFT: *The King George V Family Order was established in 1911. His Majesty is portrayed in the uniform of Admiral of the Fleet wearing the Star and Riband of the Garter and the Badge of the Royal Victorian Order. The miniature is surrounded by large brilliant-cut diamonds and surmounted by a diamond Imperial crown, within which can be seen a crimson enamelled cap of maintenance. Hidden by the crown is a platinum brooch pin. The back of the Order is gold, and set on it is the royal cypher in diamonds and the date 1911. The pale blue riband bow is the same colour as that of the Royal Guelphic Order of Hanover. King George IV instituted this Order in Britain in 1820, but it came to an end in 1837 since Salic law held that the throne of Hanover could not be inherited by Queen Victoria on the death of her uncle King William IV.*

OPPOSITE, RIGHT: *The King George VI Family Order. Established in 1937, His Majesty wears the uniform of Admiral of the Fleet, the Star and Riband of the Garter and the Royal Victorian Chain. In the border, baguette diamonds are placed between every two brilliant-cut stones. The Imperial crown on top is of a slightly different design than that of the King George V Order. The back of the Order is gold as is the raised royal cypher and the date 1937. The riband bow is pale pink.*

BELOW: *Queen Elizabeth the Queen Mother in her official eightieth-birthday portrait in 1980. Attached to her blue Garter Riband is the King George VI Family Order and the Queen Elizabeth II Family Order, established in 1953. The Queen's portrait shows her in evening dress and wearing the King George IV State Diadem and the Star and Riband of the Garter. A baguette diamond is set between every three brilliant-cut diamonds in the border and on top is a diamond Tudor crown over a red enamel cap of maintenance. The back is 18-carat gold, with the royal cypher and St Edward's Crown superimposed in gold and enamel. The chartreuse yellow riband bow is two inches wide. Queen Elizabeth's bracelet is the one made from Queen Mary's necklace (page 68).*

# THE ORDER OF THE GARTER

'The Most Noble and Amiable Company of St George named the Garter' is the oldest
Order of Christian chivalry in the world, and was established by King Edward III on
St George's Day, 23 April 1348. During the previous year he had celebrated military
victories over the Scots and French and, perhaps hoping to emulate the chivalric ideals
of the legendary King Arthur and his Knights of the Round Table, he conceived the idea of
a group of twenty-six close companions, 'co-partners both in peace and war', the
number to be unalterable but always including the Sovereign and the Prince of Wales. The
Order's symbol and motto are believed to have arisen from an incident at a ball given
by the King at Windsor Castle to celebrate the fall of Calais. While he was dancing with
his cousin, Joan, Countess of Salisbury, her blue garter fell to the floor. As those
watching began to laugh at her embarrassment, the King picked up the garter and tied it on
his own leg, saying, 'Honi soit qui mal y pense' – 'Evil be to him who evil thinks'
– adding that henceforth the wearing of the garter would represent such honour that the
recipients would be the most worthy in the land. A garter embroidered with his words
became the emblem of his new Order and remains so to this day. Membership is the greatest
personal gift that the Monarch can bestow and is only possible upon the death of one
of the twenty-four Knights.

Queen Elizabeth I reformed the Order's ceremonial procedures, and always wore the
Mantle and Collar on the feast day of St George. No king or Prince of Wales was ever
painted without his Garter Collar, and Queen Anne was the first Queen Regent to
wear the Badge and Riband on all ceremonial occasions. Only a few weeks after Queen
Victoria acceded to the throne on 20 June 1837, she went to Westminster to dissolve
Parliament wearing the blue Riband and diamond insignia of the Garter; she had already
established the habit of wearing the Riband every night at dinner. For her Coronation,
on 28 June 1838, she wore a flexible woven gold bracelet bearing the words Honi soit qui
mal y pense, as her jewelled Garter armlet for some reason had not yet been
completed. On 14 January 1840 Lord Torrington and General Charles Grey left England
for Gotha to escort the twenty-year-old Prince Albert back to England for his
wedding. He was invested with the Order of the Garter on 23 January in Gotha. At
Buckingham Palace on 9 February, the day before their wedding, the couple
exchanged gifts and Queen Victoria gave Prince Albert a Garter of very fine diamonds, a
diamond Garter Star set with a cross of five rubies and a Badge of the Order
composed of fine diamonds round an onyx swivel centre, with St George on one side and St
Andrew on the other. She wrote in her diary:

'Lord Melbourne admired the diamond Garter which Albert had on, and

*said "Very handsome." I told him it was my gift; I also gave*
*him (all before dinner) a diamond star I had worn, and badge.'*

After Prince Albert's death in 1861, the Queen took the set of Garter regalia she had given
him as a wedding gift in 1840, and wore it for the rest of her life. On 12 February
1901, four centuries after King Henry VII's mother was the last Lady of the Garter, King
Edward VII issued a special statute under the seal of the Order that conferred on
Queen Alexandra the 'title and dignity of a Lady of that Most Noble Order, and fully
authorising Her Majesty to wear the Insignia thereof'.

However, the Queen apparently viewed the Garter as a piece of jewellery rather than an
honour. On one occasion the royal family and the members of the Household were all
waiting for her to appear for an Evening Court at Buckingham Palace. When she finally
entered the drawing room the King immediately noticed that she had pinned her
diamond Garter Star on the right side of her bodice instead of on the left. When questioned,
she replied that she thought it looked nicer that way. Trying hard to restrain his
temper, the King asked her to go back upstairs and put it on properly, as the Order of the
Garter was not simply a beautiful ornament and must be worn correctly. She did as
she was told and after another long wait they were ready to enter the Throne Room. King
George V made Queen Mary a Lady of the Order on 3 June 1910, his birthday;
following his example King George VI gave Queen Elizabeth the Order on his forty-first
birthday, 14 December 1936. Queen Elizabeth immediately sent around a note to
Queen Mary at Marlborough House to tell her the news:

'Bertie discovered that Papa gave it to you on his birthday and
the coincidence was so charming that he has now followed suit and given
it to me on his birthday.'

Part of the Garter regalia, the hat, Mantle and gold Collar, is worn only once a year
when a chapter meeting of the Knights is held in the Throne Room of Windsor Castle before
they all walk in procession down the hill to a service in St George's Chapel. During
the reign of the present Queen this has almost invariably taken place on the third Monday in
June. The Garter Knights and Ladies of the Order wear full-length dark-blue velvet
Mantles lined with white taffeta, with crimson velvet hoods lined with white silk hanging
down behind. The colour of the Mantle was changed some time between 1564 and
1637 to a deep aubergine purple, but no one knows why. The headdress is a large black
velvet hat decorated with a plume of three white ostrich feathers. Worn over the
shoulders outside the Mantle is the heavy gold Garter Collar: twenty-four plaques, each
depicting the Garter surrounding a red enamel Tudor rose, joined by twenty-four knots
of chased gold. Suspended as a pendant from the Collar is the 'Great George', a heavy
jewelled gold and enamel Badge depicting St George, on a white horse with lance in
hand, slaying the dragon.

OPPOSITE: *A royal set of Garter insignia. The dark-blue velvet garter has the Order's
motto set in diamond letters. It is worn by men on the left leg below the knee and by women
on the left arm above the elbow. Below it, pictured on the left, is the eight-pointed
Star of the Order. The design of the Star is the same for all the Knights, but those
belonging to the royal family are made of diamonds, with a ruby cross of St George
in the centre encircled by a blue enamel garter with the motto picked out in diamonds. This
is worn pinned to the left breast. On the right of the photograph is the 'Lesser
George', the Badge of the Order, again depicting St George slaying the dragon and set in a
frame of diamonds with the motto encircling the figure. This pins the Garter Riband
at the right hip.* RIGHT: *Queen Mary photographed in 1935 for King George V's Silver
Jubilee. To commemorate her Coronation in 1911, the 'Marys of the Empire' – those
bearing the name she chose as Queen (she was christened Victoria Mary Augusta Louise
Olga Pauline Claudine Agnes) – had banded together to present her with the*

complete set of Garter insignia. On her left arm is the diamond-encrusted blue velvet Garter, on her breast the diamond-set Star, and on her right hip the Lesser George, its cameo of St George and the dragon carved in sardonyx and set with diamonds and rubies. (For a better view see page 109.) The cornflower-blue Garter Riband she is wearing is the only sash of an Order (apart from the Thistle and the St Patrick) that is worn over the left instead of the right shoulder. The explanation for this dates back to King Charles II. One of his mistresses, Louise de Kéroualle, Duchess of Portsmouth, bore him a son, whom he made the first Duke of Richmond and Gordon. One day while playing with the boy the King took off his Garter Badge, which was then worn around the neck, and draped it around the baby, slipping his left arm through the Riband to keep it in place, and thus began the tradition. Until the Hanoverian succession in 1714 the Riband was pale blue, but during the time the Stuarts lived abroad in exile it was changed to a cornflower blue so that there could be no doubt as to its legitimacy as the genuine Order, and from this comes the expression, 'true blue'. ABOVE, RIGHT: Her Majesty the Queen painted in her Garter regalia by Edward Halliday in 1958, later president of the Royal Society of Portrait Artists. On her Mantle, which formerly belonged to her father, is the Sovereign's Badge made of jewelled metal; the other Knights have slightly larger embroidered badges. King George VI made Princess Elizabeth a Lady of the Order on 11 November 1947, and at a pre-wedding dinner party and ball given at Buckingham Palace on the following Monday, 17 November, she wore the blue Riband and Garter Star for the first time. For ceremonial evening occasions the Queen always wears the Garter Sash, and Star and Lesser George, except in Scotland where she wears the Order of the Thistle. On a State visit when she is presented with an Order of the country (she has more than forty to date), she wears the foreign Order as a mark of courtesy. ABOVE, LEFT: Prince Philip was made a Knight of the Garter on 19 November 1947, the day before his marriage to Princess Elizabeth. For most State banquets, as here in 1974, he wears knee breeches and black silk stockings, with the Garter on his left leg, and the Garter Riband, Star and Lesser George.

# GLOSSARY

**AIGRETTE:** A jewelled hair ornament in the shape of a curved feather. From the French word for a tuft of feathers.

**BAGUETTE:** A narrow rectangular stone. From the French word for a small stick.

**BANGLE:** An inflexible round bracelet.

**BAR BROOCH:** A long narrow brooch usually worn horizontally.

**BAROQUE PEARL:** A large pearl of irregular shape.

**BEAD:** A small, usually spherical, object of any material, perforated so that it can be strung.

**BORDURE:** A wide jewelled border used to outline a bodice.

**BRILLIANT:** A form of cutting discovered by the Venetian Vincenzio Peruzzi in the late-seventeenth century. In a perfect round brilliant there are fifty-eight facets, thirty-three above the girdle and twenty-five below.

**BRIOLETTE:** An oval or drop-shaped stone, faceted all over and often pierced at the top.

**CABOCHON:** A polished unfaceted stone, domed with a flat base.

**CARAT:** The unit of weight for precious stones. One carat is ⅕ gramme. Also used as a measure of the quality in gold, with pure gold being 24 carats.

**CHANDELIER:** A style of earrings with swinging pendants.

**CHOKER:** A necklace, often with a number of strands, worn high round the throat, also known as dog-collar or *collier*.

**CLIP:** A brooch attached by a hinged clasp instead of a pin.

**CLOISONNÉ:** Coloured enamel used to cover the surface of a jewel.

**CLUSTER:** A group of stones with one central gem.

**COLLET:** A setting in which a gem is enclosed in a band of metal.

**COLLIER RÉSILLE:** A choker necklace with a web-like design.

**CORSAGE BROOCH:** A large ornamental brooch pinned centrally on the bodice.

**CROSS PATTÉE:** The name for the specific shape of the crosses traditionally used on royal crowns.

**DEMI-PARURE:** Three matching pieces of jewellery, usually a brooch, earrings and necklace.

**DIADEM:** Originally the helmet band worn by a military commander, it later referred to a plain gold band denoting high office. In jewellery terms it is usually used to describe an especially high or impressively jewelled tiara.

**DROP or PENDANT:** A style of earrings with one single hanging stone.

**EMERALD-CUT:** A style of cutting; oblong- or square-cut stones with facets polished diagonally across the corners.

**ETERNITY RING:** A ring set all round with a continuous row of small stones.

**FACET:** The surface of a stone cut to reflect and refract light to the maximum degree.

**FESTOON:** A curved loop between two points.

**FILIGREE:** Very fine lace-like ornamental wire-work.

**FLORET:** A small, flower shape with individual stones representing the petals. From the French word for little flower.

**FRINGE:** A necklace or tiara consisting of graduated hanging or upright spikes. From the Latin word for border.

**GIRANDOLE:** A style of earrings with three pendant stones hanging from one large central stone. It can also refer to a brooch that has a central stone with others hanging from it. Derives from *girandola*, revolving fireworks or jets of water.

**MARQUISE or NAVETTE:** A stone cut in a narrow, pointed oval shape.

**MILLEGRAIN:** A setting in which the metal gripping the stone is decorated with a row of tiny grains or beads.

**NEGLIGÉ PENDANT:** Two drops of uneven length on a necklace or brooch.

**PARURE:** A matching set of jewellery, consisting of a tiara, necklace, brooch, bracelet and earrings.

**PAVÉ-SET:** A style of setting stones so closely together that no metal shows.

**PEAR-SHAPED:** A stone cut in the shape of a teardrop.

**PENDANT:** Any hanging object, but usually refers to a jewel or other small ornament hanging from a chain worn round the neck.

**RIVIÈRE:** A single-stranded necklace of equal-size diamonds or other precious stones. From the French word for river.

**ROSE-CUT:** A style of cutting diamonds that dates back to the mid-seventeenth century. The stone has a flat base and rises to a point at the top.

**SAUTOIR:** A long necklace, often having a tassel on the end.

**SOLITAIRE:** A single stone set in a ring.

**SPINEL:** A gemstone that can appear in a variety of colours.

**STAR SAPPHIRE:** A sapphire of such formation that when cut as a cabochon it displays a six-rayed star.

**STOMACHER:** An elaborate ornament covering the bodice of a dress from breast to waist.

**STUD:** A style of earrings set with a single stone and without either a pendant drop or the addition of other stones.

**SUITE:** A matching set of jewellery.

**TIARA:** A formal headdress made of precious metal and set with stones, kept in place by its wire mount.

# BIBLIOGRAPHY

AIRLIE, Mabell, *Thatched with Gold* (Hutchinson, London, 1962)

ALEXANDRA, Queen of Yugoslavia, *For A King's Love* (Odhams, London, 1956)

ALLEN, Charles, and DWIVEDI, Sharada, *Lives of the Indian Princes* (Century, London, 1984)

ALMEDINGEN, Martha Edith von, *The Empress Alexandra 1872–1918: A Study* (Hutchinson, London, 1961)

ALSOP, Susan Mary, *Lady Sackville* (Weidenfeld & Nicolson, London, 1978)

AMIES, Hardy, *Still Here* (Weidenfeld & Nicolson, London, 1984)

ANTRIM, Louisa, *Louisa, Lady in Waiting* (Jonathan Cape, London, 1979)

ARGENZIO, Victor, *The Fascination of Diamonds* (Allen & Unwin, London, 1966)

ARGYLL, Margaret, Duchess of, *Forget Not* (W.H. Allen, London, 1975)

ARMSTRONG, Nancy, *Jewellery, An Historical Survey of British Styles and Jewels* (Lutterworth, Guildford, 1973)

ARNOLD, Janet, *Sweet England's Jewels from Princely Magnificence, Court Jewels of the Magnificence 1500–1630* (Debrett's Peerage with the Victoria & Albert Museum, London, 1980)

ARONSON, Theo, *Princess Alice, Countess of Athlone* (Cassell, London, 1981)

ARONSON, Theo, *Royal Family, Years of Transition* (John Murray, London, 1983)

ASHDOWN, Dulcie, *Princess of Wales* (John Murray, London, 1979)

ASQUITH, Cynthia, *The Duchess of York* (Hutchinson, London, 1928)

ASQUITH, Margot, *The Autobiography of* (Methuen, London, 1985)

ATHLONE, H.R.H. Princess Alice, Countess of, *For My Grandchildren* (Evans, London, 1966)

AUSTRALIAN NEWS & INFORMATION BUREAU, *Royal Visit to Australia of Her Majesty Queen Elizabeth II and His Royal Highness The Duke of Edinburgh 1954* (Angus & Robertson, London, 1954)

BALLARD, Bettina, *In My Fashion* (David McKay, New York, 1960)

BALSAN, Consuelo Vanderbilt, *The Glitter and The Gold* (Heinemann, London, 1953)

BARDENS, Dennis, *Princess Margaret* (Robert Hale, London, 1964)

BARKER, Brian, OBE, *When The Queen was Crowned* (Routledge & Kegan Paul, London, 1976)

BARROW, Andrew, *Gossip: A History of High Society from 1920–1970* (Hamish Hamilton, London, 1978)

BARROW, Andrew, *International Gossip: A History of High Society 1970–1980* (Hamish Hamilton, London, 1983)

BARRY, Stephen P., *Royal Secrets, The View from Downstairs* (Villard, New York, 1985)

BARRY, Stephen P., *Royal Service, My Twelve Years as Valet to Prince Charles* (Macmillan, New York, 1983)

BARWICK, Sandra, *A Century of Style* (Allen & Unwin, London, 1984)

BATCHELOR, Vivien, *H.R.H. The Princess Margaret Gift Book* (Pitkin, London, 1952)

BATTISCOMBE, Georgina, *Queen Alexandra* (Constable, London, 1969)

BATTISCOMBE, Georgina, *The Spencers of Althorp* (Constable, London, 1984)

BEATON, Cecil, *Self Portrait with Friends* (Weidenfeld & Nicolson, London, 1979)

BEDFORD, John, Duke of, *A Silver-Plated Spoon* (Reprint Society, London, 1950)

BENCE-JONES, Mark, *The Viceroys of India* (Constable, London, 1982)

BENNETT, Daphne, *King Without a Crown, Albert Prince Consort of England 1819–1861* (Heinemann, London, 1977)

BENNETT, Daphne, *Margot* (Gollancz, London, 1984)

BENTHAM-SMITH, Christopher, *God Bless The Princess of Wales* (Corgi, London, 1982)

BENTLEY, Nicolas, *The Victorian Scene* (Weidenfeld & Nicolson, London, 1968)

BERNIER, Olivier, *Louis The Beloved: The Life of Louis XV* (Weidenfeld & Nicolson, London, 1984)

BIRMINGHAM, Stephen, *Duchess: The Story of Wallis Warfield Windsor* (Macmillan, London, 1981)

BIRT, Catherine, *Her Majesty Queen Elizabeth* (Pitkin, London, 1950)

BIRT, Catherine, *H.R.H. Princess Margaret* (Pitkin, London, 1949)

BIRT, Catherine, *Royal Sisters* (Pitkin, London, 1949)

BLAND, Olivia, *The Royal Way of Death* (Constable, London, 1986)

BLOOM, Ursula, *The House of Kent* (Robert Hale, London, 1969)

BLOOM, Ursula, *Princesses In Love* (Robert Hale, London, 1973)

BOLITHO, Hector, *George VI* (Eyre & Spottiswoode, London, 1937)

BOLITHO, Hector, *Their Majesties* (Max Parrish, London, 1952)

BOOTHROYD, Basil, *Philip: An Informal Biography* (Longman, London, 1971)

BOWEN, Marjorie, *Crowns and Sceptres: The Romance & Pageantry of Coronations* (John Long, London, 1937)

BRADLEY, John, Ed., *Lady Curzon's India: Letters of a Vicereine* (Weidenfeld & Nicolson, London, 1985)

BROAD, Lewis, *Queens, Crowns and Coronations* (Hutchinson, London, 1952)

BROOKE-LITTLE, John, *Royal Ceremonies of State* (Country Life, London, 1980)

BROUGH, James, *Margaret: The Tragic Princess* (W.H. Allen, London, 1978)

BROWN, Michèle, *Queen Elizabeth II: The Silver Jubilee Book 1952–1977* (David & Charles, London, 1976)

BRYAN, J., and MURPHY, Charles V.U., *The Windsor Story* (Granada, London, 1979)

BUCKLE, George Earle, Ed., *The Letters of Queen Victoria, Vol. I 1862–1869* (John Murray, London, 1926)

CAFFREY, Kate, *The 1900's Lady* (Gordon & Cremonesi, London, 1976)

CARTER, Ernestine, *With Tongue in Chic* (Michael Joseph, London, 1974)

CARTER, Ernestine, *The Changing World of Fashion* (Weidenfeld & Nicolson, London, 1977)

CATHCART, Helen, *Anne and The Princess Royal* (W.H. Allen, London, 1973)

CATHCART, Helen, *The Duchess of Kent* (W.H. Allen, London, 1971)

CATHCART, Helen, *Lord Snowdon* (W.H. Allen, London, 1968)

CATHCART, Helen, *The Married Life of the Queen* (W.H. Allen, London, 1970)

CATHCART, Helen, *The Queen In Her Circle* (W.H. Allen, London, 1977)

CATHCART, Helen, *The Queen Mother* (W.H. Allen, London, 1965)

CATHCART, Helen, *The Queen Mother Herself* (W.H. Allen, London, 1979)

CATHCART, Helen, *Royal Lodge, Windsor* (W.H. Allen, London, 1966)

CHANNON, Sir Henry, *Diaries* (Weidenfeld & Nicolson, London, 1967)

CHURCHILL, Randolph S., *The Story of the Coronation* (Derek Verschoyle, London, 1953)

CLARK, Brigadier Stanley, OBE, *Palace Diary* (Harrap, London, 1958)

CLARK, Brigadier Stanley, OBE, *The Royal Tour of Australia* (Pitkin, London, 1954)

CLARK, Brigadier Stanley, OBE, *The Royal Tour, Part 2* (Pitkin Pictorials, London, 1954)

CLARK, Brigadier Stanley, OBE, *The Royal Tour Outward Bound* (Pitkin Pictorials, London, 1954)

COATS, Peter, *Of Generals and Gardens* (Weidenfeld & Nicolson, London, 1976)

COATS, Peter, *Of Kings and Cabbages* (Weidenfeld & Nicolson, London, 1984)

COCKS, Anna Somers, *An Introduction to Courtly Jewellery* (Compton Press, Salisbury, 1980)

COLLIER, Richard, *The Rainbow People* (Weidenfeld & Nicolson, London, 1984)

COLVILLE, John, *Footprints In Time* (Collins, London, 1976)

COOLICAN, Don, *The Story of the Royal Family* (Colour Library, Guildford, 1982)

COOMBS, David, *Antique Collecting for Pleasure* (Ebury, London, 1978)

*The Coronation Album, H.M. Queen Elizabeth* (Pitkin Pictorials, London, 1953)

*The Coronation Book of Queen Elizabeth II* (Odhams, London, 1953)

*The Coronation in Pictures: Complete Camera Record of the Mighty Pageant* (Allied Newspapers, London, 1937)

COSTER, Ian, *H.R.H. The Princess Margaret Gift Book Vol. II* (Pitkin, London, 1954)

COWLES, Virginia, *The Last Tsar and Tsarina* (Weidenfeld & Nicolson, London, 1977)

COWLES, Virginia, *The Romanovs* (Penguin, London, 1974)

CRAWFORD, Marion, *Happy and Glorious* (George Newnes, London, 1953)

CRAWFORD, Marion, *The Little Princesses* (Cassell, London, 1950)

CRAWFORD, Marion, *Queen Elizabeth II* (George Newnes, London, 1952)

CRAWFORD, Marion, *The Queen Mother* (George Newnes, London, 1951)

*Crowning the King: The History, Symbolism and Meaning of the Coronation Ceremony* (Allied Newspapers, London)

CULLEN, Tom, *The Empress Brown: The Story of a Royal Friendship* (Bodley Head, London, 1969)

CUNLIFFE, Lesley, *Great Royal Disasters* (Arthur Barker, London, 1986)

CURRAN, Mona, *Jewels and Gems* (Arco, London, 1961)

DAVENPORT, Cyril, *Jewellery* (Methuen, London, 1905)

DAVIES, Phyllis, *H.R.H. The Princess Margaret Comes of Age* (Pitkin, London, 1951)

DAVIES, Reginald, *Elizabeth Our Queen* (Collins, London, 1976)

DEMPSTER, Nigel, *H.R.H. The Princess Margaret: A Life Unfulfilled* (Quartet, London, 1981)

DE ROTHSCHILD, Guy, *The Whims of Fortune* (Granada, London, 1985)

DE ROTHSCHILD, Mrs James, *The Rothschilds at Waddesdon Manor* (Collins, London, 1979)

DEVON, Stanley, *The Royal Canadian Tour* (Pitkin Pictorials, London, 1951)

DIMBLEBY, Richard, *Elizabeth Our Queen* (University of London Press, London, 1953)

DONALDSON, Frances, *Edward VIII* (Weidenfeld & Nicolson, London, 1974)

DONALDSON, Frances, *Edward VIII: The Road to Abdication* (Weidenfeld & Nicolson, London, 1978)

DONALDSON, Frances, *King George VI and Queen Elizabeth* (Weidenfeld & Nicolson, London, 1977)

DOWNSHIRE, John, *Philip, Duke of Edinburgh* (Dennis Yates, London, 1950)

DUFF, David, *Albert and Victoria* (Frederick Muller, London, 1972)

DUFF, David, *Alexandra: Princess & Queen* (Collins, London, 1980)

DUFF, David, *Elizabeth of Glamis: The Story of The Queen Mother* (Magnum, London, 1977)

DUFF, David, *George and Elizabeth: A Royal Marriage* (Collins, London, 1983)

DUFF, David, *Queen Mary* (Collins, London, 1985)

DUFF, David, *The Shy Princess* (Frederick Muller, London, 1958)

DUNCAN, Andrew, *The Reality of Monarchy* (Pan, London, 1970)

EDGAR, Donald, *Happy and Glorious: The Silver Jubilee 1977* (Arthur Barker, London, 1977)

EDGAR, Donald, *Palace* (W.H. Allen, London, 1983)

EDGAR, Donald, *The Queen's Children* (Arthur Barker, London, 1978)

EDGAR, Donald, *A Royal Family: Edward VII–Elizabeth II* (Artus, London, 1979)

EDWARDS, Anne, *Matriarch: Queen Mary and the House of Windsor* (William Morrow, New York, 1984)

*Elizabeth Crowned Queen: The Pictorial Record of the Coronation* (Odhams, London, 1953)

ELLIS, Jennifer, *The Duchess of Kent* (Odhams, London, 1952)

ELSBERRY, Terence, *Marie of Romania* (Cassell, London, 1972)

EPTON, Nina, *Victoria and Her Daughters* (Weidenfeld & Nicolson, London, 1971)

ESHER, Viscount, G.C.B., G.C.V.O., *The Girlhood of Queen Victoria: A Selection from Her Majesty's Diaries Between the Years 1832 and 1840, Vol. II* (John Murray, London, 1912)

FERRIER, Neil, *The Queen Elizabeth Coronation Book* (London, 1953)

FISHER, Graham and Heather, *Charles and Diana: Their Married Life* (Robert Hale, London, 1984)

FISHER, Graham and Heather, *Monarch: The Life and Times of Elizabeth II* (Robert Hale, London, 1985)

FISHER, Graham and Heather, *Monarchy and the Royal Family* (Robert Hale, London, 1979)

FISHER, Graham and Heather, *The Queen's Life and Her Twenty-Five Years of Monarchy* (Robert Hale, London, 1977)

FISHER, P.J., *Jewels* (Batsford, London, 1965)

FLOWER, Margaret, *Victorian Jewellery* (Cassell, London, 1967)

FORD, Colin, *Happy and Glorious: 130 Years of Royal Photographs* (National Portrait Gallery, London, 1977)

FREDERICA, Queen of the Hellenes, *A Measure of Understanding* (Macmillan, London, 1972)

FREGNAC, Claude, *Jewellery: From the Renaissance to Art Nouveau* (Octopus, London, 1973)

FRISCHAUER, Willi, *Margaret: Princess Without A Cause* (Michael Joseph, London, 1977)

FULFORD, Roger, *Dearest Mama: Letters Between Queen Victoria and The Crown Princess of Prussia, 1861–1864* (Holt, Reinhart & Winston, New York, 1969)

FULFORD, Roger, *The Pictorial Life Story of King George VI* (Pitkin, London, 1952)

FULFORD, Roger, *The Prince Consort* (Macmillian, London, 1949)

GARNETT, Henry, *Our Royal Family, Vol. II, Part 3* (Worcester Press, Worcester, 1952)

GARRETT, Evelyn, *H.R.H. The Princess Elizabeth* (Pitkin, London, 1950)

GARRETT, Richard, *Mrs Simpson* (Arthur Barker, London, 1979)

GAUTIER, Gilberte, *Cartier: The Legend* (Arlington, London, 1983)

GIBSON, Peter, *The Concise Guide to Kings and Queens: A Thousand Years of European Monarchy* (Webb & Bower, Exeter, 1985)

GLOUCESTER, Princess Alice, Duchess of, *Memoirs* (Collins, London, 1983)

GLYNN, Prudence, *In Fashion* (Allen & Unwin, London, 1978)

GORE, John, *King George V: A Personal Memoir* (John Murray, London, 1941)

GRAY, Charles, *The Early Years of the Prince Consort* (William Kimber, London, 1967)

GRAY, Pauline, *The Grand Duke's Woman* (Macdonald & Jane's, London, 1976)

HALL, Carolyn, *The Thirties In Vogue* (Octopus, London, 1984)

HALL, Trevor, *Diana: Princess of Wales* (Colour Library, Guildford, 1982)

HALL, Trevor, *In Celebration of The Queen's Visit to Canada* (Colour Library, Guildford, 1984)

HALL, Trevor, *The Queen Mother and Her Family* (Colour Library, Guildford, 1983

HALL, Trevor, *The Royal Family Today* (Colour Library, Guildford, 1983)

HALL, Trevor, *Royal Family Yearbook* (Colour Library, Guildford, 1982; Vol. II, 1983; Vol. III, 1984)

HAMILTON, Alan, *The Royal Handbook* (Mitchell

Beazley, London, 1985)

HANMER, Davinia, *Diana: The Fashion Princess* (Park Lane Press, London, 1984)

HARDY, Alan, *Queen Victoria Was Amused* (John Murray, London, 1976)

HARRISON, Rosina, *Gentlemen's Gentlemen* (Arlington, London, 1976)

HARTCUP, Adeline, *Love and Marriage in the Great Country Houses* (Sidgwick & Jackson, London, 1984)

HARTNELL, Norman, *3 May 1985–21 July 1985 Art Gallery and Museums, Brighton* (South Leigh Press, Haslemere, 1985)

HARTNELL, Norman, *Royal Courts of Fashion* (Cassell, London, 1971)

HARTNELL, Norman, *Silver and Gold* (Evans, London, 1955)

HAWKINS, Astley, *The Royal Tour of Southern Rhodesia* (Pitkin, London, 1953)

HEDLEY, Olwen, *Queen Charlotte* (John Murray, London, 1975)

HIBBERT, Christopher, *Edward VII: A Portrait* (Allen Lane, London, 1976)

HIBBERT, Christopher, *Queen Victoria in Her Letters & Journals* (John Murray, London, 1984)

HICHANS, Phoebe, *All About The Royal Family* (Macmillian, London, 1981)

HOBHOUSE, Hermione, *Prince Albert: His Life and Work* (Hamish Hamilton, London, 1983)

HOEY, Brian, *H.R.H. The Princess Anne* (Country Life, London, 1984)

HOEY, Brian, *The Queen and Her Family* (Pitkin Pictorials, London, 1983)

HOLDEN, Anthony, *Charles Prince of Wales* (Weidenfeld & Nicolson, London, 1979)

HOLDEN, Anthony, *The Queen Mother: A Birthday Tribute* (Sphere, London, 1985)

HOLME, Bryan, *The Journal of The Century* (Secker & Warburg, London, 1976)

HOLMES, Martin, F.S.A., and SITWELL, Major-General, HDW. CB. CVO. MC. FSA., *The English Regalia: Their History, Custody and Display* (HMSO, London, 1972)

HONEYCOMBE, Gordon, *TV-AM Official Celebration of the Royal Wedding* (Weidenfeld & Nicolson, London, 1986)

HONEYCOMBE, Gordon, *The Year of The Princess* (Michael Joseph/Rainbird, London, 1982)

HOWARD, Philip, *The British Monarchy in the Twentieth Century* (Hamish Hamilton, London, 1977)

HOWARTH, Patrick, *When The Riviera Was Ours* (Routledge & Kegan Paul, London, 1977)

HOUGH, Richard, *Edwina* (Weidenfeld & Nicolson, London, 1983)

HOUGH, Richard, *Louis and Victoria The First Mountbattens* (Hutchinson, London, 1974)

HOUGH, Richard, *Mountbatten: Hero of Our Time* (Weidenfeld & Nicolson, London, 1930)

HUGHES, Graham, *The Art of Jewellery* (Studio Vista, London, 1972)

HUTH, Angela, *The Englishwoman's Wardrobe* (Century, London, 1986)

INNES, Sir Thomas of Learney, K.C.V.O., *The Queen's Coronation Visit to Scotland* (1953)

IRONSIDE, Janey, FRCA, *A Fashion Alphabet* (Michael Joseph, London, 1968)

JACKMAN, S.W., *The People's Princess: A Portrait of H.R.H. Princess Mary, Duchess of Teck* (Kensal Press, Windsor, 1984)

JENKINS, Alan, *The Rich Rich: The Story of The Big Spenders* (Weidenfeld & Nicolson, London, 1977)

JONES, William, F.S.A., *Crowns and Coronations: A History of Regalia* (Chatto & Windus, London, 1902)

JUDD, Denis, *King George VI* (Michael Joseph, London, 1982)

JUDD, Denis, *The Life and Times of George V* (Weidenfeld & Nicolson, London, 1973)

JUNOR, Penny, *Diana, Princess of Wales* (Sidgwick & Jackson, London, 1982)

KEAY, Douglas, *Queen Elizabeth The Queen Mother: A Celebration of 80 Glorious Years* (IPC Magazines, London, 1980)

KEAY, Douglas, *Royal Pursuit* (Severn House, London, 1983)

KENNEDY, Carol, *Harewood, The Life and Times of An English Country House* (Hutchinson, London, 1982)

KENT, Princess Michael of, *Crowned in a Far Country: Portraits of Eight Royal Brides* (Weidenfeld & Nicolson, London, 1986)

KING, Stella, *Princess Marina: Her Life and Times* (Cassell, London, 1969)

*Kings and Queens: The Queen's Gallery Buckingham Palace* (London, 1982)

KONOLIGE, Kit, *The Richest Women In The World* (Macmillan, New York, 1985)

KROLL, Maria, and LINDSAY, Jason, *The Country Life Book of Europe's Royal Families* (Country Life, London, 1979)

KURTH, Peter, *Anastasia: The Life of Anna Anderson* (Jonathan Cape, London, 1983)

LACEY, Robert, *Majesty: Elizabeth II and The House of Windsor* (Hutchinson, London, 1977)

LACEY, Robert, *Princess* (Hutchinson, London, 1982)

LAIRD, Dorothy, *Her Majesty Queen Elizabeth and H.R.H. The Duke of Edinburgh and Their Children* (Pitkin, London, 1954)

LAIRD, Dorothy, *How The Queen Reigns: An Authentic Study of The Queen's Personality and Life Work* (Hodder & Stoughton, London, 1959)

LAMBERT, Angela, *Unquiet Sons* (Macmillan, London, 1984)

LAMBTON, Anthony, *Elizabeth and Alexandra* (Quartet, London, 1985)

LANE, Peter, *The Queen Mother* (Robert Hale, London, 1979)

LAWFORD, Valentine, *Horst: His Work and His World* (Alfred A. Knopf, New York, 1984)

LEES-MILNE, James, *Ancestral Voices* (Chatto & Windus, London, 1975)

LEES-MILNE, James, *Midway On The Waves* (Faber & Faber, London, 1985)

LEETE-HODGE, Lornie, *The Country Life Book of Diana Princess of Wales* (Country Life, London, 1982)

LEINSTER, Rafaelle, Duchess of, *So Brief a Dream* (W.H. Allen, London, 1973)

LESLEY, Cole, *The Life of Noel Coward* (Jonathan Cape, London, 1976)

LESLIE, Anita, *Edwardians In Love* (Hutchinson, London, 1972)

LEVER, Christopher, *Goldsmiths and Silversmiths of England* (Hutchinson, London, 1975)

LINDSAY, Loelia, *Cocktails and Laughter* (Hamish Hamilton, London, 1983)

LIVERSIDGE, Douglas, *The Mountbattens* (Arthur Barker, London, 1978)

LIVERSIDGE, Douglas, *The Queen Mother* (Arthur Barker, London, 1977)

LONGFORD, Elizabeth, *Elizabeth R* (Weidenfeld & Nicolson, London, 1985)

LONGFORD, Elizabeth, *The Queen Mother* (Weidenfeld & Nicolson, London, 1981)

LONGFORD, Elizabeth, *Victoria R.I.* (Weidenfeld & Nicolson, London, 1964)

LOWRY, Suzanne, *The Princess in The Mirror* (Chatto & Windus, London, 1985)

McDOWELL, Colin, *A Hundred Years of Royal Style* (Muller, Blond & White, London, 1985)

McLEOD, Kirsty, *The Wives of Downing Street* (Collins, London, 1976)

MAGNUS, Philip, *King Edward The Seventh* (John Murray, London, 1964)

MARGETSON, Stella, *The Long Party* (Saxon House, Aldershot, 1974)

MARGETSON, Stella, *Victorian High Society* (Batsford, London, 1980)

MARIE LOUISE, Her Highness Princess, *My Memories of Six Reigns* (Evans, London, 1956)

MARLBOROUGH, Laura, Duchess of, *Laughter from a Cloud* (Weidenfeld & Nicolson, London, 1980)

*Marriage of Her Royal Highness The Princess Anne and Captain Mark Phillips, List of Wedding Presents* (St James's Palace, London, 1973)

MARTIN, Ralph G., *Charles & Diana* (Putnam's, New York, 1985)

MARTIN, Ralph G., *The Woman He Loved: The Story of The Duke and Duchess of Windsor* (W.H. Allen, London, 1974)

MARTIN, Theodore, *The Life of His Royal Highness The Prince Consort, Vol. I,* (Smith, Elder & Co., London, 1875)

MASSIE, Robert K., *Nicholas and Alexandra* (Atheneum, New York, 1967)

MASTERS, Brian, *Great Hostesses* (Constable, London, 1982)

MATHESON, Anne, *Princess Anne: A Girl of Our Time* (Frederick Muller, London, 1973)

MENKES, Suzy, *The Royal Jewels* (Grafton, London, 1985)

MICHAEL, Prince of Greece, *Crown Jewels of Britain and Europe* (Dent, London, 1983)

MILLER, H. Tatlock, *Royal Album* (Hutchinson, London, 1951)

MINNEY, R.J., *The Edwardian Age* (Little, Brown, Boston, 1964)

MONTGOMERY-Massingberd Hugh, *Diana The Princess of Wales* (Fontana, London, 1982)

MORRAH, Dermot, *Princess Elizabeth Duchess of Edinburgh* (Odhams, London, 1950)

MORRAH, Dermot, *The Work of The Queen* (William Kimber, London, 1958)

MORROW, Ann, *The Queen* (Granada, London, 1983)

MORROW, Ann, *The Queen Mother* (Granada, London, 1984)

MORTIMER, Penelope, *Queen Elizabeth: A Life of The Queen Mother* (Viking, London, 1986)

MOSLEY, Diana, *The Duchess of Windsor* (Sidgwick & Jackson, London, 1980)

MUNN, Geoffrey, *Castellani and Giuliano: Revivalist Jewellers of The Nineteenth Century* (Trefoil, London, 1984)

MURPHY, Sophia, *The Duchess of Devonshire's Ball* (Sidgwick & Jackson, London, 1984)

NADELHOFFER, Hans, *Cartier: Jewellers Extraordinary* (Thames & Hudson, London, 1984)

NASH, Roy, *Buckingham Palace: The Palace and The People* (Futura, London, 1980)

NICHOLSON, J. Haig, *H.R.H. The Princess Margaret In The British West Indies and The Bahamas* (Pitkin, London, 1955)

NICKOLLS, L.A., *The First Family: A Diary of The Royal Year* (Macdonald, London, 1950)

NICKOLLS, L.A., MVO, *Our Gracious Queen: A Diary of The Royal Year* (Macdonald, London, 1958)

NICKOLLS, L.A., *The Queen's Year* (Macdonald, London, 1955)

NICOLSON, Harold, *Diaries and Letters 1930–1964* (Penguin, London, 1984)

NICOLSON, Harold, *King George The Fifth: His Life and Reign* (Constable, London, 1952)

NOEL, Gerard, *Ena: Spain's English Queen* (Constable, London, 1984)

NORMAN, Philip, *Grandma Norman and The Queen* (Granta, Cambridge, 1985)

OWEN, Jane, *Diana: Princess of Wales, The Book of Fashion* (Colour Library, Guildford, 1983)

PACKARD, Anne, *Her Royal Highness the Duchess of Kent* (Pitkin, London, 1950)

PACKARD, Anne, *H.R.H. The Princess Margaret 20th Birthday Book* (Pitkin, London, 1950)

PACKARD, Anne, *Royal Family Golden Album Vol. 2.,*

(Pitkin, London, 1950)

PACKARD, Anne, *The Royal Tour of Canada* (Pitkin Pictorials, London, 1951)

PAKULA, Hannah, *The Last Romantic: A Biography of Queen Marie of Romania* (Weidenfeld & Nicolson, London, 1985)

PALMER, Alan, *Crowned Cousins: The Anglo-German Royal Connection* (Weidenfeld & Nicolson, London, 1985)

PARKER, Eileen, *Step Aside For Royalty* (Bachman & Turner, Maidstone, 1982)

PARKINSON, Norman, *Lifework* (Weidenfeld & Nicolson, London, 1983)

PATIENCE, Sally, *The Queen Mother* (Lutterworth, Guildford, 1977)

PAYN, Graham, and MORLEY, Sheridan, *The Noel Coward Diaries* (Weidenfeld & Nicolson, London, 1982)

PEACOCKE, Marguerite, *Queen Mary: Her Life and Times* (Odhams, London, 1953)

PEARSON, John, *The Ultimate Family: The Making of The Royal House of Windsor* (Michael Joseph, London, 1986)

PENDEREL-BRODHURST, J., *The Life of His Most Gracious Majesty*, 4 Vols. (Virtue, London, post–1910)

PERRY, George, *Diana: A Celebration* (Windward, London, 1982)

PICKNETT, Lynn, *Royal Romance: An Illustrated History of The Royal Love Affairs* (Marshall Cavendish, London, 1980)

PLOWDON, Alison, *The Young Victoria* (Weidenfeld & Nicolson, London, 1981)

PLUMB, J.H., *Royal Heritage* (BBC, London, 1977)

PONSONBY, Sir Frederick, *Recollections of Three Reigns* (Eyre & Spottiswoode, London, 1951)

POPE-HENNESSY, James, *Queen Mary* (Allen & Unwin, London 1959)

POULTON, Richard, *Victoria: Queen of a Changing Land* (World's Work, Tadworth, 1975)

POUND, Reginald, *Albert* (Michael Joseph, London, 1973)

PURTELL, Joseph, *The Tiffany Touch* (Random House, New York, 1972)

QUENNELL, Peter, *A Lonely Business: A Self Portrait of James Pope-Hennessy* (Weidenfeld & Nicolson, London, 1981)

REDWOOD, Sydney, *The Crown Jewels and Coronation Chair* (Westminster Press, London, 1936)

REGAN, Simon, *Margaret: A Love Story* (Everest, London, 1977)

*Retrospective Louis Cartier, Masterworks of Art Deco* (Exhibition Catalogue, 1982)

RICHARDS, Guy, *The Work for The Czar* (Sphere, London, 1972)

RICHARDSON, Joanna, *Victoria and Albert: A Study of a Marriage* (Dent, London, 1977)

ROBERTS, Cecil, *The Pleasant Years 1947–1972* (Hodder & Stoughton, London, 1974)

ROBYNS, Gwen, *The Royal Ladies* (Leslie Frewin, London, 1969)

ROITH, Cynthia, *Bygones: Love and Marriage Tokens* (Transworld, London, 1972)

ROSE, Kenneth, *King George V* (Weidenfeld & Nicolson, London, 1983)

ROSE, Kenneth, *Kings, Queens & Courtiers: Intimate Portraits of The Royal House of Windsor From its Foundation to the Present Day* (Weidenfeld & Nicolson, London, 1985)

RUSSELL, Audrey, *A Certain Voice* (Ross Anderson, London, 1984)

RUSSELL, Peter, *Butler Royal* (Hutchinson, London, 1982)

RUTTER, Owen, *Portrait of a Painter: The Authorized Life of Philip de Laszlo* (Hodder & Stoughton, Lon-

don, 1959)

ST AUBYN, Giles, *Edward VII: Prince and King* (Collins, London, 1979)

ST JOHN NEVILL, Barry, *Life at the Court of Queen Victoria 1861–1901* (Webb & Bower, Exeter, 1984)

ST JOHN PARKER, Michael, *Queen Victoria* (Pitkin Pictorials, London, 1976)

ST JOHNS ROGERS, Adela, *The Honey Comb* (New American Library, New York, 1969)

SAVILLE, Margaret, *Her Majesty Queen Elizabeth and H.R.H. The Duke of Edinburgh and Their Children* (Pitkin, London, 1953)

SAVILLE, Margaret, *H.R.H. Princess Anne* (Pitkin, London, 1950)

SAVILLE, Margaret, *Royal Family Picture Annual, Vol. II, Coronation Year* (Pitkin Pictorials, London, 1953)

SAVILLE, Margaret, *Royal Sisters* (Pitkin Pictorials, London, 1953)

SCARISBRICK, Diana, *Jewellery* (Batsford, London, 1984)

SHAW, Betty Spencer, *Queen Elizabeth The Queen Mother* (Hodder & Stoughton, London, 1956)

SHAW, Betty Spencer, *Royal Wedding* (Macdonald, London, 1947)

SHAW, Martina, *Princess: Leader of Fashion* (Colour Library, Guildford, 1983)

SHERIDAN, Lisa, *Our Princesses In 1942* (John Murray, London, 1942)

SINCLAIR, David, *Queen and Country: The Life of Elizabeth The Queen Mother* (Dent, London, 1979)

SITWELL, Edith, *Victoria of England* (Faber & Faber, London, 1935)

SITWELL, Osbert, *Queen Mary and Others* (Michael Joseph, London, 1974)

SMITH, Charles, *Fifty Years with Mountbatten* (Sidgwick & Jackson, London, 1980)

SMITH, Jane S., *Elsie de Wolfe: A Life In The High Style* (Atheneum, New York, 1982)

SMITH, Nina Slingsby, *George: Memoirs of a Gentleman's Gentleman* (Jonathan Cape, London, 1984)

SOMERSET, Anne, *Ladies-in-Waiting: From The Tudors to The Present Day* (Weidenfeld & Nicolson, London, 1984)

SPINK, Kathryn, *Invitation to a Royal Wedding* (Colour Library, Guildford, 1981)

STRACHEY, Lytton, *Queen Victoria* (Penguin, London, 1971)

SUMMERS, Anthony, and MANGOLD, Tom, *The File on The Tsar* (Gollancz, London, 1976)

The Sunday Express Magazine, *A Week In The Life of The Royal Family* (Weidenfeld & Nicolson, London, 1983)

TALBOT, Godfrey, *The Country Life Book of Queen Elizabeth The Queen Mother* (Country Life, London, 1983)

TALBOT, Godfrey, O.B.E., and THOMAS, Wynford Vaughan, *Royalty Annual* (Preview, London, 1952)

TEAGUE, Michael, *Mrs L.: Conversations with Alice Roosevelt Longworth* (Duckworth, London, 1981)

THOMSON, Malcolm, *The Duke of Edinburgh: A Pictorial Biography* (Odhams, London, 1953)

THORNTON, Michael, *Royal Feud: The Queen Mother and The Duchess of Windsor* (Michael Joseph, London, 1985)

TWINING, Lord, *A History of the Crown Jewels of Europe* (Batsford, London, 1960)

VACHA, Robert, Ed., *The Kaiser's Daughter, Memoirs of H.R.H. Viktoria Luise, Princess of Prussia* (W.H. Allen, London, 1977)

VADGAMA, Kusoom, *India In Britain* (Robert Royce, London, 1984)

VANDERBILT, Cornelius Jr, *Queen of the Golden Age* (McGraw-Hill, New York, 1956)

VANDERBILT, Gloria, and FURNESS, Thelma, *Double Exposure* (David McKay, New York, 1958)

VAUGHAN-THOMAS, Wynford, *Royal Tour 1953–54* (Hutchinson, London, 1954)

VICKERS, Hugo, *Cecil Beaton* (Weidenfeld & Nicolson, London, 1985)

VICKERS, Hugo, *Debrett's Book of The Royal Wedding* (Debrett's Peerage, London, 1981)

VICKERS, Hugo, *Gladys Duchess of Marlborough* (Weidenfeld & Nicolson, London, 1979)

VINCENT, John, *The Crawford Papers* (Manchester University Press, Manchester, 1984)

VREELAND, Diana, *D.V.* (Alfred A. Knopf, New York, 1984)

WARWICK, Christopher, *King George VI and Queen Elizabeth* (Sidgwick & Jackson, London, 1985)

WARWICK, Christopher, *Princess Margaret* (Weidenfeld & Nicolson, London, 1983)

WARWICK, Christopher, *Two Centuries of Royal Weddings* (Arthur Barker, London, 1980)

WATSON, Vera, *A Queen at Home* (W.H. Allen, London, 1952)

WESTMINSTER, Loelia, Duchess of, *Grace and Favour* (Weidenfeld & Nicolson, London, 1961)

WHEELER-BENNETT, John W., *King George VI: His Life and Reign* (Macmillan, London, 1958)

WHISTLER, Lawrence, *The Laughter and The Urn: The Life of Rex Whistler* (Weidenfeld & Nicolson, London, 1985)

WHITAKER, James, *Settling Down* (Quartet, London, 1981)

WHITING, Audrey, *Family Royal* (W.H. Allen, London, 1982)

WHITING, Audrey, *The Kents: A Royal Family* (Hutchinson, London, 1985)

WHITTLE, Tyler, *The Last Kaiser* (Heinemann, London, 1977)

WINDSOR, The Duchess of, *The Heart Has Its Reasons* (Universal-Tandem, London, 1969)

WINDSOR, H.R.H. The Duke of, *A King's Story* (Cassell, London, 1951)

WINN, Godfrey, *The Young Queen: The Life Story of Her Majesty Queen Elizabeth II* (Hutchinson, London, 1952)

WINN, Godfrey, *The Younger Sister: An Intimate Portrait Study of H.R.H. Princess Margaret* (Hutchinson, London, 1951)

WOODHAM-SMITH, Cecil, *Queen Victoria* (Hamish Hamilton, London, 1972)

WULFF, Louis, M.V.O., *Elizabeth and Philip: Our Heiress And Her Consort* (Sampson Low, Marston, London, 1947)

WULFF, Louis, M.V.O., *Her Majesty Queen Mary* (Sampson Low, Marston, London, 1949)

WULFF, Louis, M.V.O., *Queen of Tomorrow: An Authentic Study of H.R.H. The Princess Elizabeth* (Sampson Low, Marston, London, 1946)

WULFF, Louis, M.V.O., *Queen of Tomorrow* (Sampson Low, Marston, London, 1949)

WULFF, Louis, M.V.O., *Silver Wedding* (Sampson Low, Marston, London, 1948)

YOUNG, Sheila, *The Queen's Jewellery* (Ebury, London, 1968)

YOUNGHASBAND, Major General Sir George, K.C.M.G., K.C.I.E., C.B., *The Jewel House* (Herbert Jenkins, London, 1921)

ZIEGLER, Philip, *Diana Cooper* (Hamish Hamilton, London, 1981)

ZIEGLER, Philip, *Mountbatten* (Collins, London, 1985)

In addition to the abovementioned works, the author has consulted a wide range of newspapers and magazines.

# INDEX

Pages on which illustrations appear are in *italics*.

Adams, Marcus, photos by, *25*
Adelaide, Queen, 9, 80, 101, 158, 177
Adolphus, *see* Cambridge
Ailesbury, Prince, Marchioness of, 45
Airlie, Countess of, 36, 116
Albert, King of the Belgians, *66*
Albert, Prince, 22, 28, *41*, 97, 99, 138, 163
  family background, 158
  jewellery designed by, 10, 11, 27, 35, 138, 158
  as Knight of the Garter, 82–83
  statue of, 119
  wedding, 29, 45, *182*; *see also under* Victoria
Albert Victor, Prince, Duke of Clarence, 12, 20, 30, 31, 138
Alexander II of Russia, 116
Alexander II of Scotland, 168
Alexander III of Russia, 14, 116, 153, 157
Alexander VI, Pope, 178
Alexandra, Empress of Russia, 14, 116
Alexandra, Princess (of Kent), 8, 37, 97, 100, 111–12, 119, 139
  engagement ring, 145
Alexandra, Queen, 17, 18, 90, 121
  Coronation, 11, 29, 58, *95*, *108*, *122*, *126*, *151*, 161, 163
  death, 11, 13, 16, 86
  diamonds, 30, 32, 35–37, *44*, *45*, 58, *70*, 73, *96*
  emeralds, 86, 87, *96*
  family of, 13–15, 106, *153*, 157
  neck scar, 99
  Order of the Garter and, *183*
  pearls, 99, 101, *108*
  pearls and diamonds, 33, 111, 112, *122*, *126*, *128*, *129*, 134, *135*, *164*
  personal characteristics, 11, 12, 20, 30, 31, 58
  wedding gifts, 36, *45*, *64*, 65, 86, *96*, *122*, *129*, 138
Alice, *see* Andrew; Athlone; Gloucester
Amalie Auguste, Princess of Bavaria, 95
amethysts, 20, *22*, 26
Andrei, Grand Duke of Russia, 117
Andrew, Prince, Duke of York, 36, 59, *96*, 97, 102, 158, 139
Andrew, Princess of Greece, 17, 37, 47, 85
Angeli, Heinrich von, *133*
Anne, Princess, Mrs Mark Phillips, 47, 78, *107*, 112, *159*, 180
  as baby and child, *25*, *69*, *96*, *102*
  engagement ring, 145
  wedding and gifts, 21, 35–36, *43*, 97
Anne, Queen, 9, 23, *46*, 47, 99, *182*
  pearls, 98, *104*
Anne Boleyn, Queen, 97, 99
Antrobus, Philip, jeweller, 85
aquamarines, 21, 23
Armills, *176*, 176–77
Armstrong-Jones, Antony, *see* Snowdon
Armstrong-Jones, Lady Sarah, *96*, 158
Art Deco style, 60, 93, *94*, 140
Ascot racecourse, 23
Asprey, jewellers, 147
Asquith, Margot, 11
Asscher, diamond works, 72–75, 90
Athlone, Countess of (Princess Alice of Albany), 13, 88, 100
Augusta, Grand Duchess of Mecklenburg-Strelitz, 45, 65, 90, 111, 113, *114*, 146
Augusta, Princess of Hesse, *see* Cambridge
Australia, 8, *25*, 52, 57, 84, 97, 138
  Queen's visits, 34, 76, 134
Ayub Khan, President of Pakistan, *159*

Bahrain, Sheikh of, 102
Balmoral, 58–59, *64*
Beaton, Cecil, 32, 170
Beatrice, Princess, 102
Beatrix, Queen of the Netherlands, 105
Beaufort, Duchess of, 100
Beauharnais, Eugène de, 95
Birley, Oswald, painting by, *68*
Blum, Maître, 87
Boer War, 27, 72
Botha, Louis, 72, 73
Boucheron, jewellers, 87
Bowes-Lyon, Lady Elizabeth, *see* Elizabeth, Queen Mother
bracelets
  King William IV buckle, 32, *80*
  Prince Philip wedding, *85*
  Princess Marie Louise's, *137*
  Queen Alexandra's (four-row pearl), *108*
  Queen Alexandra's snake, 32, *96*
  Queen Mary's (five-row pearl), *109*
  Queen Mary's Art Deco, *94*
  Queen Mary's Cambridge chain bracelet (emerald), 88, 90, *91*
  Queen Mary's Indian bangle, *82*, 83
  Queen Mary's link, *81*
  Queen Mary's Rose of York, *142*, *143*
  Queen Mother's quartet, *141*
  Queen Victoria's cuff, 32, *55*
  Queen's eighteenth birthday, *157*
  Queen's fifth wedding anniversary, *144*
  Queen's modern baguettes and brilliants, *84*
Brazil, 21, 26
Briefel & Lemer, jewellers, 34, 102
brooches
  Cullinan V heart, *76*
  Cullinan VII and VIII, *77*
  Duchess of Cambridge's pendant, *133*
  Duchess of Teck's corsage, *132*
  Empress Marie Feodorovna's, *152*, *153*
  Empress Marie Feodorovna's oval, 37, *50*, *51*
  King William IV, 31, 32, *70*, *71*
  Lesser Stars of Africa, 73, 74, *75*
  Prince Albert, 145, *150*, *151*
  Prince Philip's naval badge, *69*, *144*
  Queen Alexandra's baroque pearl, 111, *135*
  Queen Alexandra's triple drop, *128*, *129*
  Queen Mary's bar, *131*
  Queen Mary's Dorset bow, 63, 134, *135*
  Queen Mary's Kensington bow, *134*, *135*
  Queen Mary's Rose of York, 35, *146*
  Queen Mary's Russian, *156*, 157
  Queen Mary's true lover's knot, *68*, 69
  Queen Mary's Warwick sun, *134*, *135*
  Queen Mary's 'Women of Hampshire' pendant, *130*
  Queen Mother's flower, *136*
  Queen Mother's leaf, 139, *154*
  Queen Mother's maple leaf, *62*
  Queen Victoria's bar, 32, *64*, *65*, *150*
  Queen Victoria's bow, 31, 32, 58, *59*, *75*, *95*, *129*
  Queen Victoria's cluster (pearl and diamond), *118*, *128*, *129*
  Queen Victoria's waterfall, 32, *64*
  Queen Victoria's wheat ear, 35, *78*
  Queen's Cartier clips, 23
  Queen's flower basket, *60*
  Queen's flower spray, *155*
  Queen's ivy leaf, *61*
  Queen's jardinière, *60*
  Queen's set of flower clips, *155*
Bruce, Robert, 178

Burma, 69
Butler & Wilson, jewellers, 36, 100

Cambridge, Prince Adolphus, Duke of, 88, 113, 146, 158
Cambridge, Princess Augusta, Duchess of, 65, 88, 113, *133*, 146
Cambridge, Prince George, Duke of, 13, 111
Cambridge and Delhi Durbar parure, 13, 76, 88–93, *88*, *89*, *91–93*
Campbell-Bannerman, Sir Henry, 72
Canada, 16, 22, 62, 87, 97, 106, 121
Canrobert, General, 138
Caroline, Queen, 98, 104
Carrington, jewellers, 62, 161
Cartier, jewellers, 30, 60, 87, 97, 116, 139, 146
  Queen and, 23, 34, 40, 61, 82, 102, 124, 147, *155*, *157*
  Queen Mother and, 32, 33, *141*, 147, *154*
Catchpole and Williams, jewellers, 31–32
Catherine de Medici, 98, 168
Channon, Henry 'Chips', 17, 42
Charles I, 160, 161, 168
Charles II, 160, 161, 167, 168, 171, 174
  Order of the Garter and, 184
  Scottish Coronation, 178
Charles, Prince of Wales, 18, 34, 60, 147
  gifts to wife, *79*, 93, 97, 99, 145
  Investiture, 86
Charlotte, Queen, 9, 10, 146
China, 18, 21
Christian IX of Denmark, 14, *152*
Christian X of Denmark, 14–15
Churchill, Winston, 72, 171–72
Clement VII, Pope, 98, 168
Collingwood, jewellers, 36, 111, 112, 115, 134
Colville, John, 104–105
Connaught, Prince Arthur, Duke of, 27, *41*
Conyngham, Lady, 168, 180
coral jewellery, 24, *25*, 26
Coronation Regalia, 160, 161, *163*, 166–77, *179*
Coster's, jewellers, 28
Coward, Noel, 149
Crawford, Marion, 162, 179
Cromwell, Oliver, 161, 167, 168, 174, 178
Crown Regalia, 9, 11, 74, 98, 160–63, *164–84*
crowns, *see* Imperial State; King George State Diadem; St. Edward's; tiaras
Cullinan diamonds, 18, 27, 31, 72–77, *73–77*, 90–93
  in Coronation Regalia, *167*, 168, 171–72
  Queen Mary and, 13, 59, 66, 70, 74–75, *75–77*, 80, 81, 88, 91 *92*, 161, *164*, 171
Cumberland, Thyra, Duchess of, *152*
Cumberland, Prince William Augustus, Duke of, 9

Dagmar necklace, *126*, *127*
Dalhousie, Lord, 27
Deacon, Gladys, 11
De Beers Consolidated Mines, 31, 33, 35, 49, 102
de Laszlo, Philip, 11
Delhi Durbar, 13, 66, 76, 90, 161–62
  parure, *see* Cambridge and Delhi Durbar parure
diamonds, 26–37, *38–85*, 98
  pearls and, combined, 110–12, *113–37*
  *See also* Cullinan; Koh-I-Noor
Diana, Princess of Wales, 24, 87, 99–100, 111, 180
  engagement gifts, *79*, 86, 97, 145
  pictured, *52*, *56*, *57*, *79*, *84*, *93*, *105*, *115*
  wedding gifts, 36, *52*, *57*, *79*, 93, 99, *115*, 147
  wedding ring, 97
Didrichsen, Jules, 127
Disraeli, Benjamin, 29

Dorset bow brooch, *63*, 134, *135*
Duleep Singh, Maharajah, 28

earrings
   Duchess of Kent's (amethyst), 22
   Duchess of Teck's (pearl and diamond), *120*
   King George VI chandelier, *53*
   King George VI Victorian, *148, 149*
   Princess Augusta's Cabochon emerald drop, *88*
   Queen Alexandra's cluster, 112, *122, 123*
   Queen Mary's button, 112, *124, 125*
   Queen Mary's Cambridge earrings (emerald), *88, 89, 91*
   Queen Mary's cluster (diamonds), *48, 49*
   Queen Mary's cluster (rubies), *140*
   Queen Mary's floret, *44*
   Queen Mary's pendant, *118*
   Queen Mother's drop, *46*, 110
   Queen Mother's pendant, *33, 64*
   Queen Victoria's collet necklace and, 17, 27, 32, *54, 55*
   Queen Victoria's drop, 112, *121*
   Queen Victoria's fringe, 87, *95*
   Queen Victoria's stud, *50, 51*
   Queen's pear drop, 8, *52*
East India Company, 27, 28, 54, 101, 139
Edgar, King, 177
Edward I, 160
Edward II, 174
Edward III, 90, 161, 167, 182
Edward VI, 176
Edward VII, 11, 12, 71, 87, 122, 129, 140
   Coronation, 95, 134, 161, 166, *169*, 175, 179
   Cullinan diamond and, 18, 72, 73, 90, 167
   death, 13, 74, 86, 110, 121
   Family Order, 180
   marriage, 36, 86, 99
   Order of the Garter and, 183
   wedding ring, 97
Edward VIII, 16, 46, 86–87, *143*, 173
   Investiture as Prince of Wales, 90, *93*
Edward of Woodstock, Prince of Wales, 167
Edward the Confessor, King, 163, 168, 174
Egbert, King, 160
Elgin, Lord, 72
Elizabeth I, 9, 19, 27, 98, 162, 168, 176
   death, 177
   Order of the Garter and, 182
Elizabeth II, 18–19, 30
   amethysts, 20, *22*
   aquamarines, 21, *23*
   ascension to the throne, 17, 33–34, 149
   as baby, *25*, *102*, 133
   Coronation, 21, 32, 34, 40, 55, *80*, 88, 101, 102, 143, 145, 161, *169–73, 171, 175, 176, 176–77*
   Coronation tours, 18, 19, 34, 48, 49, *178*
   diamonds, 8, 29, 31–37, *40, 45*, 46, *47*, 49, *51–53, 55–57, 59–61, 63, 64*, 66, 68, 74, *75–78*, 80, *81, 84*
   emeralds, 87, *91, 92, 94, 95*
   engagement ring, 17, *85*
   Family Order, *181*
   jewellery collection, generally, 17
   as Lady of the Garter, 17, *121, 184*
   as mother, *25*, 60, *69*, *102*, 155
   at parents' Coronation, 103, *179*
   pearls, 8, 100, 101, *102, 103, 105, 106, 108, 109, 120*
   pearls and diamonds, 112, *115, 117, 119, 120, 121, 123, 125, 127, 128, 130–33, 135–37*
   as Princess, 17, 22, 33, 35, 40, 48–49, *60–63, 85, 96*, 102, *103, 120, 136*, 139, *148, 154, 155*, 157, 162, *179*
   rubies, *68*, 138–39, *140, 141, 143, 144*
   sapphires, 8, 139, 147, *148, 149, 151, 152, 154–57*

Silver Jubilee, *141*
State visits, 18, 21, 22, 34, 35, *55*, 57, 62, 66, 75, *76, 77, 84, 95*, 108, 119, 121, 124, *128, 132, 134, 135*, 152, 158, *see also* subhead Coronation tours
turquoises, 158, *159*
twenty-first birthday, 17, 33, *61*, 82
watches, 40, 79, 81, 97, 125
wedding, 33, 34, 40, 42, *43*, 74, *104*, 104–105, 121
wedding gifts, 17, 34, 40, *47*, 53, *63*, 66–69, 79, 82, 85, 87 102, *104*, 124, 132, 140, 142, *143*, 147, 149
wedding ring, 97
Elizabeth, Queen Mother, 16–17, 30, 31, 53, 86, 99
   amethysts, 20
   aquamarines, 21
   coral, 24, *25*
   Coronation, 32, 54, 55, 71, 80, 81, 103, 127, 161, *179*
   diamonds, 8, 29, 31–36, 42, *43*, 46, 54, 55, 58, *59, 62, 64, 69, 70, 71*, 80, *179, 181*
   eightieth birthday, *64, 181*
   emeralds, 86–88
   engagement ring, 110, 145
   husband's funeral, 173
   as Lady of the Garter, 183
   pearls, 100–101
   pearls and diamonds, *46*, 110, 119, 122, 129, *136, 137*
   rubies, 138, 139, 140, *141*
   sapphires, 106, 139, 145, 146–47, *151, 152, 154*
   Silver Wedding anniversary, 129, 138
   tours abroad, 16–17, 22, 25, 32–33, 34, 40, 48–49, 61, 62
   turquoise, *141*, 158
   wedding and honeymoon, 87, 100
   wedding ring, 97
Elizabeth, Queen of the Belgians, 66
Elizabeth, Queen of Bohemia, 99
Elliot, Walter, 173
emeralds, 86–87, *88–96*
   *See also* Cambridge and Delhi Durbar parure
Ernest Augustus, King of Hanover, 9, 10
Eugénie, Empress of France, 138

Fabergé, 12, 14, 131
Faisal, King of Saudi Arabia, 57, *137*
Family Orders, *180*, 180–181
Fellowes, Lady Jane, 36
Ferguson, Sarah, *see* York
Fisher, Archbishop Geoffrey, 177
France, 40, 124, 129, 138
Frederick VII of Denmark, 127
Frederick the Great, 162

Garrard, Crown Jeweller, 58, 69, 73
   Queen Alexandra and, 45, 122, 129
   Queen Mary and, 88, 113, 161
George I, 9, 99, 180
George II, 9, 104
George III, 9, 12, 22, 71, 78
   Coronation, 173
   fringe tiara of, 32, 37, *41–43*
   mentioned, 88, 113, 146
George IV, 11, 27, 180, 181
   Coronation, 163, 166, 168, 172, 175
George V, 31, 32, 86, 90, 158, *170*, 183
   ascension to the throne, 12, 80, 110
   Coronation, 13, 73, 88, 166–68, *171*, 175
   at Delhi Durbar, 13, 161–62
   as Duke of York, *135*
   Family Order, 180, *181*
   first Opening of Parliament, 74, *169*
   funeral, 173
   mentioned, 25, 35, 87, 141, 145

Romanov relatives and, 14–16
Silver Jubilee, 101, 103, *184*
wedding ring, 97
George V of Hanover, 10
George VI, 17, 35, 53, 102, 104, *143, 170*
   ascension to the throne, 86, 138
   Coronation, 32, 76, 88, 103, 161, 166, 175, *179*
   death and funeral, 33, 149, *172*, 173
   as Duke of York, 25, 46, 141, *143*
   Family Order, *180, 181*
   first Opening of Parliament, 139
   Order of the Garter and, 183, 184
   sapphires as favourite of, 147, 149, 157
   Silver Wedding anniversary, 129, 138
   tours abroad, 16–17, 22, 25, 32, 33, 40, 48–49, 61, 62
   World War II years, 16, 101, 162
Girl Guide Movement, 34
Giuliano, Arthur and Carlo, jewellers, 147
Giuliano, Federico, 139
Gloucester, Princess Alice, Duchess of, 100, 111, 115, 145
   diamonds, 37, 48, 63, 81
   wedding and gifts, 21, 87, 96, 134, 158
Gloucester, Birgitte, Duchess of, 24, 78, 87, 97, 100, 111, 115
   diamonds, 30, 37, 48, 63, 81
   turquoises, 8, 158
Gloucester, Prince Henry, Duke of, 145, 158
Gloucester, Prince Richard, Duke of, 37, 99
Gloucester, Prince William of, 150
Godman necklace, *95*
gold jewellery, 97
Great Exhibition of 1851, 127, 139
Greville, Charles, 168, 177
Greville, Lady Eve, 39
Greville, Mrs Ronald, 87, 101
Grey, General Charles, 28, 182
Grey, Lady de, 101
Grima, Andrew, 112

Halifax, Lord, 10
Halliday, Edward, painting by, *184*
Hanoverian jewels, 8, 9–11, 16, 17, 27, 99, *102*
Hardy, jeweller, 15, 16
Harewood, 6th Earl of, 145, 179
Hartnell, Norman, 16, 21
Hayter, Sir George, paintings by, *164, 169*
Helen, Grand Duchess of Russia, *see* Nicholas
Hennell & Sons, jewellers, 15, 106
Henrietta Marie, Queen, 160–61, 168
Henry II of France, 98
Henry II, 160
Henry V, 167–68, 177
Henry VII, 183
Henry VIII, 97, 98, 99, 138, 176, 179
Hopkins, Harry, 16, 17
Hopwood, Sir Francis, 72
Hunt and Roskell, jewellers, 124
Huntington, Lieutenant, 173
Hussein, King of Jordan, 158
Hyderabad, 26, 27
   Nizams of, 18, 69, 82, 143

Imperial Crown of India, 161–62
Imperial State Crown, 74, 98, 162, 166–73, *167, 172*, 175
India, 29, 65, 86, 138, 139
   diamonds, 26–28
   Queen Mary and, 18, 76, 82, 90
   Imperial Crown of, 161–62
Iveagh, Lord and Lady, 62

Jacobs, Erasmus, 26
James I, 98–99, 160, 177

James II, 168, 172
James IV of Scotland, 178
James V of Scotland, 178
James, Mrs Arthur, 32
Japan, 147
Jardine, Lady, 34
Jordan, 158
Joséphine, Empress of France, 95
Juliana, Queen of the Netherlands, 35
Julius II, Pope, 178

Kensington bow brooch, *134*, *135*
Kent, Prince Edward, Duke of, 37, 146
Kent, Prince George, Duke of, 37, 100, 139, 145, 146
Kent, Katharine Duchess of, 37, 65, 78, 81, 111,
    pearls, 99, 100
    sapphires, 145, 146
Kent, Princess Marina of, *see* Marina
Kent, Prince Michael of, 37, 97, 100, 145, 146
Kent, Princess Michael of, 37, 50, 78, 100, 111,
    145, 146
Kent, Princess Victoria, Duchess of (Queen Victoria's
    mother), *22*, 158, 177
Kent demi-parure, 20, *22*
Kenya, 34, 149
Kéroualle, Louise de, 184
Khalid, King of Saudi Arabia, 57
King George IV State Diadem, 27, *163–65*, 166, *181*
Koh-I-Noor diamond, 18, *27–29*, 65, 74–75, 81, 161
    pictured, *51*, *55*, *59*, *80*, *95*

Lahore diamond, *54*, *55*
Laing and Sons Ltd, 121
Lane, Ken, jeweller, 36, 99
Lane, Richard James, drawing by, *121*
Lang, Cosmo Gordon, 175
Lehzen, Baroness, 24
Leopold, King of the Belgians, 158
Linley, Viscount, *96*
Lloyds of London, 34
Louis XIV of France, 160
Louise, Princess (Edward VII's daughter), 13
Louise, Princess (Victoria's daughter), 102

McCorquodale, Lady Sarah, 36, 99
MacDonald, Margaret 'Bobo', 17
Malan, Daniel F., 172
March, T.C., 28
Marchant, Harry, 85
Marcos, Imelda, 112
Margaret, Princess, 88, 97, 110, 141, 149, 162
    diamonds, 32–35, *46*, 71
    engagement ring, 139
    pearls, 101, *103*
    pictured, *22*, *46*, *96*, *103*, *136*, *179*
    rubies, 139, 155
    sapphires, 81, 106, 147
    turquoise, *111*, 158
Marie Antoinette, Queen of France, 36, 87
Marie Feodorovna, Empress of Russia, 14–15, 37,
    *106*, 116, *152*, 157
    estate of, 15–16, 31, 50, 81, 106, 153
Marie Louise, Princess, 33, 37, *137*
Marina, Princess, Duchess of Kent, 97, 100, 111, 117,
    139, 146
    diamonds, 37, 50, 65, 81
    engagement ring and wedding, 145
Mary I (Mary Tudor), 98, 176
Mary, Princess of Burgundy, 26
Mary, Princess Royal, Countess of Harewood, 16, *77*,
    145, 179
Mary, Queen, 15, 17, 25, 36, 158, 179
    Coronation, 32, 54, *55*, 58, 75, *80*, 88, 127,
        134, 161
    death, 17, 102, 110, 115

diamonds, 29–33, 35, 37, *38–40*, 42–45, 48, 49,
    *51*, *55*, 58, *63*, *64*, *66–68*, 80–83, 86, *135*, *181*,
    *see also under* Cullinan
dress style, 12, 111
emeralds, 18, 76, 87, *88–92*, 94, 96
engagement to Albert, Duke of Clarence, 12,
    30, 138
family background, 12, 13
jewellery acquisitions, summarized, 13, 16, 18
mourning jewellery, 110, *121*
Order of the Garter and, 183–84, *184*
pearls, 100, 101, *106*, *109*
pearls and diamonds, 110–22, *124*, *125*, *127*, *128*,
    *130*, *131*, *133–35*
rubies, *140*, *142*, *143*
sapphires, 65, 146, *151*, *152*, *156*, *157*
Silver Jubilee, *94*, *109*
trips abroad, 13, 62, 82, *134*
wedding, 11, 31, 88, 97
Mary Adelaide, Princess, *see* Teck
    pictured, *88*, *120*, *132*
Mary Queen of Scots, 98, 168
Maud, Queen of Norway, 13, 86
Maximilian, Archduke of Austria, 26
Mears, Kenneth, 37
Mecklenburg-Strelitz, Grand Duchess, *see* Augusta
Melbourne, Lord, 10, 169, 182–83
Menzies, Sir Robert, 34, 177
Mew, Frederick A., 33, 102
Michael, Prince and Princess, *see* Kent
Montagu-Douglas-Scott, Lady Alice, *see* Gloucester
Morshead, Sir Owen, 162
Mountbatten, Lord Louis, 85

Napoleon I, 95
Napoleon III, 138
Narraway, William, photo by, *46*
necklaces
    Empress Marie Feodorovna's, *106*, *107*
    Godman, 95
    King Faisal, *56*, 137
    King George V jubilee, 101, *103*
    King George VI and Queen Elizabeth bandeau, *140*
    King George VI festoon, *53*
    King George VI Victorian, *148*, *149*
    King Khalid, *57*
    President Ayub Khan of Pakistan, *159*
    Queen Alexandra's *collier résille*, 30, *45*
    Queen Alexandra's Dagmar, *126*, *127*
    Queen Alexandra's Indian, *96*
    Queen Anne and Queen Caroline, 98, *104*,
        104–105
    Queen Mary's choker, *68*, *181*
    Queen Mary's 'Ladies of England', *38*, 40, *134*
    Queen Mary's 'Ladies of India', 18, *90*, *91*
    Queen Victoria's collet, 17, 27, 32, *54*, *55*, 80
    Queen Victoria's Golden Jubilee, 112, *118*, *119*,
        122, 129
    Queen's first, *25*, 158
    Queen's first pearl, *102*
    Queen's four row choker, *105*, *106*
    Queen's fringe, 32, *66*
Nepal, 119, 132
Netherlands, 35, 75
New Zealand, 18, 25, 48, 108, 110
Nicholas II of Russia, 14, 116
Nicholas, Princess of Greece, 37, 91, 100, 111,
    117, 139
Nicolson, Harold, 10, 173
Nightingale, Florence, 34
Normanton, Helena, 87
Noyes, Newbold, 87

Ogilvy, Hon. Angus, 37, 112, 119, 139
Olga, Grand Duchess of Russia, 14–16

Olga, Queen of Greece, 139
opals, 138
Opening of Parliament ritual, 163, 166, 169
Oppenheimer, Mary, 49
Orb, *171*, 172, *172–73*
Order of the Garter, 17, *121*, 182–84, *182–84*
Over-Seas League, 34

pearls, 98–101, *102–109*
    diamonds and, combined, 110–12, *113–37*
Pedro the Cruel of Castile, 167, 168
Philip II of Spain, 98
Philip, Prince, Duke of Edinburgh, 36, 47, 149
    as designer of jewellery, 10, 85, 139, 144
    engagement and wedding, 33, 85, 104–105
    as Knight of the Garter, *184*
    naval badge, 69, 144
    pictured, *23*, *43*, *52*, *62*, *63*, *77*, *94*, *120*, *144*, *155*,
        *157*, *184*
    trips with Queen, 21, 33–34, 62, 75, *77*
    wedding, 17, 33, 104–105
Phillips, Captain Mark, 21, 35, 36, *43*, 112, 145
Ponsonby, Sir Frederick, 14, 15–16
Portugal, 22
Premier Diamond Company, 72
Punjab, 28, 101, 139

Qatar, Amir of, 57, 101, 134, 139

Rashid, Sheikh of Dubai, 147
Revelstoke, Lord, 72
Richard II, 176
Richard III, 168
rings
    Coronation, 177
    engagement, 17, *79*, *85*, 110, 139, 145
    wedding, 97
Robbins, Ellis, 34
Romanov jewels, 13–15, 31, 37, 50, 81, 91, 106,
    116–17, 153
Roosevelt, Eleanor, 16, 17
Roosevelt, Franklin D., 16
Rose of York jewellery, 35, *142*, *143*, 146
Rosebery, Lord, 10
Ross, William, engraving after miniature by, *22*
Rothschild, Alice de, 32
rubies, 54, 55, 68, 138–39, *140–44*, 167–68
Rundell, Bridge and Rundell, Court Jewellers, 166,
    168, 177

St Cyr, Claude, 35
St Edward's Crown, 161, 166, 169, *174*, 174–75, 181
Salisbury, Lady, 45, 182
sapphires, 65, 81, 106, 145–47, *148–57*, 168
Saudi Arabia, 36, 57, 147
Sceptre, 170–72, *171*, *172*
Scotland, 168, 178, 184
Scott, Sir Walter, 178
Scottish Regalia, *178*
Shakespeare, William, 162
Shand Kidd, Hon. Mrs, 36
Sierra Leone, 34, 50, 55, 77
Simpson, Mrs Wallis, *see* Windsor
Smuts, Jan Christiaan, 49
Snowdon, Lord, 35, 36, 139
Solomon, Richard, 72, 74
Solomon Islands, 153
Sophia, Electress of Hanover, 99
South Africa, 26–27, 30, 72–74, 172
    visits to, 31, 32–33, 48–49, 61, 66
Spencer family, 36, 45, 52
Sri Lanka, 84
stomachers
    Queen Mary's, 31, 66, 67
    Queen Victoria's, 54, *55*, *126*, *164*

Stopford, B., 116–17
Strathmore, Earl of, 31–32
Stuart, Hon. James, 32
Stuart sapphire, 168
Stucley, Lady, 35
Sussex, Duke of, 138, 158
Swiss Federal Republics watch, 79

Talbot, Sir Gilbert, 174
Teck, Prince Adolphus of, 112
Teck, Prince Alexander of, 13, 88, 112
Teck, Prince Francis of, 88, 93, 112
Teck, Prince Francis, Duke of, 12–13
Teck, Princess Mary Adelaide, Duchess of, 12–13, 31, 71, 88, 93, 111, 158
Thynne, Lord John, 172
tiaras
    Cambridge lover's knot, 113, 114
    Grand Duchess Vladimir's, 37, 90, 91, 116, 117
    King George III fringe, 32, 37, 41–43
    Poltimore, 35
    Princess Andrew's meander, 35, 47
    Princess Anne's festoon, 95, 106, 107
    Princess Mary Adelaide's diamond crescent tiara, 88
    Queen Alexandra's Russian Kokoshnik, 37, 44, 45
    Queen Mary's Delhi Durbar, 88, 90
    Queen Mary's 'Girls of Great Britain and Ireland', 38–40, 124
    Queen Mother's fan-motif, 110, 141, 158
    Queen Mother's scroll, 32, 35, 46
Timur ruby, 54, 55, 139
Torrington, Lord, 182
Turkey, 27, 161
turquoises, 26, 158, 159

Van Cleef & Arpels, jewellers, 87
Vanderbilt, Consuelo, 116
Vanderbilt, Cornelius Jr, 11
Victoria, Princess (Edward VII's daughter), 13, 86
Victoria, Princess (Victoria's daughter), 99, 102, 138
Victoria, Queen, 8, 9–14, 24, 29, 35, 158
    Coronation, 160, 161, 163, 166, 168, 169, 172–73, 175, 177, 182
    death, 11
    descendants, 13, 14, 27, 33, 41, 47, 88, 97, 102, 137
    Diamond Jubilee, 10–11, 29, 55, 96, 110, 118, 119, 135
    diamonds, 27–32, 50, 51, 54, 55, 58, 59, 64, 65, 74, 78, 80, 95, 150, 161, 164
    emeralds, 87, 95
    Family Order, 180, 181
    Golden Jubilee, 10, 29, 70, 112, 119, 129
    Hanoverian jewels and, 9–10, 11, 27, 181
    jewellery containing family pictures, 10, 80, 97
    jewellery left to the Crown by, 11, 13, 16, 17, 22, 30, 32, 41–43, 54, 55, 65, 71, 78, 80, 86, 95, 99, 104, 110, 118, 121, 138, 139, 140, 150, 163
    Koh-I-Noor and, 27, 29, 95, 161
    Order of the Garter and, 182–83
    pearls, 98, 99, 101, 102
    pearls and diamonds, 112, 118, 121
    pictured, 41, 51, 55, 64, 78, 118, 121, 151, 164, 169
    Prince Albert brooch of, 145, 150, 151
    rubies, 138, 139
    statue of, 70
    taste in jewellery and dress, 10–11, 27, 29, 37, 127
    wedding, 27, 29, 36, 37, 145, 150, 182
Viktoria Luise, Princess of Germany, 164
Vladimir, Grand Duchess of Russia, 37, 91, 111, 116
Vroomen, Leo de, 99

Vyner, Sir Robert, 161, 171, 172, 174

Wales, Princes and Princesses of, see Edward, Alexandra, Charles, Diana, etc.
Walpole, Horace, 104
Warwick sun brooch, 134, 135
watches, 40, 79, 81, 97, 124, 125, 147
Watson, Sir Francis, 95
Webb, David, 87
Wellington, Duchess of, 130
Wellington, Duke of, 28, 41
Wells, Captain Frederick, 72
Welsh Guards emblem, 124
Westminster, Bendor, Duke of, 72
William I (William the Conqueror), 160, 174
William III, 168, 172
William IV, 9, 27, 78, 98, 101, 168
    brooch made by, 31, 32, 70, 71
    buckle bracelets of, 32, 80
    Coronation Regalia, 166, 175, 177
William, Prince, 32, 97
Williamson, Francis John, statue by, 70
Williamson, John T., 102
Windsor, Duchess of, 86–87
Windsor, Duke of, see Edward VIII
Windsor, Lady Helen, 146
Winston, Harry, 57, 87, 146
Winterhalter, Franz, 16, 27, 32, 54, 145
    painting by, 41
Woolf, Virginia, 31
World War II, 16, 100, 101, 145, 162
World Wide Shipping Group, 35, 106

Xenia, Grand Duchess of Russia, 14, 15

York, Sarah, Duchess of, 36, 59, 78, 97, 139

# PHOTOGRAPH CREDITS

The author and publisher would like to thank the following for permission to reproduce illustrations and for supplying photographs.

The following photographs are reproduced by gracious permission of **Her Majesty Queen Elizabeth II**. Copyright reserved, 39, 41, 42, 44 above, 54, 58, 68 left, 91 above, 96 above left, 113, 118 below, 120 above left, 132 above right, 133 below left, 163, 167; The following photographs are reproduced by gracious permission of **Her Majesty Queen Elizabeth II**. Copyright reserved. Photographs by **Maurice Foster**, 23 left, 44 below, 48, 50, 52 above, 53 above left, above right, 56 above, 60 above left, above right, 61 above, 63 above, 65, 67, 68 above right, 71, 73, 74, 76 above right, 77 above left, 78 left, 83, 84 left, 85 above left, above right, 89, 92 above centre, below centre, 95 centre, 118 above centre, 122 above, 126 below, 130 below, 133 above, 134 above, 140 above left, right, 141 above left, 142, 144 above, 148 above, 150, 153, 154 above left, 155 above left, above right, 156 above, 157 above, 180.

**Marcus Adams**, 25 below, 96 below left, 102 right; **Marcus Adams/Popperfoto**, 25 above right; **Associated Press**, 51 below right, 61 below, 122 below right, 130 above left, 155 below right; **Author's Collection**, 95 right; **Baron/Camera Press**, 63 below right, 66 right, 91 below left, 104 below, 148 below, 155 below left; **Bassano**, 70 above right; **BBC Hulton Picture Library**, 22 above left, 23 below right, 38 above left, 43 above left, above right, 45 above left, 49 left, 51 above left, above right, 55 above left, above right, 56 below left, 59 below, 60 below left, 62 left, 63 below left, 64 above left, above right, below left, 70 above centre, below right, 75 left, 76 above left, 78 above right, below right, 79 above right, 82 left, 88, 92 above left, above right, 94 below, 95 left, 96 above centre, 104 above, 106 above left, below right, 108 left, 109 left, 114 above left, above right, below left, 116 right, 118 above left, above right, 120 above right, below left, below right, 121, 122 below left, 125 above left, above right, 126 above left, above right, 128 above left, below right, 129, 132 above left, 133 below centre, 135 above left, 137 right, 142 left,

151 above left, above right, below left, below centre, 152 above right, 154 above right, 156 below left, below right, 164 below left, below right, 169, 170, 172, 176; **Cecil Beaton**, 55 below left; **Cecil Beaton/Camera Press**, 69, 171; **BIPNA**, 184 left; **Bippa**, 40 below left, 62 right, 106 below left, 125 below, 128 below left, 159 above; **Anthony Buckley/Camera Press**, 45 below, 81 below; **Camera Press**, 40 right, 92 below left, 171; **Central Press Photos Ltd**, 76 below, 102 left, 179; **Colorific**, 131 right; **Courtauld Institute of Art**, 70 above left; **Daily Herald**, 132 below; **Daily Sketch**, 55 below right, 77 below; **General Photographic Agency**, 38 below; **Tim Graham**, 40 left, 41 below right, 57 left, 79 below, 84 above right, below right, 152 below; **Edward Halliday/Camera Press**, 184 right; **Anwar Hussein**, 56 below left, 59 below right, 93 right, 119; **Karsh/Camera Press**, 75 right, 143 right; **Lafeyette**, 93 left; **Serge Lemoine/BBC Hulton Picture Library**, 107; **Patrick Lichfield/Camera Press**, 64 below centre; **London News Agency**, 131 left; **Donald McKague/Camera Press**, 117; **Mansell Collection**, 80 below, 103, 124, 134 below, 136 above, 141 above right, 152 above left; **National Portrait Gallery**, London, 25 above left; **Desmond O'Neill**, 159 below; **Norman Parkinson/Camera Press**, 64 below right, 96 above right, 181; **Pathe Gazette**, 22 above right; **Photographic News Agencies**, 23 above right, 53 below, 123; **The Photo Source**, 2, 46 above right, 51 below left, 127, 135 below, 136 below, 140 below left, 151 below right, 182; **Planet News Ltd**, 70 below left, 144 below, 154 below; **Popperfoto**, 38 above right, 43 below left, 45 above right, 66 left, 81 above left, above right, 82 right, 91 below right, 94 above, 106 above right, 114 below right, 164 right, 174; **Press Association**, 43 below right, 46 below, 47, 57 right, 105 left, 133 below right, 137 left, 141 below, 149, 178; **C.H. Pricam**, 79 above left; **Reuter/Press Association**, 77 above right, 80 above left, 85 below, 96 below left, 108 right, 115 above, 130 above right, 157 below, 175; **John Shelley**, 22 below, 68 below right, 105 right, 115 below, 135 below; **Snowdon/Camera Press**, 165; **Soper**, 128 above right; **Sport and General**, 46 above left, 59 below left, 92 below right; **Syndication International**, 60 below right; **The Times**, 49 right; **Topham**, 80 above right; **Vandyk**, 109 right, 183; **Wartski**, 166 left.